Walt Disney World
for
Lovers

Rick and Gayle Perlmutter

PRIMA PUBLISHING

*To our mothers,
who taught us how to enjoy life.
And to our children,
who we hope learned it from us.*

PRIMA PUBLISHING and its colophon, which consists of the letter P over PRIMA, are trademarks of Prima Communications, Inc.

Library of Congress Cataloging-in-Publication Data

Perlmutter, Rick.
    Walt Disney World for lovers / by Rick & Gail Perlmutter.
        p.   cm.
    Includes index.
    ISBN 0-7615-0321-8
        1. Walt Disney World (Fla.)—Guidebooks.   2. Young adults—Florida—Walt Disney World—Recreation—Guidebooks.   I. Perlmutter, Gail.
    II. Title.
    GV1853.3.F62W3463   1995
    791'.06'875924—dc20   95-31313
                                                              CIP

95 96 97 98 99 DD 10 9 8 7 6 5 4 3 2 1

Printed in the United States of America

Maps by Shane Acker

The prices herein reflect 1996 figures. Rates for resorts, prices for meals, and ticket costs are all subject to change by Walt Disney World.

How to Order
Single copies may be ordered from Prima Publishing, P.O. Box 1260, Rocklin, CA 95677; telephone (916) 632-4400. Quantity discounts are also available. On your letterhead, include information concerning the intended use of the books and the number of books you wish to purchase.

$\mathcal{C}$ontents

PART 2:
What to Do Once You Get There

PART 3:
The Ultimate Romance at Walt Disney World

$\mathscr{I}$ntroduction

Just what makes this the guidebook for you?

There are Walt Disney World guidebooks for children, for families, and for the budget-minded. This book has a different slant. We have written it especially for couples wishing to spend a romantic and special vacation at Walt Disney World.

Whether you are going to Disney World to celebrate your honeymoon, your anniversary, or simply to celebrate being in love, this guide is what you are looking for. If you have never, in your wildest dreams, imagined Disney World as a romantic place, then we have a surprise for you. Hidden inside the Walt Disney World that everyone knows is a secret place, where couples can go to enjoy a luxurious resort, fine dining and excellent wine, outstanding nightlife, and all the excitement of the most magical and fun place on earth. This "hidden" Disney World is relaxing and romantic. It is the perfect destination for lovers. This Disney World is where we go to enjoy each other's company in the pampered and intimate surroundings of any one of a dozen absolutely first-class hotels.

For us, Disney is breakfast in bed. It is a place where we can enjoy a sunset stroll on a deserted sand beach, hold hands over a cup of espresso at a sidewalk cafe, or take a midnight soak in a hot tub. Disney is live jazz after a dinner of fresh grilled Pacific salmon. It is a boat ride on a lake at sunset, a movie, a champagne cocktail after dinner, or dancing until the wee hours. Disney World is a balcony overlooking a fireworks show or a picnic lunch in a wildlife sanctuary. Disney World is all this and the excitement of a parade, the enchantment of the Disney–MGM Animation Studio Tour, or the thrills of Splash Mountain. For incurable romantics such as ourselves, Disney is the perfect place to make an exit from the real world and its demands. Disney World is nearly 30,000 acres large. It is, we are sure, the biggest and most diverse resort area anywhere in the world. Five championship golf courses, tennis, boating, horseback riding, swimming, health clubs, nature preserves, an island of nightclubs, and nearly 200 dining opportunities make the Walt Disney World resorts the most unique and complete vacation area on Planet Earth. Throw in Epcot, Disney–MGM Studios, the Magic Kingdom, and a host of other attractions such as Typhoon Lagoon, Blizzard Beach, River Country, and Pleasure Island, and you will see why Walt Disney World is known as the Vacation Capital of the World. It is the last word in resorts and, for couples, a real land of enchantment.

The "World" is so big that going there without some kind of plan is like going to Europe without any plan beyond a pair of air tickets to Paris. You need a strategy, which this guidebook will provide.

This book will help you with virtually every phase of your Disney vacation. Since where you will be staying will be one of the most important elements of your time together, we have created the most complete guide to the Walt Disney World resorts ever written. We will help you select the resort that best suits your needs and guide you through every phase of planning your special time at Disney, to make your vacation an easy one. (If you had wanted difficult, you'd be camping out in the jungles of Panama.) We'll tell you how to find the level of comfort, convenience, and luxury that suits you both.

And since you have neither an oil well nor a gold mine in your backyard, we'll show you how to get as much for your money as possible. If by chance you do have a gold mine in your backyard or if you are planning that once-in-a-lifetime event, we will give you the whole lowdown on the very best Disney has to offer. And how suite it can get! We will show you how to plan the ultimate Disney experience. For the last word on anniversaries, weddings, or honeymoons, Disney is *the* place. In our guide to Disney's Fairy Tale Weddings, we'll show you the options available for a unique, unforgettable Disney wedding. We will also describe some of the weddings that have been staged at Disney, from the small and intimate to the lavish and extravagant.

Wondering if you should opt for a package or make all of your own plans? We'll provide you with more than enough information to make this decision with confidence. Traveling with the kids? No problem. You can still have a wonderfully romantic time. We will tell you everything you need to know about doing things as a family and how to get away on your own for those special times together.

And once you have arrived, we will help you avoid the pitfalls common to Disney visitors. We will help you find your own special rhythm that will keep the two of you feeling comfortable, pampered, and relaxed: three of the ingredients essential to romance.

For your dining adventures, we have gone beyond anything done before. We will provide you with first-hand information about the World's many wonderful dining establishments. We have seen, done, and eaten it all, and if you are looking for the rarest of steaks, the freshest of fish, or simply the best cup of coffee, we'll let you in on all of our secrets.

For your Disney adventures, you'll get some real insider information, the kind of stuff that you can get only by spending a lot of time looking for it, which is exactly what we have done. From Adventureland to parasailing, from Star Tours to Wine Flights, from high tea to fireworks, we promise not to leave a Disney stone unturned. Looking for that something special? An exotic dinner, a stroll along a quiet beach at sunset, or a quiet cafe for lunch? If you expect Walt Disney World to be more than just some great rides, then take a good look at what we have written here.

If you are lovers of any age, looking for the time of your lives, then this guidebook is for you. Take the "road less traveled," the path to a magical and romantic adventure. Let us show you the Walt Disney World for lovers.

It's a Matter of Attitude

We didn't always think of Disney World as a romantic place. There was a time when going to Disney meant thrill-packed days of running from attraction to attraction, spending hours waiting in long lines, gulping down counter food, and exhausting ourselves trying to do and to see everything. Our days were filled with fun, but we found ourselves stumbling back to our hotel room at night with just enough energy left to ask, "What will we be able to fit in tomorrow?" It was fun, but it wasn't romance. Then we learned how to do it right.

We discovered that our days at Disney could become opportunities to enjoy the tranquil luxury of a top resort that just happens to be located in this incredible vacation place. We have managed this transition by not only learning *what* to do at Disney World and when to do it, but also by changing our *attitudes*. In short, we have learned how to find and to sustain a relaxed and romantic mood while visiting Disney.

Finding Romance at Walt Disney World

Daylight was fading as we made our way across the deserted beach. The blazing reds and brilliant ochers of the fleeting sun ignited the fiery clouds and spilled onto the lagoon, setting it afire with shimmering lights. The sand beneath our bare feet still held the warmth of the day. Hand in hand, we passed empty cabanas to a large swing, where we sat together, savoring those final moments of daylight.

Dinner at a nearby restaurant had been elegant and intimate. We had decided to kick off our shoes and find some place to enjoy the sights and sounds of the evening when we discovered the secluded swing. We watched the boats make their way across the lagoon. We could hear the people aboard them, laughing and talking. Their voices and the thrumming of engines faded as the boats disappeared in the distance. There was something special about being here, away from everything. It seemed dreamy and blissful.

We sat silently, swinging slowly. There was nothing to say after what had seemed to be yet another perfect day. This was a contentment so powerful that we simply shared it in a knowing silence. Just when we were sure that it couldn't possibly get better, fireworks began to flash in the sky across the water. We could hear the dull thuds of rockets as they exploded over Cinderella's Castle, igniting the sky with clouds of gold and showers of red. Huge and brilliant flowers of sparks blossomed in the darkening sky only to be carried gently away in the breeze. We watched in awe as we realized that the entire display was being mirrored on the surface of the lagoon before us. We squeezed each other's hand just a bit harder.

It *was* a special moment for us. Relaxing, romantic, *magical*. It was that kind of moment that we take vacations hoping to find. If we were going to rate it as a romantic experience, we would consider it special and sublimely romantic.

Romance is a personal thing, and we do not pretend to know what will make everyone experience it. We do feel that there are ingredients conducive to romance, as well as elements that are incompatible with it. Things romantic involve an enhanced chemistry of togetherness. This kind of intimacy can occur when you are alone on a beach at sunset, or it can happen in a crowded theater. It is a special feeling of closeness that transports you together to a place away from the everyday. It is something special and out of the ordinary, that seems to occur just for the two of you.

As you read through this guidebook, look for heart symbols (♥). The more ♥ you see, the more likely we think you will be able to ignite this chemistry. We have tried to savor a place for its ability to enhance our own feelings of togetherness, for its potential to elevate us above the everyday and to let us know that this special thing is happening just for us. Not surprisingly, Disney has a real knack for creating these moments. Sometimes romance just happens, and sometimes we can help it happen.

♥	**A hint of romance**
♥♥	**An air of romance**
♥♥♥	**Intimate and enchanting**
♥♥♥♥	**Unforgettable, sublimely romantic**

What You Can Do Before You Leave Home

CHAPTER 1

$\mathcal{M}$aking the Decisions

In this chapter, we will cover a host of topics on making your special vacation together easier and more relaxed and, we hope, setting the stage for some real romance. We will help you make the big decisions regarding your upcoming Disney romance vacation: when to go and where to stay. If you are making your romantic holiday a family affair, we'll give you lots of information about the special accommodations for families and how the two of you can go off by yourselves for some special time together. We will also describe the many tickets and passes, the variety of discounts available, and how to fit everything neatly into your budget. In short, we'll help you to prepare for your special Disney World vacation.

The Ever-Changing Walt Disney World

If you think that it's the same old Walt Disney World year after year, you should try writing a guidebook. Team Disney is always looking for new things to do and new ways to do old things. New attractions are constantly being unveiled, and everything from rides to resorts are undergoing upgrades and rehabs. It is a continual process of change, and, short of weekly bulletins, there is no way to keep up with everything.

What this means is that the really important stuff in this guidebook will stay timely. Here and there, you will likely find a few changes in schedules, pricing, and other details. You may discover a show or attraction that did not exist when we were researching this guide, or you may discover that something we have described has been eliminated.

As writers, this process of change poses a small problem. As Disney enthusiasts, we relish this state of flux, because it means constant improvement. Virtually every time we visit Disney World, we have new and better things to look forward to. And, of course, this is good news for you, too. We can assure you that the Walt Disney World that you may have visited several years ago is not the same place today. In the last year alone, we have seen such new creations as the Disney Institute, *Honey, I Shrunk the Audience*, *Alien Encounter*, and the BoardWalk. And there's more to come. For a picture of upcoming changes at Walt Disney World, see Appendix D of this book.

The prices in this guidebook reflect 1996 figures. Rates for resorts, prices for meals, and ticket costs are all sure to rise slightly over time. What we have given you will provide a clear idea of the relative expense at Walt Disney World. Any future changes should be small ones.

When to Go

When the two of you head off to Disney, you will discover more seasons there than the old and familiar summer, fall, winter, and spring. These seasons describe the weather, but the Disney seasons take into account other important considerations such as crowds, holidays, and special events.

Seasons of the World

The Disney folks speak in terms of the regular season, the value season, and the holiday season. Regular season is those times of year that the park is operating at full tilt. Schools are out of session and the parks, resorts, and other Disney attractions are all at their busiest. Holiday season refers only to the period of time from about the week before Christmas to the last day of December. During the brief holiday season, resort rates are actually higher than at any other time of year.

Value season is what remains of the year. During these off-season times, almost every place in Disney World is less crowded. Many of the Disney resorts offer discounted rates and attractive vacation packages. These less-busy seasons occur throughout the year. Here's how the three seasons run:

REGULAR SEASON AND HOLIDAY SEASON

- Mid-February to late April; the end of the first week of June to mid-August; approximately one week before Christmas to December 31
- More people, bigger crowds, longer lines
- Few, if any, discounts
- Holiday season means higher resort rates and even bigger crowds

- Parks open early and stay open late
- Numerous special events such as fireworks and parades

$\mathcal{V}$ALUE SEASON

- Beginning of January to mid-February; late April to the end of the first week of June; mid-August to one week before Christmas
- Fewer people; every place is less crowded
- Numerous special rates, offers, and discounts
- Parks open later and close earlier
- Fewer special events such as fireworks and parades

Good Times to Visit

During the course of the year, there are many special and seasonal events. Whether it's the Fourth of July or Chinese New Year, the folks at Disney love a party. Most of these events are memorable. Besides the usual holidays are celebrations of Mother's Day, Mardi Gras, a spring garden festival, a summer swing music celebration, and even a fall kite festival. For more information and dates of special events, call Disney Information at (407) 824-4321. If you are planning to visit Disney World on a big holiday, such as Independence Day, be forewarned: park attendance hits record highs on these days.

Our favorite time of year has always been during the three weeks after Thanksgiving and before Christmas. At least several of the premium Disney resorts offer greatly reduced rates, and the World is dressed in its finest holiday attire. There are special events, such as the Jolly Holidays Dinner Show, nightly tree-lighting ceremonies, wandering carolers and musicians, and the Very Merry Christmas Party. It is beautiful, festive, and fun. During these weeks, you may enjoy all the benefits of the holiday season without the crowds.

Other times of year attract fewer people as well. The week following Labor Day is the slowest of the Disney year. January to mid-February are nice months and the weather is generally quite nice. The final week of August, though hot, is not usually crowded. The entire fall, except for Thanksgiving weekend, is a wonderful time for a Disney visit.

$\mathcal{O}$UR RECOMMENDATIONS

- If possible, go during value season.
- Take advantage of numerous resort discounts, fewer crowds, and discount vacation packages.

Weather

Weather-wise, central Florida is a mixed bag, encompassing all of the four seasons without the severity of, say, New England. Winters are usually cool and balmy with occasional cold snaps. If you are coming from colder climes, you will likely find the winter weather at Disney World to be most agreeable. Summers in Florida range from hot to HOT. Spring and fall land somewhere in between with a mix of warmer and cooler days, a sort of leftovers time.

OUR SUMMER RECOMMENDATIONS

- Prepare for heat: brings lots of light, loose clothing, hats, and bathing suits.
- Make full use of Disney pools and water attractions.
- Be ready for brief afternoon thundershowers.

OUR WINTER RECOMMENDATIONS

- Expect any kind of weather except very hot; be prepared clothing-wise; try layering clothes.
- Don't forget your bathing suits: most pools and water attractions are heated, and there are always the spas (hot tubs).
- Avoid holidays or college break periods, to keep crowds low.

OUR SPRING AND FALL RECOMMENDATIONS

- Pack for almost any weather except very cold or very hot.

Here's a month-by-month look at weather and crowds:

January

Weather: Be prepared: expect occasional cold spells, with cool nights and balmy days. Average high: 70°. Average low: 50°.

World Conditions: After January 1, everything slows down beautifully. An excellent time for a romantic visit.

February

Weather: A very likely month for wintery cold snaps. Still, February can be a nice month for weather. Expect more balmy days and cool evenings. Average high: 72°. Average low: 51°.

World Conditions: Attendance is low through the first week and average for the remainder of the month. Things begin to pick up a bit in the last few days of February. Value season lasts until about the tenth of this month. After this, the regular season begins and runs until late April. Parks are open late for the busy President's Day week.

March

Weather: March can be a blustery month with a mix of weather. It's usually one of the wetter winter months. Rarely will March be very cold. Average high: 76°. Average low: 56°.

World Conditions: Attendance begins to pick up, getting busy during the spring break season. This month is all regular season.

April

Weather: This is a nice month! The climate is usually breezy, with warm days and balmy nights. Average high: 82°. Average low: 60°.

World Conditions: This is a busy month through Easter, after which the crowds go home. The weather is great and the parks are less crowded. Regular season lasts until about April 21, after which value season begins.

May

Weather: Another month of splendid weather. The days become a bit warmer than April but only occasionally does it get hot. This is spring in central Florida. Average high: 88°. Average low: 66°.

World Conditions: Fewer crowds and wonderful spring weather make this a great time for your romantic Disney getaway. Just watch out for the busy Memorial Day weekend and you'll have it made. A solid month of value season!

June

Weather: Summer begins to arrive and with it . . . HEAT. Evenings are still fairly pleasant. Average high: 90°. Average low: 71°.

World Conditions: The first week is not too crowded, but after that, watch out. The summer season begins full-tilt and the hoards arrive.

Value season usually ends around the end of the first week. School gets out and the regular season begins, lasting until the third week in August.

July

Weather: This is summer—expect it to be HOT. Afternoon thundershowers are fairly common. Average high: 92°. Average low: 73°.

World Conditions: Summer is in full swing now, and Disney World is about as crowded as it gets. The weekend of the fourth is the busiest of the year. If there is one month to avoid, this is it. Regular season all month long.

August

Weather: This is definitely a hot month: hot days, hot nights. A good chance of afternoon thundershowers, too. Average high: 92°. Average low: 76°.

World Conditions: The first two weeks are very busy and then the crowds begin to leave. By the last week of the month, things are starting to get pretty nice. Regular season lasts until about the August 18, then value season begins. It's still hot but getting to be a good time to visit due to fewer people.

September

Weather: Don't forget, it's still summer here in Florida, which means more hot days and hot nights. Also, the rainy season begins. This mostly means afternoon thundershowers, nothing like the monsoons of India. Average high: 89°. Average low: 72°.

World Conditions: The week after Labor Day is the slowest week of the year at Walt Disney World. The rest of the month is also slow: few crowds, short lines. Value season all month long.

October

Weather: Still warm, but the real heat of the summer has passed. Nights are beginning to get balmy. Average high: 82°. Average low: 68°.

World Conditions: A nice month for a visit. The weather is pleasant and the crowds are still elsewhere. Another month of discounts: it's value season.

November

Weather: The weather is really starting to get nice now. Days are balmy and evenings are cool. Don't forget your bathing suit. Average high: 76°. Average low: 57°.

World Conditions: This is a nice month to visit, with few crowds until Thanksgiving week (a good week to stay home). After this: our favorite time of year. Value season all month.

December

Weather: This is usually a very nice month but occasionally cold. Average high: 72°. Average low: 52°.

World Conditions: It's value season for about the first three weeks. Crowds are less than normal until about December 19, when the official holiday season begins. After this, the World is very crowded. Swimming suits are still useful, especially in a hot tub.

Deciding Where to Stay

Yes, this is the big decision. Selecting where to stay will set the backdrop and mood of your entire visit. Convenience, luxury, and even romantic atmosphere are all very much related to your resort.

Basically, you have two choices if you are visiting Walt Disney World: you can stay inside the World or you can stay outside. Inside, known to cast members (the Disney Folks) as "on-property," means staying in one of the many and varied Disney resorts. Staying outside, or "off-property," means staying in one of the many hotels or motels located in the surrounding areas, such as Kissimmee, Lake Buena Vista, or Orlando.

There are, indisputably, many fine hotels and even a few resorts in the areas surrounding Walt Disney World. Many of them may be cheaper than staying inside Disney, but they all share one thing in common: they are *not* in Disney World.

Outside, you will be staying at least several miles from the fun. Even though an off-property motel may advertise that it is "five minutes from Disney," this doesn't mean that it will take you only five minutes to make the trip. The motel may actually be a five-minute drive from Disney's front gate, but by the time you add parking, walking, traffic, and a host of other impediments, we seriously doubt that you will be able to leave your off-property room in the morning and get to the park of your choice in less than 45 minutes.

If you stay off-property, you'll quickly discover that all of this going back and forth eats up valuable vacation time. And staying outside usually means that it isn't very practical to drop back to your hotel room for an hour's rest or an afternoon together. If you are driving, the dense crowds at the gates in the morning and at closing time spell H-A-S-S-L-E.

If this doesn't sound so discouraging, consider what it is like to stay inside Disney. Every bed on property is located in what Disney calls a "themed resort." At a Disney resort, you will find yourselves the pampered guests at accommodations that have been carefully themed to enfold you in the very Disney magic that you have come looking for. Each Disney resort has its own specially designed atmosphere. Everything at Dixie Landings, for example, reflects the Mississippi River theme of the resort. The look of the resort, the Bayou cuisine of its restaurants, the dress of the cast members, the room furnishings—everything down to the smallest detail enriches that theme. Each resort is designed to enhance your Disney visit, to make it easier and more fun. Once you have left the theme parks and returned to your resort, you will not feel as though you have left Disney World. It will mean exciting days and luxurious and intimate nights.

And this is really just the beginning. Disney resort guests get special benefits such as early admission into the theme parks, special passes, and full use of Disney transportation.

But, you are thinking, it costs a fortune to stay at a Disney resort. Not true. There are now Disney resorts for virtually every budget, with prices beginning at $69 per night. If you take a close look into the off-property "bargains," you will find that regular season prices in basic motels will be this much, frequently more. Even the most basic Disney resort compares favorably to most of the more expensive off-property lodgings.

So, are we trying to talk you into staying in a Walt Disney World resort? You bet we are! We want you to have to best possible vacation, and staying on property is the way. We feel sure that there is a Disney resort for you and staying in it will make your romance vacation what it should be: fun, easy, and relaxing.

How Much Will It Cost?

There is a place to stay at Walt Disney World to satisfy virtually any desire. From the basic All-Star Resorts to the Victorian elegance of the Grand Floridian, the folks at Disney have it all covered. There are campsites, trailers, suites, multiroom villas, treehouses, vacation homes, and much more. There is a tremendous offering of truly luxurious places in a range from $69 to $250 per night, up to $1,500 for the Captain's Deck at the Yacht Club (yes, that's per night!).

Types of Disney Resorts

There are three types of Disney resorts: premium, moderate, and economy.

As you would expect, the rooms are larger and have more lavish furnishings in the premium, full-amenities resorts. Amenities mean services and, here at Walt Disney World, you will get what you pay for. The choice of recreational activities is always greater at the premium resorts. Each offers room service as well as bell service, and many provide a nightly turndown service. Some even feature luxurious bathrobes.

While the moderate resorts do not enjoy a level of luxury equal to that of the premium resorts, the rooms are comfortable, spacious, and well appointed. And there are numerous recreational activities. The economy resorts feature even smaller rooms and simpler furnishings; besides swimming pools, recreation is minimal.

While each Disney resort features food service, the premium resorts tend to provide an interesting variety of restaurants. The moderate resorts each have one table-service restaurant and a food court, while the economy resorts offer only food courts.

The grounds and lobbies of the premium resorts are the most lavish and elaborately styled. Each moderate resort is beautifully themed and is an enchanting place to spend your romance vacation. Simply, the premium resorts offer more of everything.

There is one important advantage to rooms in the premium resorts. The entrance to each room is through a hallway inside the resort. This makes for large windows that look out onto landscaped resort grounds, often onto a lagoon, a forest, or even a castle. Many premium rooms also feature balconies or patios. The moderate and economy resorts, on the other hand, have outside walkways. Windows open onto these and, with the curtains open, the result is a lack of privacy. With the drapes closed, you get a feeling of being closed in. There are no balconies or patios at either the moderate or economy resorts.

The following lists the Disney resorts by type.

$\mathcal{P}$REMIUM RESORTS

Prices begin at $159 per night

- The Contemporary
- The Polynesian
- The Grand Floridian
- The Yacht and the Beach Clubs
- The Wilderness Lodge
- The Swan and the Dolphin
- The Disney Institute
- Fort Wilderness Campground Resort, Wilderness Homes
- The Village at the Institute
- The Vacation Club

$\mathcal{M}$ODERATE RESORTS

Prices range from $95 to $134

- Port Orleans
- Dixie Landings
- The Caribbean Beach

$\mathcal{E}$CONOMY RESORTS

Prices range from $69 to $79

- All-Star Music
- All-Star Sports

The Disney World of Discounts

If the Disney resort that sounds best to you seems out of reach, you'll be happy to know that list prices at Disney are like list prices everywhere else. Disney offers a large variety of discounts for both resorts and vacation packages. Experience has shown us, however, that these discounts must be pursued. They are usually not widely advertised or generally known. With a bit of research, though, you should be able to find something that suits your needs.

To begin with, discounts are affected most by the season. Of course, we are talking about value season. During the regular and holiday seasons, discounts become hard to come by and, if you are able to get one, it will not be as large as during value season. So, if you are looking for a deeply discounted resort or package rate, begin by planning an off-season visit.

The following sections describe sources of Disney discounts.

Disney Central Reservations Office (CRO)

Yes, discounts are available through the regular reservation process. Simply ask the reservationist about specials or special deals for the dates that you have selected. Remember that most discounts are scheduled for value season. Try a variety of dates to see what you can get. Call Disney Central Reservations at (407) W-DISNEY (934-7639).

The Magic Kingdom (MK) Club

Membership to the Magic Kingdom Club is available to state employees (usually any state), employees of hospitals, large corporations, or businesses, and often university employees.

If you are not eligible, you may purchase a Magic Kingdom Club Gold Card for $65. Walt Disney Company stockholders may obtain a Magic Kingdom Gold Card for $50. The Gold Card offers the same discounts as well as a few extras not included with the regular MK Club membership.

The Magic Kingdom Club is the most widely-used discount. Check with your employer's human resources or personnel department to see if one is available for you. Using it can mean big savings. Even if you have to pay the $60 for a Gold Card, you will likely discover that the card will pay for itself in a single visit, especially during value season. Call or write:

Magic Kingdom Gold Card
P.O. Box 3850
Anaheim, CA 92803
(800) 248-2665

DISCOUNTS AND PRIVILEGES

- Disney resort discounts are available on a variety of selected packages and resort rooms: 10% discounts during regular season and discounts of 20% to 30% during value season.
- Additional discounts include Disney admission tickets and passes, golf, dinner shows, select theme park restaurants, merchandise at Disney World shops and Disney stores (nationwide), cruise vacations, and rental cars.

The Magic Years Club

This is the Magic Kingdom Club for persons 55 years of age and older. The cost of membership is $40 per person. Membership lasts for five years and only one of you needs a card.

Call or write:

The Disney Magic Years Club
P.O. Box 4709
Anaheim, CA 92803
(714) 490-3250

DISCOUNTS AND PRIVILEGES

- All of the discounts given with the Magic Kingdom Club card
- Discount parking tickets
- 50% discount at Discovery Island
- Toll-free reservation number
- Discount dining coupons
- Disney totebag, key chain, and luggage tag

American Express

The official credit card of Walt Disney World, American Express offers an ever-changing assortment of promotional packages, each aimed at encouraging you to use your card to pay for your Disney vacation. These packages seem to vary throughout the year. Some are bargains, some are not. Simply checking-in with your American Express card will get you a free portrait with Mickey and a fanny pack. Call American Express Disney Reservations at (407) 827-7200.

𝒟ISCOUNTS AND PRIVILEGES

- An assortment of promotional add-ons, packages, and extras
- 10% discounts on boating activities and select dinner shows

Walt Disney World Annual Passport

The Annual Passport is available to anyone willing to spend $250 for it (about $210 for children). Besides providing an entire year's worth of admission to the three theme parks—Magic Kingdom, Epcot, and Disney–MGM Studios—it can be a source of outstanding resort discounts, both during the regular and value seasons.

Only one of you needs a passport to get the resort discount, and you may book your discounted room before you even buy it. Just be prepared to present either your pass or its voucher at check-in. There is even a discount on the Annual Passport for both Magic Kingdom Club members and Florida residents. To obtain information and book reservations for Annual Passport discounts, call Disney Central Reservations and tell them you are a passholder. Discounts during value season are always greater than those offered during regular season. Call Disney Central Reservations at (407) W-DISNEY (934-7639).

𝒟ISCOUNTS AND PRIVILEGES

- A hodgepodge of resort discounts, some very good. Some resort discounts may be as much as 50% off of regular resort rates.
- Bearer gets unlimited admission to the three theme parks for one full year.

American Automobile Association (AAA)

Because this organization functions as a travel agency, it offers a variety of resort and package discounts to its members. Some are quite good. These are worth looking into.

𝒟ISCOUNTS AND PRIVILEGES

- Resort rate and vacation package discounts (available to AAA members only)

Delta Airline Dream Vacations

Delta is the official airline of Walt Disney World and offers its own assortment of Disney vacation packages. Some are on property, and others are not. These are sold in conjunction with airline tickets, usually to Orlando. Because Delta's packages and promotionals change throughout the year, we suggest that you call for their current offerings. Call Delta Airlines Dream Vacations at (800) 872-7786.

DISCOUNTS AND PRIVILEGES

• A variety of vacation packages that include airfare with Delta

Your Local Travel Agent

Several years ago, Disney began discounting vacation packages to travel agents. This has enabled travel agents everywhere to be competitive in a previously closed market.

Florida Resident Discounts

Mickey loves Floridians. After all, he lives in Florida, doesn't he? A number of benefits are afforded to Florida residents. Usually offered during value season, discounts include resort rates, packages, and admission tickets. If you are Florida residents planning a visit, you will certainly wish to take advantage of one. Simply call Disney Central Reservations at (407) 934-7639 and ask when Florida residents' specials are being offered.

Discounts are available to anyone with a Florida driver's license or other proof of residency, such as a rent receipt or a utility bill.

The Disney Dining Experience   This little-known organization is available only to Florida residents. Briefly, membership provides a 20% discount in a large selection of Disney restaurants. The Disney Dining Experience discount is good for food as well as alcoholic beverages and includes the cardholder and his or her entire party. The cost is $40. If you enjoy dining at Walt Disney World, this card will pay for itself in short order.

DISNEY DISCOUNT TIPS

• Be comparative shoppers. Look around for the best deal. Check out every source possible.
• Don't pass up a good deal waiting for a great one. You can make a reservation and cancel it later when a better deal arrives.

- When talking with a CRO reservationist, be sure to ask a lot of questions. Carefully explain what you are looking for. These people know a lot, but they also seem trained to not offer the cheapest alternative unless you ask for it.
- For best-room availability, try calling Central Reservations around 10 A.M., eastern time. This really works.

Doing It All on Your Budget

We are sure that you, like most couples, are planning your Disney vacation to fit a budget. It is important that you know ahead of time how much your Disney vacation is going to cost so that you will be able to enjoy yourselves without worry. Nothing can ruin a vacation like the nagging concern that you are overspending. If you have elected to purchase one of the all-inclusive packages, then you will be enjoying one of its greatest advantages: you will already have a very good picture of what your Disney vacation will cost.

If you are making your own plans, you will have to do some figuring to know what your Disney adventure is going to cost.

The Major Expenses

After the expense of getting to Walt Disney World, the major expenses fall into three categories: resort expenses, admission ticket costs, and food expenses.

Resort Expenses   Resort and admission expenses are the expenditures easiest to factor. Take a look at our guide to the Disney resorts in Chapter 2 and see which resort looks good to you. Modest price increases are yearly events at Disney, so you might want to check with Central Reservations to make sure that you have the most current rates. Don't forget to add a combined Florida state sales and resort tax of 11% to your room.

Admission Ticket Costs   Admission tickets will also be a simple matter to calculate (See "Admission Options" later in this chapter). Once you have made your admission choice, you should have a clear figure to deal with.

Food Expenses   Figuring your food expenses will be a bit more complicated. Whatever your tastes and habits may be, you should know that dining out, three meals a day, at Disney World will constitute a significant part of your vacation budget. Just how big a part will depend on you. It is *possible* for a couple to eat at Walt Disney World for $60 per day. However, it will have to be done very carefully. A $60 per day food allowance will require dining largely at the more inexpensive, counter-service restaurants with one moderately priced meal per day. Dining exclusively in the fast-food eateries is not our idea of a romantic vacation.

For a more realistic figure for a couple's food expenses, we suggest planning on $110 per day. Allowing for this amount, you will be fairly free to eat in all of the moderately priced restaurants and even include one or two expensive restaurants during your vacation. Needless to say, a larger budget will mean more lavish meals in fancier restaurants. Please note that this $110 does not include alcoholic beverages in significant amounts. For tips on where to dine, how to eat at the finer restaurants without spending a fortune, bargain meals, and a host of other information, see what we have to say about the Disney dining experience and the Disney restaurants in Chapter 6. Remember, of the big three expenses, food is really the only one that can be difficult to predict.

Putting It All Together: What Will It Cost?

Now that you have some idea of what the major costs will be, all that remains is to add them up and to see what you can get. To give you a good idea of the scope of possibilities, we have constructed a sample budget. (Note that the value season version of the sample budget includes a 50% room discount with Annual Passport.) Remember that it does not include anything extra that you elect to spend on memorabilia or alcoholic beverages. Other extras such as dinner shows should also be taken into consideration. For the most part, we have elected to use Length of Stay Passes to provide admission to the Disney attractions. We have also included taxes and tips.

A Four-Night Stay for Two at the Beach Club

Garden view room	$1,200
Meals	440
Length of Stay Passes	373
TOTAL	$2,013

Value Season Version of Beach Club Four-Night Stay

Garden view room	$550
Meals	440
Annual Passport for one (includes all add-ons)	339
Length of Stay Pass for one	186
TOTAL (saves nearly $500)	$1,515

𝒯IPS FOR DOING IT BEST ON A BUDGET:

- Take advantage of off-season specials and lower rates to get the most for your money. Plan ahead.
- Try a variety of resorts and admission ticket combinations before making your final decision.

Admission Options: Which Ticket Is for You?

While it is not necessary to purchase your admission passes before you arrive, it is wise to know which will be the best choice. Disney offers a confusing assortment of tickets and passes. If you are opting for a vacation package that includes admission to the Disney attractions, then you will not have to choose among these. For descriptions, comparisons, and recommendations to help you select what is best for you, see Table 1 on pages 20–21.

Getting Your Tickets, Passes, or Passports

If you elect to get either an Annual Passport or a Florida Resident's Seasonal Passport, you would be wise to do it before you arrive at Walt Disney World. All of the other passes and tickets are easily available at your resort's Guest Services.

For either of the two passports, you can go to any of the 200 Disney stores across the United States. There, you may purchase a voucher that can be converted into the actual pass once you arrive at Walt Disney World. This process can only be done at one of the Guest Services at a front gate of one of the three theme parks. It is very simple, especially if you arrive 30 minutes before the park opens. Passport vouchers can also be purchased by telephone with a credit card, by calling (407) W-DISNEY, or from many travel agents.

Vacation Packages: Are They for You?

Like the Disney characters, Walt Disney World vacation packages come in many shapes and sizes. Typically, they include at least room accommodations and admission tickets. Many include much more. Some offer airfare to Orlando and others offer meals as well as unlimited recreation. There are even plans that include virtually everything that you might want to do at Walt Disney World, from golf and boating to a champagne breakfast in bed. There are family packages, holiday packages, golf and sports packages, honeymoon and wedding plans, and the ultimate in vacation experiences, Disney's Grand Plan. This assortment of packages is priced for either value season or regular season.

There are basically two sources for packages to Walt Disney World: the first is independent agents and tour guides, and the second is Disney. Independent packages usually provide accommodations in off-property locations. Many also include air or bus transportation. Most provide Disney admission tickets and frequently little else. This is the type of package deal that you are likely to find in your local newspaper. If you are considering one of them, we can only warn you to be very careful. Off-property accommodations are often not what they're described to be or what they look like in photos. And once you get to Walt Disney World, you may be amazed at what these "all-inclusive" package deals don't include.

Vacation plans created by Team Disney will be our focus. With these, you will be able to stay in one of the many themed Walt Disney World resorts or, if you prefer, in a good-quality non-Disney hotel.

The Nuts and Bolts of Packages

Disney vacation plans are figured on a per person, per day cost. Youngsters are accounted for at either of two cost levels: juniors (10 to 17 years old) or children (3 to 9 years old). Children under 3 years of age are free. Different packages and prices are available for the entire spectrum of Disney resorts. If you opt for a vacation package, you should know that after your initial deposit, the balance of your package cost is due no later than 21 days before the first day of your vacation.

The first step in the quest for your vacation package should be to call the Walt Disney World Travel Company. Request their catalogue of vacation packages. This booklet will give you all of the basic package

Ticket	Price		Cost per Day	Features	Drawbacks	Recommendations
One-Day/ One-Park Pass A = adult C = child	A C	$37 $30	$37 $30	Admission to one park: Magic Kingdom, Epcot, or Disney–MGM Studios	No park hopping Limited use of WDW transportation	Good for 1-, 2-, or 3-day visit if on a tight budget or staying off property Use to fill in extra days with other passes
Four-Day Value Pass	A C	$124 $97	$31 $24.50	Admission to one theme park per day Unused days do not expire	No park hopping Admission to other attractions is extra	For a mere $10 more, get Four-Day Park Hopper and have more fun
Four-Day Park Hopper Pass	A C	$137 $109	$34.25 $27.25	Can hop three major parks Unused days do not expire	Admission extra to: Water Parks ($24) Pleasure Island ($17) River Country ($16) Discovery Island ($11)	A good value Stay five days with this pass and spend one day at Typhoon Lagoon for only $24.00
Five-Day World Hopper Pass	A C	$186 $148	$37.20 $29.60	Unlimited admission to all Disney attractions (Typhoon Lagoon, Discovery Island, River Country, Pleasure Island, Blizzard Beach) Admission to additional attractions good for seven days after first use of pass Park hopping to ALL parks and attractions Unused admissions to three parks that do not expire	If you are staying on property, this pass is more expensive than the equivalent Length of Stay Pass Seven days of admission to additional attractions, expires seven days after the first use of this pass Limited use of WDW transportation	A good value only if you use admission to additional attractions Use this pass for a 6- or 7-day stay, and use 7-day admissions to: Typhoon Lagoon Discovery Island Pleasure Island River Country Blizzard Beach to fill in "extra" days

	Price	Break-even	Features	Additional notes	Value
Annual Passport	A $229 C $199	Break-even on Day 6 of stay	Unlimited admission to three parks for one full year Seasonal resort discounts to 50% Park hopping to three parks Unlimited use of WDW transportation	Additional attractions not included Yearly unlimited admission add-on for each attraction or Annual Super Pass for all eight attractions Also extra attractions by daily admission rate	Great value for visits of seven days or longer Outstanding bargain when used with resort discount during value season
Florida Resident's Seasonal Passport	A $129 C $109	Break-even on Day 3 of stay	Unlimited admission to three parks for 272 days of value seasons throughout the year Seasonal resort discounts up to 50% Allows park hopping Limited use of WDW transportation	Florida residency required Not valid on holidays or during busier seasons Additional attractions: unlimited yearly admission add-ons available Add-ons available	The best value for Floridians Get this pass, go during off season, have a great time, and SAVE!

Length of Stay Pass	A / C		Includes admission to all Disney attractions (Typhoon Lagoon, Discovery Island, River Country, Pleasure Island, Blizzard Beach) Allows park hopping Additional days available Valid until midnight of last day of stay	Available only to Disney resort guests Not available to guests of the Swan or the Dolphin or at Hotel Plaza Hotel/Resorts	Cost-effective only if you use admission to additional attractions Get this pass and do everything!
1-Night/2-Day	$88/70				
2-Night/3Day	$129/102				
3-Night/4-Day	$167/154				
	$41.75/38.50				
4-Night/5-Day	$194/173				
	$38.80/34.60				
5Night/6-Day	$218/173				
	$36.33/29				
6-Night/7-Day	$242/192				
	$34.57/27.40				
7-Night/8-Day	$260/207				
	$32.50/25.90				

combinations and their list prices. To get your booklet, call the Walt Disney World Travel Company at (800) 828-0228.

Walt Disney World Travel Company is not the only source of vacation packages. A growing number of companies deal in Disney vacation packages. What they offer and how much they charge vary greatly. Armed with the Walt Disney World Travel Company basic price booklet, you will be ready to shop around and select a package that is priced right.

ᏚOURCES FOR DISNEY VACATION PACKAGES

- WDW Central Reservations Office (CRO): (407) W-DISNEY (934-7639)
- Walt Disney World Travel Company: (800) 828-0228
- The Magic Kingdom Club: (407) 824-2600
- American Automobile Association: call your local AAA travel agent
- Delta Airlines Dream Vacations: (800) 872-7786
- AT&T True Rewards: (800) 298-5061
- American Express: (407) 827-7200
- Your local travel agent

Three Types of Package Vacations

There are three basic types of resort packages: Classic, Deluxe, and the Grand Plan. The Classic package is the most basic. It offers room accommodations, passes to all Disney attractions, one character breakfast per person, and limited use of recreational activities such as canoes and bicycles. A five-night Classic package for two at the Yacht or the Beach Clubs would cost $1,970.

To the basic features of the Classic, both the Deluxe and Grand Plan packages add such a host of amenities that further expenses may simply not be necessary. The Deluxe package ♥♥♥ includes accommodations at any of the premium resorts for three or more nights, passes to all Disney attractions, three meals daily in any of more than 70 Disney restaurants (including nearly all of our favorites), use of all Walt Disney World recreational facilities (including unlimited golf and tennis), and a private portrait session with Mickey. Also a part of this plan is free use of the Wonders of Walt Disney World, a children's educational program for juniors (ages 10–15 years).

A five-night Deluxe vacation package at the Yacht or the Beach Clubs would cost around $2,800 for two. The same package at the Wilderness Lodge is $2,400.

The Grand Plan ♥♥♥♥ provides an even greater level of luxury and even more features. For about $95 per couple per night above the cost of the Deluxe package, this package adds in-room dining, private tennis and golf lessons, health club use, a video camera to use in the theme parks, six hours each day of baby-sitting services or supervised children's activities, and special room amenities. It also adds Victoria & Albert's to the already impressive list of restaurants.

Either the Deluxe or the Grand Plan packages will give you a sublime Disney experience, during which you would both feel privileged and pampered. Expensive, yes. But, if you can afford it, the experience will be unforgettable.

The following sections describe some specialty vacation packages.

The Golf Getaway

The Golf Getaway package offers resort accommodations, unlimited golf, a complimentary golf clinic, and round-trip transportation to any of the five Disney courses (already offered by the premium resorts). Admission to Disney attractions is not included. Packages begin around $700 per couple for two nights.

The Jolly Holidays

We have found this package to be one of the most attractive, as it is available just prior to the winter holidays, which is an exciting time to visit. The Jolly Holidays package is often an outstanding value and includes a spectacular live dinner show, resort accommodations, and passes to all attractions. Dates for these plans usually run from late November to several days before Christmas.

The Fall Fantasy Package

The period for these three-night packages runs from late August to mid-November. During this time there are a number of fall activities, such as the jazz and art festivals. This plan includes daily breakfast, resort accommodations, and a coupon book, good for $500 in special values. It does not include admission to Disney attractions. Resort discounts can be good.

The Sunshine Getaway

One of Disney's newer seasonal packages, this one is available from January 1 to mid-February and includes accommodations, a character breakfast, and a book of coupons. Theme park tickets are available as an add-on to the package.

Special Event Packages

There are a host of special events every year at Walt Disney World, from the Indy 200 auto race to the Night of Joy Christian Music Celebration. Each offers its own package. Other events include the Disney/Oldsmobile Golf Classic, the annual Sci-Fi Convention, the Walt Disney World Marathon, and the Disneyana Convention. For details and dates, call Disney Central Reservations at (407) 934-7639.

In addition, here are some possibilities to further customize your package:

Add the Food 'n Fun Plan

Adding this feature gives each of you two meals a day at select Disney restaurants. There is no spending limit, and gratuities and tax are included. The "fun" comes from being able to indulge yourselves in the use of select forms of recreational activities. Zip around the lake in your own watersprite, enjoy a lazy cruise in a canopy boat, or go horseback riding.

This option is available only with a package plan. Food 'n Fun will add about $60 per day per person and about $17 per day for children 3 to 9 years of age.

We were once great lovers of this plan, but recent cutbacks have dampened our enthusiasm for it. The number of restaurants has been reduced, and many are only options for breakfast or lunch. While the recreational side of this pass has not suffered as much, Food 'n Fun is no longer the outstanding deal that it once was.

Upgrade Your Package to a Suite or Concierge Service   We have been told countless times by Central reservationists that a package cannot be applied to a suite or to a concierge room. Like other things in life, it depends on who you talk to. To begin with, a package can only be upgraded to a suite by the "suite people," and they will not speak to you. These folks only deal with a certain branch of Central Reservations called Disney Special Programs at (407) 824-7200. All you have to do is to call this number and explain that you want to reserve a package and that you want it in a specific suite or that you'd like it upgraded to concierge.

Are Packages a Bargain?

The first question to ask yourselves about vacation packages is: "Can we do better by ourselves?" This can usually be answered by adding up the features of a package plan and comparing the total to what you are able to get on your own. Generally, most Classic packages seem to save a small amount of money over the same features purchased separately. If you have managed a particularly good deal on a resort room, however, you may find that no package can compete with it.

The all-inclusive packages are, most certainly, expensive. They do, however, provide a special and lavish way to experience the magic of Walt Disney World. Either the Grand Plan or the Deluxe package would be just the thing for a special romantic getaway or anniversary. One of the less-tangible pluses of an all-inclusive package is the carefree and relaxed feeling it provides.

What makes a package worthwhile economically is making use of all it has to offer. The more you use the recreational features of the classic package, the more worthwhile it becomes. The same can be said for either the Deluxe or Grand Plan packages or any of the specialty packages. None of these packages are economical unless you make good use of all their features.

The Romantic Family Trip

If having children meant the end to romance for married couples, then everyone would be an only child. We hope that if you have children, romance is alive and well in your lives. If it isn't, may this be your wake-up call. With a bit of planning, you will be able to visit Walt Disney World as a family and still have romantic moments for just the two of you.

Making a family trip to Disney World is a large undertaking, one that will take even more planning than a visit for two. It will be more expensive, and there will be a greater number of logistical concerns, especially if you are traveling with very young children or an infant. Consider, though, that it's a free ride for kids under 3 years of age at Disney World. No admission tickets are necessary, they do not count as people in resort rooms, and they eat for free at buffet meals.

Walt Disney World has been imagineered with families in mind. When it comes to meeting the needs of a family, the facilities are nearly limitless.

Making Plans: When to Go

The best time to visit Walt Disney World is during the off season. Unfortunately, this means while schools are in session. Yes, we are suggesting that you take the kids out of school for your Disney vacation.

Fall is the perfect time for Walt Disney World. It is still early in the school year and it should be an easy time to arrange a short absence. Off season is also the value season. Hotel rates, packages, and admission tickets are all available at discounted rates. While people are still at the parks, they will be significantly fewer in number. You will see much more, do much more, have a more relaxed time of it, and spend less money. Need we say more?

Accommodations: An Even Bigger Decision for a Family

For us, staying off property with children is even less appealing than doing it by ourselves. There's a lot of travel, a host of logistics, and a lot of lost time. It's a lot easier to get the kids back to a Disney resort for an afternoon of rest than it is to get them back to a motel on Highway 192.

Along with the choice of off property or on, you will be faced with the decision of how to accommodate all of you. There are more options than you think.

One Room, One Family   Sharing a room with your family will not make having a romantic time impossible, it simply makes things more of a challenge. Getting a room in a Disney resort is expensive enough. Getting two may be a fatal blow to an already stretched budget. While we cannot speak for accommodations outside of Disney World, we can tell you that children younger than 17 stay for free at all Disney resorts. Standard resort rooms feature two large beds, and cribs are available at every Disney resort at no extra cost.

Most Disney resorts permit a maximum of four people in each room. The Wilderness Lodge, besides its standard room with two queens, has a number of rooms with one queen bed and a set of bunk beds, which is a more interesting option for a family of four. Many of the premium resorts allow five. This is usually managed with two queen beds and a daybed/sofa. One moderate resort features accommodations for five. A trundle bed comes standard at Dixie Landings, but only in the non-king rooms of Alligator Bayou. If you have a family larger than five, you'll have to do something besides share a standard resort room.

One Family, Two Rooms   Two rooms is another way to go. All Disney resorts offer connecting rooms, and some feature a room with two beds connected to a room with one king-size bed. This sounds to us like the perfect layout for a small family. If you are considering sharing a room at one of the premium resorts, we would suggest that, for about the same expense, you get two rooms at one of the more moderately priced resorts, such as Port Orleans or the Caribbean Beach.

A Suite for a Family   Suites offer yet another route to accommodate a family. Virtually all of the premium resorts offer a selection of suites, some with as many connecting rooms as you might care to add. While these can be the perfect place for a family, they can be very expensive.

Family-Sized Accommodations   Special family accommodations are yet another great option. For about the cost of a room at the Yacht and the Beach Clubs, you could get a one-bedroom villa at the Vacation Club. Here you would have your own king-size master bedroom with an oversized private Jacuzzi, a large living room with a fold-out queen bed and sofa, a full kitchen, bath, dining area, balcony or porch, and even a laundry room. And these places are simply luxurious. For an additional amount, a second room with two queen beds and a bath could be added.

The Village at the Institute also offers a variety of family accommodations. The Treehouse Villas or Fairway Villas can each sleep six in luxurious and woodsy surroundings for under $400 nightly. Deep discounts are available off season, some reducing the prices to that of a single premium resort room. Maids come in to clean and even do your dishes. Now that's a vacation.

On the budget end of the spectrum is a Wilderness Home at Fort Wilderness. Here you could enjoy a double bed for yourselves in your own room and bunks for the kids. The Wilderness Homes also enjoy maid service. Again, your dishes will be taken care of. Pretty nice for traveling on a budget.

Family Necessities

If you have an infant, bring all the baby supplies that you might need. Though widely available at Disney, choices are limited and prices are high. We would also suggest bringing snacks and drinks for the kids. Boxed juice drinks and refillable plastic drink cups with straws will come in handy too. And, if you are able, bring your own folding stroller. While these are easily and inexpensively rentable at the theme parks, you will frequently find yourselves standing in line to get one. Besides, a stroller will come in handy at your resort and while shopping at the Village Marketplace. Be sure to mark it with your name and your resort.

Preparing the Kids

When our kids were young, we took them to Walt Disney World as a surprise. "Let's go out for donuts," we told them as we dragged them out of bed at 6 A.M. All the way to the front gate (it was 120 miles), we pretended that we had no intention of actually going in. We just want to *look* at it, we told them. Meanwhile the kids whined and cried. By the time that we'd gotten our tickets, they were beginning to smell a rat. Or at least, a Mouse.

This was certainly a memorable adventure but, in reality, none of us were prepared for our visit, and pandemonium reigned supreme. We suggest that you do a few simple things to prepare your children for the kind of visit to Walt Disney World that you wish to make. Get them set to enjoy spending some leisure time at the resort and, if you plan to take advantage of the many and varied children's activities, you might prime them for these. We are sure that you know just how to do it.

You might also ask Central Reservations what attractions will be closed (in rehab, as insiders say) during your visit. Better to head off expectations now than later.

Setting Your Pace

Let your family know that this visit will not include spending every waking moment trying to cram in one more attraction. You'll spend plenty of time in the theme parks but you'll also take time to relax around the pool and to explore other areas of Walt Disney World. Take them for a boat ride or explore Discovery Island. Try to keep to your child's regular schedule. If naps are the rule at home, then they should be at Disney too. Try to eat and snack at the normal times also.

Logistical Concerns

If you have children, you know what an art it is to travel with them. We always enjoyed finding ways to make travel with our kids easier and more fun. When our children were younger, we traveled so much that they were in correspondence school, but that's another story.

Disney World is built to accommodate families, so you should find facilities for almost every situation. Each of the three theme parks has a baby-care center where you will find facilities for heating formula, rocking chairs for breast feeding, and a large assortment of expensive baby supplies. Diaper-changing stations are available in both men's and women's restrooms throughout Walt Disney World.

Getting Some Time Alone Together

Being here in "The Happiest Place on Earth" will be paradise for you and your family. There are lots of things to do here together, and there should be no shortage of time to enjoy each others' company. We have always found that being here with our kids somehow made us feel even more like a family. Having this kind of fun together is something that none of you will ever forget. A Disney vacation will bring you nearer to your children and it will make you, as a couple, feel closer. If this isn't romance, we don't know what is.

Still, having time together is both natural and healthy for a couple in love. You may wish to spend an evening together, perhaps have a romantic dinner and go out for some grown-up entertainment. No problem. Depending on the age of your children, there are a number of alternatives.

If you are traveling with an infant or very young children, KinderCare, Disney's sitting-service, will be your best alternative for an afternoon or evening out. With older children, the options increase to include activities ranging from Disney activity centers to educational programs.

KinderCare   This service provides in-room baby-sitting. These trained sitters will show up with toys and games to entertain your kids. Since this is done in your resort room, your children will feel more "at home." While these sitters are not permitted to take your kids on any Disney transportation, they are allowed to walk them around your resort or to a nearby restaurant.

Reservations should be made at least 24 hours in advance. Cost is $9 per hour for one child, $10 for two, and $11 for three. Charges for four or more children will be dependent on their ages. If you have a sitter for eight hours or more, you will be required to provide a meal. For information or to make arrangements ahead of time, call KinderCare at (407) 827-5444.

Disney Children's Activities Centers   If your child is at least 3 years old and potty-trained, then one of these "clubs" will be your best bet. Each will provide your child with a memorable evening of entertainment and his or her very own Disney experience. There are five such centers for the children of Disney resort guests. We have heard many wonderful things about these centers and can tell you, first hand, that children love them—ours did, during our visit to the Polynesian years ago. For more information or to make reservations at the Disney clubs, call (407) WDW-DINE (939-3463).

In addition to Disney kid's clubs, both the Swan and the Dolphin offer children's activity clubs, and there is a children's center at the Hilton Resort at Hotel Plaza as well. Because all of these clubs are very busy, we recommend that you make your reservations in advance.

The Neverland Club   The Neverland Club at the Polynesian is open nightly from 5 P.M. to midnight and features a dinner buffet from 6 to 8 P.M. Foods usually include chicken strips, pizza, hot dogs, and ice cream. Activities include a live animal show from Discovery Island, video games, films, and a picture with Goofy. $8 per hour per child with a three-hour minimum. This imaginative Peter Pan experience begins with a trip through an open window out of Wendy's bedroom and into Neverland—fun and memorable.

The Cub's Den   The Cub's Den at the Wilderness Lodge also offers a buffet dinner. The cost here, though, is only $6 per child per hour and includes a Discovery Island animal show, video, games, and movies. The menu usually includes hamburgers, hot dogs, pizza, macaroni and cheese, corn on the cob, and peanut-butter-and-jelly sandwiches. Hours are 5 P.M. to midnight, with dinner from 5:30 to 7:30 P.M. Open to guests of all Disney resorts, this western-themed adventure is great for boys and girls.

The Sandcastle Club   This children's center is located at the Beach Club and is available to guests at the Yacht and the Beach Clubs; it is also free to anyone dining at Ariel's. While the Sandcastle Club does not include a buffet, it has plenty for kids to do. Computers, video games, a large library, and arts and crafts are a few of the offerings here. Hours are 4:30 P.M. to midnight and cost is $4 per hour per child. Meal arrangements must be made through room service if your child is visiting during mealtime or for more than four hours.

The Mouseketeer Clubhouses   There are two Mouseketeer Club-houses: one at the Contemporary and the other at the Grand Floridian. At $4 per child per hour, these activity centers do not offer as much as either the Cub's Den or the Neverland Club and have facilities for far fewer children. While the clubhouse at the Contemporary is open to all Disney resort guests, the one at the Grand Floridian is available only to its guests. Reservations are strongly suggested and may be arranged through the Mouseketeer Clubhouses at (407) 934-6290.

Camp Dolphin and Camp Swan   Camp Dolphin is a special recre-ational program for children 3 to 12 years of age and available only to guests of either the Swan or the Dolphin. This "camp" is open from 2 to 5 P.M. and again from 6 to 10 P.M. with a dinner program. Regular hours cost $6.50. Memberships are available that reduce this hourly cost by half. Extended hours are available with a week's notice and cost around $8 per child per hour. Camp Swan is open from 4 P.M. to mid-night. It is for children 3 through 12 years of age. Arts and crafts, music, and T-shirt painting are a few of the many activities. For in-formation regarding these clubs, speak to each resort's reservations department.

Special Activities for Children

A number of special programs are also available for youngsters that are educational as well as entertaining. Some of these activities will take your children behind the scenes at Walt Disney World, while others will involve them in environmental studies at Epcot. Since these pro-grams are subject to continual updates, we suggest that you inquire about new programs as well as changes.

- The Chip and Dale Rescue Rangers Discovery Island Kidventure is available Sundays and Wednesdays for kids 8 to 14 years of age. This four-hour exploration of Discovery Island includes lunch, arts and crafts materials, and a souvenir photo. Cost is $32 per child or $25 for children of Disney resort guests. For information and reser-vations, call (407) 824-3784.

- The Wonders of Walt Disney World Educational Programs are six-hour programs available to individual children ages 10 through 15 for around $80. While these are expensive, they provide park admission, lunch, and a remarkably interesting educational adventure. There are several different themes, from wildlife and ecology to show business and art. These "seminars" are available to the general public. For information, call (407) 354-1855.
- Night Under the Sea is a slumber party at the Living Seas Pavilion at Epcot. Offered to children 7 to 11 years old, this provides an unforgettable overnight experience. The program includes an evening at Epcot, IllumiNations, and a character breakfast at the Coral Reef restaurant. Kids even get to keep their sleeping bags. At $120, this party is pretty expensive. There is a $24 discount for American Express cardholders. For information and reservations, call (407) 939-8687.

OUR RECOMMENDATIONS FOR ROMANCING WITH KIDS

- Take your vacation during the off season. It will be cheaper and more relaxing.
- Thoroughly explore the possibilities of getting your own room or your own bedroom. It will make a big difference.
- Keep your pace a relaxed one. Don't wear yourselves out. Spend time at your resort. The kids will play happily in the pool and not get cranky and overtired. Same for you.
- It is important that both of you share the chores involved in taking care of your children. It's no fun for one person to be stuck with all of the work while everyone else is vacationing.
- Make use of Disney's children's activity centers to take an evening off for yourselves. Wine, dine, and enjoy yourselves while the kids are having their own Disney adventure.
- Try a family activity such as bike riding or boating. Do something special together.

Making Your Resort Reservations

There are over 700 cast members at the Disney Central Reservations Office (CRO) taking an incredible 20,000 reservations daily. The special rates and least-expensive rooms are the first to go, so we suggest that you have plan A, plan B, and even a plan C in the event that your choice is not available. Here are the numbers to call:

Disney Central Reservations (CRO)   (407) W-DISNEY (934-7639)
- Open 8 A.M. to midnight, every day
- Handles reservations for resort rooms and vacation packages

For suites and concierge service rooms   (407) 824-7200

Magic Kingdom Club   (407) 824-2600
- Open 8 A.M. to midnight, every day

Magic Kingdom Gold Card   (800) 446-5365
- Open 8 A.M. to midnight, every day

Walt Disney World Travel Company   (407) 828-3232

Annual Passport and Florida Resident's Seasonal Passport
(407) 827-7200

Before you make your call, here are some things to think about beforehand:

- Views: A variety of views are available in all of the Disney resorts. Selecting one of these will be part of making your reservations.
- Types of beds: Most resort rooms come with two queen beds or two doubles, but as we have mentioned earlier, there are a number of king-size beds available at most of the Disney resorts. This is the time to reserve one of these if that is your choice. Making a king-size bed reservation usually means that the view cannot be guaranteed. However, you can still request a view and, when you check in, request it again.
- Room location: In our guide to the Disney resorts in Chapter 2, we describe the various choices of room locations. If you have a preference for a certain location, you should make this request when you reserve your resort room. Although no guarantee can be made, a mention of this will be attached to your reservation.
- Smoking or nonsmoking room: Be sure to mention your preference when making your call.
- Connecting rooms: If you are bringing your children along, consider a room that connects to your own. Disney reservations can guarantee connecting rooms.

- Discounts or specials: Always ask about specials or promotions when you make your reservations.
- Dinner show reservations: If you're planning on a dinner show, you should make reservations at this time.
- Special comments: If this is your honeymoon or anniversary, be sure to tell your reservationist. This will come up when you check in, and virtually all Disney resorts will do something—usually a card, a rose, and a split of champagne.

Making Reservations

You will probably want to begin your reservation odyssey by simply gathering the most current information. Once you get a Disney reservationist on the telephone, you will immediately discover that the system is designed to make reservations, not to dispense information. The very first thing that you will be asked for is a date. If you are simply shopping for prices and have no date, pick any date during value season to get those prices or any date during regular season to compare prices.

RESERVATION TIPS

- Make your reservations in the morning, around 10 A.M. For some reason, resort availability seems best at this time.
- Keep trying if at first you are unable to get what you really want. There are plenty of cancellations that produce more available rooms.
- A CRO reservationist can act as your intermediary in reserving a suite. Simply call and spell out what you want. There will be some communicating back and forth, but eventually you'll get what you want. Suite availability is usually good.
- Reservations that begin with a value season rate maintain that rate for the entire visit. The lower rate remains good as long as you wish to stay, up to the maximum reservation limit of 30 days. Since some value season discounts can be as much as 50%, simply arriving a day earlier can pay for several nights of your holiday visit.

What to Bring with You

Don't forget a liberal amount of sun screen with a minimum SPF of 15 or higher for the summer. The Florida sun can burn you even on an overcast day. We recommend not only that you bring sunscreen but that you use it, too.

Be sure that you have a handful of dollar bills for tipping, especially if you are staying in one of the premium resorts.

You can always bring your own snacks, liquor, or wine. Ice machines are convenient to all rooms, and an ice bucket and glasses are standard furnishings.

If you are interested in having some of your favorite music in your room, you might want to bring a small portable stereo. It might be just the thing for creating that special mood.

Available Items in Disney Resorts

Housekeeping will be happy to provide you with an assortment of items. Available at every resort, for no charge, will be extra pillows, blankets, iron and ironing board, and hair dryer.

If you need a refrigerator in your room, whether for pleasure or medical reasons, you should know that some resorts charge $5 per day for them and some do not. A limited number of microwave ovens are available at the Grand Floridian. Coffeemakers are standard at the Caribbean Beach and come with some of the rooms and suites at the Dolphin and most concierge rooms elsewhere.

Some of the premium resort rooms have minibutlers. These small refrigerators are stocked with wines, liquors, soft drinks, candy, and snacks. The selection is impressive. So are the prices.

Each Disney resort has a "general store" section in one of its shops. In this area, you will find sunblock, magazines and newspapers, film, insect repellent, Band-Aids, and a whole gamut of items dealing with everything from a headache to the munchies.

Your First Day at Walt Disney World

On your first day, you'll need to make arrangements to get to your resort. If you are arriving by automobile, you will be delighted to know that the roadways are well marked. Once on property, you will find that Walt Disney World has its own system of road signs. They are large and easy to read.

If you are staying in a Disney resort, all that you really need to know is which resort area your resort belongs to. Simply follow the

Magic Kingdom Resort Area

Florida highway signs to the exit for that area and then follow the red and purple Disney signs to your resort.

If you are flying or taking the train into Orlando, you may be surprised to learn that Disney World is not there. It is 20 miles south, near Lake Buena Vista. Fear not. An entire industry has evolved solely to transport guests from the airport or train station to Disney. You will find a variety of cabs, limousines, and van services that will take you directly to your resort (or not so directly, if that is your wish). Several transportation options are available.

Florida Town Cars is a service that has many repeat users. With a fleet of Lincoln town cars, this company provides a personalized option for getting to the Disney resorts from either the Orlando airport or the Amtrak station. All you have to do is to make arrangements via a toll-free number, and you will be met at the gate by a friendly driver holding a sign with your name on it (we've always wanted to do that). Round-trip fare for five persons or less is $67. You are promised the same driver on both ends of your vacation. We have heard glowing reports of this company. Arrangements and inquiries should be directed to Florida Town Cars at (800) 525-7246. Town car service seems particularly personal and even a bit romantic.

Mears is the other company providing a similar service and offers both van and town car service. Van service (round-trip) is $23 for each adult and $17 for each child. Arrangements should be made in advance with Mears at (800) 759-5219. A Mears booth can be found at the Orlando International Airport on the second level. Passengers may make arrangements upon arrival at this kiosk. Because this service is used by the Walt Disney World Travel Company for its packages, lines here can get long.

Cab fare from either the Orlando train station or airport to a Disney resort is $40 each way, making the round-trip fare no bargain.

Getting Your Own Wheels

A rental car is yet another option for transportation between airport and resort. Of course, you will be paying for the car every day that you keep it. Rental car rates vary greatly during the course of the year, from company to company, and with special deals and packages. A midsized car for one week at $120 may be twice that at another time of year.

So, is having a car while you are at Walt Disney World a good idea? This is a tough question to answer simply. If you are able to find your way around easily, then it might be a convenience to drive from your resort to other resorts, to play golf, or to go to the Village Marketplace—which are all easily reachable via Disney transportation.

Arriving at Your Disney Resort

If you are staying in a Disney resort, check-in time is 3 P.M. If you are arriving earlier than this, you will be entitled to preregister, which means that you will be able to check into your resort but you will not get your room until it is ready, sometime later in the day. During the slower times of year, we have frequently found that we could arrive early in the morning and move right into our room. This, of course, is subject to chance availability. Preregistration, however, can be done as early as 8 A.M.

As part of preregistration, you will be able to check your baggage for storage. You will also receive your resort ID cards, which will immediately enable you to charge things to your room.

If you are staying in one of the hotels or resorts outside of Disney World, what happens to you when you arrive is bound to vary considerably. Check-in times differ from one hotel or motel to the next, so be sure that you have worked out, in advance, all of the details.

Special Requests and Last-Minute Changes

If you were unable to reserve the room that you had wanted, this may be a good time to remedy that situation. When you check in, remember to ask for what might not have been available earlier. While there is no guarantee, cancellations and last-minute changes may pay off.

Your Last Day at Walt Disney World

It seems cruel to have to think about this before you even arrive at Disney, but your last day, like your first, demands a few considerations. Check-out time at Disney resorts is 11 A.M. If you plan to leave Disney World before that time, no problem. Simply get packed up and depart. Give yourselves an hour to get to the airport from your room (add a little longer during a holiday). If you are returning to the train station or to the airport, the process is pretty much the same as arriving.

If you are departing later in the day, early check-out will mean that you will have to vacate your room no later than 11 A.M. Again, you will be able to place your luggage in storage until you actually leave. Your resort ID cards and Length of Stay Passes will be good until midnight of your last day, so you will be able to carry on with your Disney adventures.

Late Check-Out

Disney resorts are usually able to grant a 1 P.M. check-out each day for a limited number of rooms. These two extra hours can make a big difference. If you want late check-out, call the front desk at your resort on your last night to see what that resort's policy is.

Some Things You Might Need to Know

A Few Tips on Gratuities

For some reason, tipping situations tend to make both tipper and tippee uncomfortable. However, knowing when to tip and what amount is appropriate should alleviate the awkwardness.

- Cab, limo, town car drivers: 15%
- Valet parking: $1 to $2
- Bellpersons: $.50 to $1 per bag
- Housekeeping, maid service: $1 to $2 per day
- Room service: 15% included in bill, add more as desired
- Housekeeping, delivery: $1
- Table-service restaurants: 15%–20%
- Cocktail service: 15%–20%

Banking Around Walt Disney World

Running out of cash at Walt Disney World should pose no problem (as long as you are still solvent). Banking facilities and automated tellers are convenient and numerous.

ATMs are located:

- Near City Hall, Main Street USA, Magic Kingdom
- At entrance to Disney–MGM Studios
- At main entrance to Epcot
- Outside Guest Services at the Village Marketplace
- Outside the Rock 'n Roll Beach Club, Pleasure Island
- At Gooding's Market, Crossroads Plaza (near Hotel Plaza)

Banking facilities can be found at several locations:

- Full-service Sun Bank on Main Street USA, the Magic Kingdom, and on Buena Vista Boulevard, directly opposite the Village Marketplace
- Foreign currency is exchanged at the Guest Services of all three theme parks, at City Hall in the Magic Kingdom, and at Earth Station in Epcot. Also at the Sun Bank on Main Street and the Marketplace and at all Disney resort front desks.
- Disney resort front desks will happily cash personal checks for all resort guests.

Food Shopping

If you are staying in one of the many Disney resorts that offers a kitchen or even if you are simply looking for a place to buy beverages and snacks, you'll probably need a supermarket. While the gourmet Pantry at the Village Marketplace is certainly handy for limited groceries, lots of baked goods, and an outstanding selection of wines, it is expensive. An alternative is not far away: Gooding's Market is a large and modern supermarket located at the Crossroads Shopping Plaza at the end of Hotel Plaza Boulevard. To find it, drive a bit past the Village Marketplace until you come to Hotel Plaza Boulevard. Turn onto it and continue through the intersection at Route 535 and into the shopping plaza. By the way, you're still on Disney property.

$\mathcal{O}$ur Guide to Walt Disney World Resorts

We are always surprised how little we are able to learn about a Disney resort before seeing it for ourselves. For example, learning just how convenient the resort really is to the parks and attractions, the atmosphere of its guest rooms, and where in the resort we should have booked our room are things we would love to know ahead of time. Once we had spent time at a particular resort, the answers to these and other questions became apparent. We learned quickly what is meant by "insider information."

This chapter is an insider's look at the resorts of Walt Disney World, written by a couple who has stayed everywhere seeking out that something special for a memorable and romantic experience.

Services Available to Disney Resort Guests

Certain services are provided by all of the Disney resorts. Note that although they are on Disney property, the Dolphin, the Swan, and all of the hotels at Hotel Plaza are not Walt Disney resorts. Therefore, the following discussion of available services will not apply to these establishments, although they may offer such services. See the following descriptions of each for a list of available services.

Resort ID Cards

When you check into your Disney resort, you will each receive a resort ID card. These cards will be your tickets to unlimited use of the Walt Disney World transportation system and free parking at any of the attractions, and, if guaranteed with a credit card, they will be your Disney credit cards. Your resort cards will allow you to cover your Disney expenses virtually everywhere simply by charging everything right to your room account.

On the morning of your departure, a fully detailed bill can be prepared to give you a complete picture of what you have spent. These cards are valid from check-in or preregistration to midnight on the day of your departure. Everything charged to them after your check-out will appear on a final bill that you will receive in the mail.

The Length of Stay Pass

For Disney resort guests only, this pass provides unlimited admission to all Disney attractions for the exact length of your Disney vacation.

Surprise Mornings

The Surprise Mornings program is a powerful perk that will admit you both to a different theme park each day, 1 1/2 hours before the general public.

Guest Services

This essential service, usually located in the lobby or main building of each resort, will be invaluable in planning and executing your stay at Walt Disney World. You can go to Guest Services to buy tickets or to make your reservations for dinner, tennis, golf, or for entertainment. Guest Services will also be your source of Disney information. Brochures, menus, and schedules for virtually everything are available here. Whether you want to know the time for a parade or ignition time for a fireworks show, your Guest Services should have it all.

Resort Newspaper

Each resort has its own little themed information newspaper that you'll receive at check-in. The Polynesian's paper is the *Island Palm Press* and Dixie Landings' newspaper is called *The Sassagoula Times*. Each paper will give you lots of information about your resort, its restaurants and shops, and its services.

First Aid

Emergency service and in-room health care are available on a 24-hour basis. Guests are responsible for any charges.

Wake-up Service

If you need to be up early, simply press the appropriate button on your room telephone to arrange a wake-up call. You won't believe who is going to make the call.

Additional Services

- Guest messaging system
- Pager rental
- Walt Disney World Foreign Language Center
- Same-day dining reservations by telephone
- Three full-service barber and beauty shops
- Luggage assistance
- Overnight use of Walt Disney World Kennels is available only to Disney resort guests. For information, call (407) 824-6568.
- Package delivery to your resort room from any Disney shop
- Sunday church services held at Luau Cove at the Polynesian
- Children's activities centers and in-room baby-sitting
- Coin-operated laundry and laundry service
- Quality two-hour film developing
- Some banking services available at the front desk of your resort
- Walt Disney World Florist is available to deliver a variety of floral arrangements, food baskets, and wine or champagne to any Disney resort room, including your own; call (407) 827-3505. Send someone you love a rose.

The Resorts by Area

There are seven resort areas at Walt Disney World. Each occupies its own little piece of Disney turf, and each has a unique offering of resorts.

THE MAGIC KINGDOM RESORTS

- The Polynesian
- The Contemporary
- The Grand Floridian
- The Wilderness Lodge
- Shades of Green

It should come as no surprise that all of the Magic Kingdom resorts are near the Magic Kingdom. If you want to be as close as possible to

Cinderella's Castle, than take a careful look at this group. The Grand
Floridian, the Polynesian, and the Contemporary are all right on the famous monorail loop that runs around the Seven Seas Lagoon. Although
they're nearby, neither the Wilderness Lodge nor Shades of Green enjoys
a location on the Seven Seas Lagoon. Shades is located over on the golf
courses near the Polynesian, and the Wilderness Lodge can be found on
Bay Lake, not far from the Contemporary.

THE EPCOT RESORTS

- The Yacht and the Beach Clubs
- The Swan
- The Dolphin
- The Caribbean Beach
- Disney's Boardwalk Resort (opens summer of 1996)

Except for the Caribbean Beach, the Epcot resorts are all premium resorts, and all are adjacent to Epcot and Disney–MGM. Convenience to all
other Disney destinations from these resorts is about as good as it gets.

The Caribbean Beach is a charming, moderately priced resort.
Neither the Swan nor the Dolphin are Disney hotels. The Swan is managed by Westin Hotels and the Dolphin is managed by Sheraton.

THE DISNEY VILLAGE RESORTS

- Port Orleans
- Dixie Landings
- The Vacation Club

The Village resorts are all located on the east side of Walt Disney World,
scattered along the man-made Sassagoula River. They are all convenient
to the two new Disney golf courses as well as to Pleasure Island and the
Village Marketplace.

THE STUDIO RESORTS

- All-Star Sports
- All-Star Music

This area, located in Disney's southwestern area, is near both
Disney–MGM Studios and Blizzard Beach. The Studio resorts are
Disney's entry into the budget market.

THE FORT WILDERNESS CAMPGROUND RESORT

- Fort Wilderness Homes
- Fort Wilderness Campsites

Not to be confused with the Wilderness Lodge, this area is a world of its own. Fort Wilderness has its own beach and a water park called River Country. There are restaurants and even a popular dinner show "out there."

THE DISNEY INSTITUTE AND THE VILLAGE AT THE INSTITUTE

The Disney Institute is nothing like the other Disney resorts and, for this reason, we put it in its very own category. For Disney guests, the Institute offers a brand new type of vacation experience. Along with the Institute, we include the old Disney Village, now known as the Village at the Institute.

THE HOTEL PLAZA RESORTS

- The Grosvenor Resort
- Buena Vista Palace
- The Hilton
- The Hotel Royal Plaza
- Travelodge Hotel
- DoubleTree Guest Suites Resort
- The Marriot Courtyard

These are not Disney resorts. They are, however, well located compared to off-property accommodations, and prices at some of them can be attractive, especially off season.

The Magic Kingdom Resorts

Disney's Polynesian Resort

This lovely "South Seas" type resort was our first experience staying at Walt Disney World. Located along a white sand beach, directly across the lagoon from Cinderella's Castle, "The Poly" enjoys one of the most spectacular views in all of Disney World.

The Polynesian Resort

The atmosphere here has been meticulously imagineered to re-create the magic of Polynesia, Disney-style. The lush grounds are dense with tropical foliage, and the lilting serenades of the South Seas are heard everywhere through a hidden sound system. Coconut palms, banana trees, gardenias, and orchids are but a few of the more than 75 species of tropical plants that make the resort grounds a veritable garden. A stroll at night here will work its powerful and romantic charm on any couple. The flickering light of torches, the lagoon's balmy breezes, and the scents of the flowering foliage all combine to create this potent piece of Polynesia.

The Great Ceremonial House lies at the center of life in Disney's South Seas. It is surrounded by a profusion of exotic plants and fish ponds. Native statues stand sentry at the entrance. Inside, the mingling of Hawaiian music and rushing water set the stage for your Polynesian adventure. Mammoth hewn beams and woven bamboo are the makings of this place, all trimmed carefully with hanging baskets of brightly colored orchids and birds of paradise.

The centerpiece of the Great Ceremonial House is its towering garden of palms, volcanic rock, and splashing water. It reaches to the domed glass ceiling three stories above. The gurgling waterfalls, brilliant blossoms, and verdant foliage produce a sensation that is both cool and soothing. Large wooden ceiling fans spin slowly, and several brightly colored macaws squawk in the branches of a tree.

The Great Ceremonial House is home for this resort's front desk, Guest Services, shops, and several of its restaurants and lounges. "Aloha" is the usual greeting here at the Polynesian, where there is a Hawaiian word for nearly everything. The real theme of this tropical paradise may be best expressed by "Ho'Onanea," which means the passing of time in ease, pleasure, and peace.

The Polynesian's guest rooms are located in the "longhouses" that surround the Great Ceremonial House. With names such as Tonga, Moorea, Bali, and Bora Bora, the longhouses offer not only a variety of locations but also an assortment of accommodations. Some of the buildings are near the Great Ceremonial House, others surround the pools, and still others can be found along the white sand beach of the lagoon. The Bali houses the Polynesian's suites, while Tonga is home to the Royal Polynesian concierge service. Given the lay of the land and the size of this resort, you will find that certain longhouses are closer to some things and farther away from others. But nothing is very far, and walking around the Polynesian is a pleasure.

There are two pools, one standard and one themed. The quiet pool is located in a lovely garden area in the center of the resort complex. The main swimming area is located along the Polynesian's beautiful beach. Nestled amidst dense tropical foliage and bordered by huge rocks and waterfalls, it is lavish and tropical. There is one small water slide, intended for children. This is a fairly small pool, considering both the size of this resort and the fact that most guests come here to swim and play. It and the rooms that surround it get pretty noisy, especially in the evening hours of summer. This pool also features an underwater sound system and a poolside bar.

Rooms at the Polynesian

After the Great Ceremonial House, the lovely guest rooms at the Polynesian should come as no surprise. Each is spacious (409 square feet) and splendidly themed. Fabrics are batiks and tapa cloths of browns and russets. Furnishings are tropical creations of wickers and bamboo. A room at the Poly does not provide a mere hint of tropical paradise but will immerse you in the romance of Polynesia.

Guest rooms each have two queen-size canopy beds and a daybed. None of the standard rooms feature king beds. Each room also has a small table and several handsome wicker chairs. A large tropical armoire hides the television and, along with the closet, provides room enough even for travelers like ourselves, who can never seem to decide what not to bring. The bathroom is comfortable with a large vanity area and shower-tub combination.

There are eleven three-story longhouses. First-floor rooms have patios, third-floor rooms have balconies, and second-floor rooms simply have sliding glass doors that open against wooden railings. Requests for your selection should be made when you reserve your room. Reminding the front desk at check-in should ensure your choice.

Standard rooms overlook the parking areas. There are also the usual variety of garden, water, pool, and lagoon views. Of course, the most expensive views overlook the white sand beach, lagoon, and Cinderella's Castle. If you can afford the difference, you will find the view memorable and romantic. At night, the lights of the monorails make their way around the lagoon and the fireworks explode above Cinderella's Castle. Garden-view rooms are beautiful as well: at night, the torchlit footpaths and dense greenery will positively transport you.

Following are 1996 room rates for the Polynesian.

1996 Room Rates for the Polynesian

Accommodation	Regular Season	Value Season	Holiday Season
Parking lot view	$215	$200	$225
Lagoon View	$305	$285	$315
Pool or Marina View	$280	$265	$290
Garden View	$250	$235	$260
Concierge garden	$325	$305	$335
Concierge lagoon	$380	$360	$395

Royal Polynesian Concierge Service

The Tonga longhouse is home to the Polynesian's concierge service. It is located right on the lagoon, and rooms on that side of the building boast exceptional views. Determined to get a first-hand experience of everything, we happily stayed here in the tropical lap of Polynesian luxury.

Royal Polynesian concierge service provided additional room amenities such as bathrobes, a coffeemaker, a full array of toiletries, and a lovely decorative gift box of Polynesian stationery.

As concierge guests, we relished the use of Tonga's lounge. Amidst the plush Polynesian furnishings, we savored a day-long offering of foods, snacks, beverages, and desserts. Each evening found us sipping cordials, nibbling desserts, and watching the fireworks over the lagoon. Like passengers on a small cruise ship, we were able to chat with other guests, some of whom we had seen at breakfast.

A small but dedicated staff was ready to spring into action for reservations, transportation, and any of our other concerns. We found the Polynesian's concierge service to be romantic and unforgettable—the perfect choice for us or for any other couple in love.

Suites at the Polynesian

The Bali Hai longhouse, located next door to the Great Ceremonial House, accommodates the Polynesian's suites. The Bali Hai is much smaller and more intimate than the other longhouses. It has only two stories and a dozen or so suites.

While all of the suites and rooms at the Bali Hai include concierge service, the concierge lounge is far enough away to make it less than convenient. To accommodate guests of the suites, a continental breakfast from room service is standard. The concierge staff is available, and use of the Tonga's concierge lounge is encouraged.

The smallest and least expensive suite here is not really a suite at all; it is a single oversized room. While considerably larger than the regular resort room, this luxurious accommodation is grand enough to accommodate a comfortable sitting area, a small desk and chair, and a dining table. The bathroom is large and offers a shower-tub and bidet. With either a single king bed or twin queens, this room comes as a garden-view room only. Marina-view versions are available on the lagoon side of the building, but they offer only dual queen-size beds. Garden kings or queens cost around $370 per night. These rooms are exceptionally nice and are on our small list of favorite Disney accommodations. The marina queen version is about $20 more per night and features a waterfront panorama.

The King Kamehameha suite is one of the most lavish in Walt Disney World. This two-level set of rooms commands a panoramic view of the marina area and lagoon. At over $1,000 per night, it is the stuff that dreams are made of. It has a large living room downstairs with a wet bar and enough space for a small wedding reception or party. The upstairs king bedroom is luxurious and perfectly themed. The bathroom features an oversized Jacuzzi tub. By adding adjoining rooms both upstairs and downstairs, this suite could accommodate the largest of families.

Transportation and Convenience

The Polynesian is right on the main monorail loop that runs around the lagoon. The monorail station at the Poly is located on the second floor of the Great Ceremonial House. It is a relatively short walk from most of the longhouses, giving this resort a real convenience to the Magic Kingdom and the other resorts around the lagoon. A boat also runs from the Magic Kingdom to the Grand Floridian and then to the Polynesian and back to the Magic Kingdom. From the longhouses along the lagoon, getting to the Magic Kingdom by boat is especially pleasant and convenient.

If you are guests at either Moorea or Pago Pago (pronounced Pongo-Pongo), you might find that the short walk from your longhouse to the ferryboat landing or monorail station at the Ticket and Transportation Center (TTC) may provide more convenient travel to the Magic Kingdom. Other Disney destinations are reachable by bus from a bus stop near the main entrance of the Great Ceremonial House. We found bus service to be quite good.

- To the Magic Kingdom: monorail, boat from dock, or ferry from TTC
- To Epcot: monorail with transfer at TTC to Epcot monorail
- To Discovery Island, River Country: boat from the Magic Kingdom
- To Disney–MGM Studios, Blizzard Beach: direct bus
- To Village Marketplace, Pleasure Island, Typhoon Lagoon: 8 A.M. to 4 P.M., by bus to TTC and transfer; after 4 P.M., by direct bus

Dining at the Polynesian

With five restaurants in the Polynesian and the many others at nearby resorts along the monorail, your dining options are considerable. Guests enjoy three table-service eateries and two snack bars. There's even a dinner show, called the Polynesian Luau. 'Ohana at Papeete Bay offers a character breakfast and Disney-style Polynesian dinner show and buffet. There's also the Tangaroa Terrace, a pleasant table-service restaurant that features buffet and a la carte offerings and serves breakfast and dinner. The Polynesian has an all-purpose restaurant, the Coral Isle Cafe. Serving three meals daily, its menu has a definite Polynesian accent. For in-room dining, 24-hour room service is available. No resort would be complete without some sort of fast-food offering, and at the Poly it's Captain Cook's Snack Isle. It's open 24 hours.

For reviews and more information about the table-service restaurants and dinner shows at the Polynesian Resort, see Chapter 6.

Lounges at the Polynesian

There are two tropical lounges at the Polynesian: the Tambu Lounge and the Barefoot Bar. Both offer a tantalizing selection of specialty drinks. The Tambu Lounge, which adjoins 'Ohana, has been recently redesigned. Appetizers are from the firepit of 'Ohana. The Barefoot Bar is the Polynesian's poolside bar.

Shops at the Polynesian

Trader Jack's is located on the second floor of the Great Ceremonial House. It offers character merchandise, toys, gifts, films, postcards, and Polynesian logo items. The Grog Hut is right next door, featuring an assortment of beers, wines, liquors, sundries, and snacks. There is an excellent selection of clothing shops on the ground floor of the central building. Whether you are looking for something special for yourselves or for a gift to bring home, these places definitely have nice stuff. Kanaka Kids, Robinson Crusoe, Esq., and the Polynesian Princess all make for interesting browsing.

Recreational Activities at the Polynesian

- Two heated swimming pools
- Watercraft rentals
- Evening fireworks cruise
- Moana Mickey's Video Arcade
- The Neverland Club children's activity center and dinner club
- 1.5-mile jogging and walking path

OUR IMPRESSIONS OF THE POLYNESIAN

- A beautifully themed resort, with rooms that are some of the best in Disney World. This is a first-class place to stay. We found it romantic and memorable. The Polynesian's motto is "Aita Peatea": there will be another day tomorrow just like today.
- All in all, convenience to the Magic Kingdom is good to very good; convenience to other Disney destinations is average. Consider using the boat to travel to the Magic Kingdom, especially if you are staying in one of the longhouses near the dock.
- The main pool is small. There is no hot tub at the Poly, which is a real shortcoming for us. The quiet pool seems a sensible alternative to the noisy central area. A major rehab planned for both pools will include several hot tubs. The timetable for this is, as yet, uncertain.

RECOMMENDATIONS FOR RESERVATIONS

- Pool-view rooms are considerably noisier than other rooms. Try a quiet pool-view room, if you must.

ROMANCE AT THE POLYNESIAN

- The rooms at the Polynesian: ♥♥♥
- Royal Polynesian concierge service or garden king room at the Bali: ♥♥♥♥

- Breakfast in bed: ♥♥♥♥
- Breakfast on your balcony or patio: ♥♥♥
- Dining at the King's Table at 'Ohana at Papeete Bay: ♥
- Strolling around the grounds after dark; exploring; sitting in the comfortable two-person swings along the beach: ♥♥♥
- Viewing the Electric Water Pageant or fireworks from Sunset Point, a small grassy area along the beach near the Oahu longhouse: ♥♥♥
- Fireworks cruise for two, available at the marina: ♥♥♥
- Renting a boat and taking a cruise: ♥♥

The Contemporary Resort

The Contemporary was Disney World's first hotel. It is an impressive display of the imagination and vision of the Man himself, Walt Disney. There's more than just a little excitement to this place. The monorails streak back and forth through the colossal lobby. Each train is filled with awed visitors, whose faces are pressed to the windows as the train glides through. The Contemporary is a marvel of steel, glass, and concrete. It is itself a Disney icon.

This may be Disney's oldest resort, but it is no dowager. Seeming as new as the day it was created, this resort keeps a firm grip on its first-rate status. The Contemporary offers a variety of spacious rooms and suites and a complete package of resort amenities. These, and its unequaled proximity to the happiest place on planet Earth, are what this exciting place is all about.

The resort's main building is the Tower. Adjacent to it are two newer additions called the Garden Wings. Each wing lies along the north and south sides of the Tower building. The ambience at the Contemporary is definitely modern. It is fast-paced and high-energy. In the 1960s, the Contemporary was the forefront of architectural innovation. Thirty years later, it has lost only some of its distinction, as the rest of the architectural world has been playing catch-up. The Contemporary is still an impressive site on the Disney horizon.

The Tower building is an enormous 15-story, A-frame structure. Its atrium-style lobby is the Grand Canyon Concourse. Tiers of guest rooms hang suspended from its sides. The ends of the building are large, open expanses of glass. Within them is an entire world of restaurants, shops, and lounges. A dazzling mosaic leaps hundreds of feet from floor to ceiling.

The Contemporary Resort

Rooms at the Contemporary

The rooms at the Contemporary, at 422 square feet, are some of the largest standard rooms at Disney. Compare them to the All-Star's 260 square feet. Each room is light, airy, and spacious. The decor is modern with a color scheme of beige trimmed with black. The bedspreads are light, with a splash of brightly colored, confetti-like patterns. There is a large, Danish modern armoire with plenty of drawer space and a television. The vanity area is large and has a single sink. The bathroom features the usual shower-tub. While well appointed and comfortable, the rooms lack the charm and fantasy that are so present at other Disney resorts.

All of the rooms in the Tower have balconies; none of the standard rooms in the Garden Wings do. Rooms in the Tower building face either the Magic Kingdom or Bay Lake with views that range from very good to astounding. Furnished with several chairs and a small table, balconies in the Tower are large and comfortable. Our room was located on the twelfth floor overlooking the Magic Kingdom. After dark, the view was spectacular. Tower rooms with panoramas of the Magic Kingdom are the most requested at the Contemporary. So, if this is your wish, reserve early.

Guest rooms in the Garden Wings have views of the parking areas, the garden, or the lake. Because the buildings are only three stories tall, the views, though pleasant, are much less dramatic than those in the Tower. The Garden Wings are not as convenient or as centrally located as the Tower, but you might enjoy a certain tranquility that you won't find in the hubbub of the Grand Canyon Concourse.

Most rooms at the Contemporary offer the usual two queen beds and a daybed/sofa. There are only 33 rooms with king beds, counting both the Tower and Garden Wings, and many of these are suites. The rooms at the Contemporary do not have minibutlers.

Following are the 1996 room rates for the Contemporary.

1996 Room Rates for Disney's Contemporary

Accommodation	Regular Season	Value Season	Holiday Season
Garden Wing, standard	$215	$210	$220
Garden Wing, garden or lake	$245	$220	$255
Tower rooms	$290	$270	$300

Concierge Service and Suites at the Contemporary

The fourteenth floor is reserved for concierge guests and access to it is limited. Needless to say, the view from these 33 luxurious rooms is "Top of the World." The concierge lounge is plush and comfortable. The day's offerings include continental breakfast, midday snacks, afternoon hors d'oeuvres and champagne, and evening cordials. Turndown service in concierge is standard. There are complimentary VCRs with an assortment of Disney movies, and guests will enjoy private check-in and check-out as well as use of the resort's health club.

The concierge floor of the Contemporary offers only an assortment of suites, and the simplest begins at $850 nightly. There are two Presidential suites. One of these offers a spacious king bedroom with a Jacuzzi bath. This is the only room with a whirlpool tub at the Contemporary. With wet bar, desk, dining table, sofa and chairs, three bathrooms, and two oversized balconies, this suite costs more than $1,000 nightly. Oh, but what a night! More than once, an Arab prince and his entourage have occupied all of the rooms on this floor.

There are also an assortment of suites in the Garden Wing. Because there is no concierge service in this area, these rooms, as you would expect, are less expensive. The Junior suite, at just under $300, is large and can be had with either a king bed or two queens. Either comes with a daybed and parlor area with sofa and chairs. These are corner rooms, which make for a splendid view and an interesting layout.

The Deluxe suites are the only rooms in the Garden Wing that have balconies, and each one has two. With 1,313 square feet, you will certainly not feel cramped in this luxurious set of rooms. A large bedroom and adjacent parlor room with pull-down bed provide enough space for a family but, at $650, two rooms in the Tower might be preferable.

Transportation and Convenience

With the Contemporary right on the monorail loop, travel to and from the Magic Kingdom is both easy and exciting. Arrivals and departures are from the monorail station on the Tower's fourth floor. Be advised that during peak hours the trip to the Magic Kingdom can take upwards of 20 minutes. There is also a short walking path to the Magic Kingdom. This is a pleasant stroll past some amusing topiary. The walk is especially convenient from the north Garden Wing.

Except for the pleasant monorail ride to Epcot, travel to other Disney destinations is not quite so much fun. It is relatively easy, though. Several areas require transferring buses at the Ticket and Transportation Center (TTC), which can be reached easily from the Contemporary by either monorail or by direct bus.

- To the Magic Kingdom: monorail or a short, pleasant walk
- To Epcot: monorail with transfer at TTC to Epcot monorail
- To Discovery Island, River Country: boat from the dock at the lakeside of resort
- To Disney–MGM Studios, Blizzard Beach: direct bus
- To Village Marketplace, Typhoon Lagoon, Pleasure Island: 8 A.M. to 4 P.M., by bus to TTC transfer; after 4 P.M., by direct bus

Dining at the Contemporary

Dining is outstanding. The resort has four restaurants, and you have many other fine choices around the lagoon. There are three full-service restaurants at the Contemporary as well as 24-hour room service and a fast-food eatery. The California Grill is one of our favorite places to dine. The Concourse Steakhouse is the Contemporary's all-purpose eatery and features a character breakfast. The Contemporary Cafe offers Disney characters at both breakfast and dinner. For more information and our reviews of the table-service restaurants at the Contemporary, see Chapter 6.

The Food 'n Fun Center is located on the ground floor, adjacent to its video arcade. It is a pretty average counter-service restaurant, offering a large selection of fast food for meals and snacks from 6 A.M. to 1 A.M. The food is acceptable, but the dining area is very noisy (remember the video arcade?).

Lounges at the Contemporary

The California Grill Bar is located right inside the restaurant and shares the Top of the World view. Besides an extensive wine list and a full complement of liquors, it offers a menu of appetizers, sushi, taster plates, and pizzas from the Grill. The Grill Bar is open from 5 P.M. to 1 A.M.

The Outer Rim Cocktail Lounge is on the fourth floor of the Tower building, overlooking Bay Lake and Discovery Island. Open from 12 P.M. to 11 P.M., this lounge offers an assortment of cocktails and appetizers. It is often crowded with guests waiting to get into the

Contemporary Cafe, however, and it is also noisy, due largely to its location in the Grand Canyon Concourse.

The Sand Bar is located in the marina complex near the pool, on the lakeside of the resort. This lounge operates seasonally.

Shops at the Contemporary

Except for the Bay and Beach and the Racquet Club, all of the Contemporary's shops can be found on the fourth floor in the Grand Canyon Concourse.

Concourse Sundries and Spirits should pretty much take care of any loose ends. Whether you are in search of souvenirs, snacks, newspapers or magazines, film or tobacco products, or nonprescription medicines, here is where you will go. Concourse Sundries has a large offering of beers, wines, and liquors. Bayview Gifts is the perfect place to stop for that little something special. Fresh flowers and unique gifts are the specialty here, so you can surprise someone you love. Other shops offer character merchandise, jewelry, and men's and women's sportswear.

Recreational Activities at the Contemporary

- Two heated swimming pools (to be refurbished late 1995, creating a themed and landscaped water playground)
- Hot tub spa (to be built early 1996)
- Kiddie pool
- The Olympiad Health Club
- Marina Pavilion with watercraft rentals
- Waterskiing, parasailing
- Six lighted tennis courts, backboards, ball machine
- Volleyball and shuffleboard
- Lakefront beach area
- Children's playground and spray fountain
- Food 'n Fun Center video arcade
- Free Disney movie every night in the theater at the Food 'n Fun Center

OUR IMPRESSIONS OF THE CONTEMPORARY

- While the Contemporary lacks the fantasy atmosphere of most other Disney resorts, it is exciting and engaging. Its theme translates as pleasantly modern. Exciting, yes, but it reminds us of a modern airport.

- Perhaps the completion of the themed pool area with hot tub will enhance this resort's romantic appeal.
- This resort is not our idea of a romantic place to stay. Unless you find this exciting and urban setting romantic, we would suggest that you consider one of the other Disney resorts.

ℛECOMMENDATIONS FOR RESERVATIONS

- Both Garden Wings are not convenient to the main building or the monorail. The north wing is, however, convenient to the tennis courts and the footpath to the Magic Kingdom.

ℛOMANCE AT THE CONTEMPORARY

- Resort theme: ♥
- Breakfast in bed: ♥♥♥♥
- Breakfast on your balcony overlooking Disney World or Bay Lake: ♥♥♥
- Having a drink at the California Grill Bar during the evening fireworks show: ♥♥♥
- The fifteenth-floor observation deck at night, especially during the fireworks shows at any of the parks: ♥♥

The Grand Floridian

Even from a distance, there is something very romantic about this place. Its red-shingled roofs, ornate turrets, and intricate latticework all seem to belong to a time long past. We confess gladly to a little thrill each time we are near it. In our hearts, this lovely resort represents an unhurried age when the quality of life was held dear and when time was something to be savored. Here amidst the stately palms and gas lamps and among the verandas and the rose gardens, old-world craftsmanship has been brought to life.

This is the Grand Floridian, and it is the jewel in the Disney crown. A stay here will immerse you in a richness and elegance that will be the stuff of your romantic dreams. Details are everything at the Grand. From flawless service to sumptuous bathrobes, the luxurious and the lavish come standard.

Arriving at the Grand Floridian is definitely exciting, and it is likely something that you will never forget. The tree-lined drive leads through

The Grand Floridian

manicured gardens and up to an entrance where a dozen costumed valets and bellpersons scurry about. Knickers, knee socks, and pastel jackets are the uniforms of the day. Once inside the huge lobby, you begin to understand why this place is called Grand. Level upon level of formal balconies surround this cavernous space, they lead the eye upward towards the domed ceiling high above. Rows of turned white posts are capped with rails of gleaming mahogany. Sunlight filters through stained-glass skylights onto sparkling chandeliers.

Fabrics, decor, and design are all in perfect harmony. Details attract your eye: A topiary Cinderella's Castle occupies one space, while above it an old-fashioned cage elevator ascends slowly. This striking Grand lobby is an awesome and even a dizzying sight. Everything about the Grand Floridian appears to be first-class, and everything most certainly *is* first-class. A stay here will be, for both of you, a celebration of everything that is special and memorable.

Set perfectly along a combed, white sand beach on the Seven Seas Lagoon, the Grand Floridian is but a stone's throw from Cinderella's front door. The monorail slips quietly from the station and whisks guests away to Disney adventures.

The Grand's five lodge buildings are neatly arranged around a large pool area. Connected by garden walkways, these buildings reflect the Victorian charm of the lavish Grand lobby and house the resort's luxurious guest rooms. Each building is named for a Florida key: Sago, Boca Chica, Conch, Big Pine, and Sugar Loaf.

Rooms at the Grand Floridian

Each charming and luxurious room in this resort is decorated much as it might have been a century ago, with marble-topped sink, ceiling fan, and antiqued armoire. Each marvelous remembrance is made complete with plush carpets, pastel floral fabrics, and lightly colored woodwork. Large glass doors open onto a spacious balcony that looks onto the lovely garden grounds. Costumed housekeepers arrive daily carrying wicker baskets of fresh linens.

Rooms here are large (400 square feet) and comfortable. They are the perfect marriage of the elegance of yesterday and of the creature comforts of today. Each has two queen-size beds, several chairs, and a small table. A daybed/sofa lends the perfect place to lounge. Every guest room features twin marble vanities in a spacious and well-lit area adjacent to the bathroom.

Because of the unusual shapes of the lodge buildings, standard room sizes and shapes vary slightly within each building. Top-floor attic rooms, while a bit smaller, feature quaint dormer balconies and vaulted ceilings. Lodge Tower rooms are a bit more expensive and are a little larger than the standard rooms; a comfortable sitting area substitutes for the balcony or patio.

Rooms at the Grand enjoy one of four views, each of which has a certain charm. The garden view is this resort's standard. Pool, marina, or lagoon views each command a variety of premium prices. Many lagoon-view rooms feature an impressive panorama of Cinderella's Castle. The sparkling water, fireworks, and Electric Water Pageant make evenings magically romantic. Whatever your choice, you will find the Grand Floridian a luxurious place to celebrate your honeymoon, anniversary, or romantic Disney vacation.

Following are the 1996 room rates for the Grand Floridian.

1996 Room Rates for the Grand Floridian

Accommodation	Regular Season	Value Season	Holiday Season
Garden view (standard)	$290	$265	$300
Pool/marina view	$310	$285	$320
Lagoon view	$335	$310	$350
Lodge tower	$365	$340	$380
Concierge (in main building)	$490	$470	$505
Honeymoon room	$490	$470	$505
Turret room	$490	$470	$505

Concierge Service and Suites at the Grand Floridian

There are 65 concierge rooms and a handful of suites at the Grand, ranging from the lavish to the magnificent. Most suites offer the extravagant concierge service, and all of the concierge rooms or suites are located on the top three floors of the main building. Access here is limited. As you would expect, the service is exceptional.

You will awaken to a continental breakfast, served in the comfortable concierge lounge on the third-floor balcony. You can either breakfast there or return to your room and enjoy it on your balcony or in bed. The rest of the day's tempting offerings include midday refreshments, afternoon tea, and hors d'oeuvres and wine in the late afternoon. In the evening, drop by the lounge, sip cordials, and share a dessert while you listen to the music of the Grand's orchestra waft up from a landing below. All concierge rooms include bathrobes and slippers and VCRs with complimentary movies. This is the life.

With rooms of such quality, it would only follow that the suites at the Grand would be just as memorable. The variety of suites range from the lovely honeymoon Turret rooms to the multilevel Roosevelt suite, where Princess Di and her boys stayed during their Disney visit. The Roosevelt's level of amenities and luxuries, at nearly $1,700 per night, are most definitely fit for a royal family.

There are two types of honeymoon "suites" at the Grand (neither are truly suites, but they have been designated such by the "suite people"). Our favorite is the Turret room. Six of these lovely rooms are located in the round towers of the main building. Each is octagonally shaped and features a small sitting area, king bed, and spectacular view. Several of the Turret rooms command panoramas of Cinderella's Castle, and from them you will be able to see and hear the Fantasy in the Sky fireworks show. It is even possible in several of these rooms to see the Castle while you lie in bed. One of these airy and spacious rooms would be the perfect place for your honeymoon or romantic celebration. The other honeymoon suites are on the secluded Clarendon level. Room amenities are typically luxurious and include a king four-poster bed, love seat, and Jacuzzi tub.

There are other suites at the Grand too, but none are such enchanting places for a couple in love. With names such as the Biscayne, the Sanibel, and the Cypress, these suites offer a variety of king and queen bedrooms and parlors, all with other possible adjoining rooms. Prices begin at around $900 per night. A handful of one- and two-bedroom suites are located on the top floors of the lodge buildings. These suites do not have concierge service, however. Basically, they are attic rooms that have adjoining parlor rooms. The parlor has a pull-out queen sofa bed in a lovely sitting area and a half-bath and television. The cost is more than $600 per night. A second bedroom can be opened onto the parlor, costing even more but providing space for a large family.

Transportation and Convenience

Guests at the Grand Floridian enjoy the same monorail and bus transportation as the Contemporary and the Polynesian. The motor launch that makes the trip from the Polynesian stops at the dock near

Narcoossee's (a restaurant) on its way back from the Magic Kingdom. We suggest that you monorail to that park and return by boat.

- To the Magic Kingdom: monorail or water taxi
- To Epcot: monorail with transfer at TTC to Epcot monorail
- To Discovery Island, Fort Wilderness, River Country: monorail or boat to Magic Kingdom, then boat
- To Disney–MGM Studios, Blizzard Beach: direct bus
- To Village Marketplace, Pleasure Island, Typhoon Lagoon: 8 A.M. to 4 P.M., by bus to TTC and transfer; after 4 P.M., by direct bus

Dining at the Grand Floridian

Some of Walt Disney World's finest eateries are located here. Victoria and Albert's ♥♥♥♥, a gourmet dining experience, is considered by many to be one of Florida's best places to eat. There is also Narcoossee's, specializing in seafood, as well as the elegant Flagler's ♥♥♥ and the wonderful Grand Floridian Cafe. These places all rate high and are among our very favorite spots in all of Walt Disney World.

As if these weren't enough, 1900 Park Fare is a delightful breakfast and dinner buffet-style restaurant. It features Disney characters galore at both meals. For snacks and fast food 24 hours a day, visit the Gasparilla Grill, which serves a large variety of counter foods that are a notch or two above the standard Disney fare. To complete the largest selection of restaurant offerings in any Disney resort, an elegant afternoon high tea ♥♥♥ is served at 3 P.M. in the Garden View Lounge. The Grand also offers round-the-clock room service. For more details regarding these and other Disney dining spots, see Chapter 6.

Yet another dining option available to guests of the Grand Floridian is the Romance Dinner ♥♥♥♥. This special service provides an unforgettable private dining experience delivered to the Grand Floridian location of your choice. Enjoy it in your room, on your balcony, on the beach, in the garden, or even out on the lagoon in one of the resort's Flote boats. Just about any location is possible. There are no set menus, but sample meals such as the Italian Romance Dinner or the Romance from the Sea hint at what is possible. Needless to say, such a dinner would be simply enchanting and, of course, expensive. The suggested menus are all around $200 for a five-course dinner for two (tax and gratuity included). For a bottle of wine, add another $30. A Flote boat would be an additional $75. This unforgettable experience, served white-glove with crisp linens and candlelit table setting, is included with the Grand Plan vacation package. For information, call room service.

Lounges at the Grand Floridian

The Grand Floridian is home to three quite different lounges. The charming Garden View Lounge is on the ground floor of the lobby building. It features not only the lavish afternoon high tea but also a full service bar from 11 A.M. to 11 P.M.

Mizner's is located on the second floor of the main building. Specialties here include ales, ports, and select brandies. Each evening, a small orchestra plays on the landing right next to this handsome and comfortable lounge.

Summerhouse is the Grand's pool and lakeside lounge and snack bar. Beer, wine, specialty drinks, and a small assortment of sandwiches are available in a Victorian beach setting.

Shops at the Grand Floridian

A good selection of shops can be found at the Grand Floridian, all of which are located in the lobby building. As you might expect, though, the emphasis is on classy and expensive. Still, you will find a good selection of Disney character merchandise, in addition to some rather fancy clothing and accessories for both men and women. Sandy Cove is the resort's gift and sundries shop, where you will find film, sunblock, and other such items.

Recreational Activities at the Grand Floridian

- One large, heated swimming pool, open 24 hours
- One large hot tub
- White sand beach on Seven Seas Lagoon
- Marina complex with watercraft rentals
- St. John's Health Club
- In-room massage, by appointment
- Jogging and walking path
- Wingfield tennis courts
- Golf shuttles to golf courses throughout the day
- Children's activity center
- Video arcade

OUR IMPRESSIONS OF THE GRAND FLORIDIAN

- The Grand Floridian is an enchanting and romantic resort. The rooms are luxurious, and a stay here will have you feeling special and pampered.
- The downside is that the Grand is expensive. Specials and discounted rooms are available, but rates are rarely outstanding. The exception to this rule is the Jolly Holiday Package.

RECOMMENDATIONS FOR RESERVATIONS

- For a good view of Cinderella's Castle, the best views are from Boca Chica, which is a smoking-optional building. The next best view is from Conch, with rooms ending in 25 to 31. After that, Big Pine rooms ending in 41–47 have great views. Both Big Pine and Conch are no-smoking buildings.

ROMANCE AT THE GRAND FLORIDIAN

- Unsurpassed theme, service, accommodations, and ambience: ♥♥♥♥
- Restaurant selection (the best in the World): ♥♥♥♥
- The Honeymoon suite or Turret room: ♥♥♥♥
- A lagoon-view room: ♥♥♥♥
- Breakfast in bed: ♥♥♥♥
- High tea at the Garden View Lounge: ♥♥
- Eating at Flagler's: ♥♥♥
- An intimate dinner at Victoria & Albert's: ♥♥♥♥
- The Romance Dinner: ♥♥♥♥
- Watching the fireworks or Electric Water Pageant from one of the swings on the beach: ♥♥♥♥
- A late-night swim in the pool or hot tub: ♥

The Wilderness Lodge

Located in the woods near the Magic Kingdom is the Wilderness Lodge. It is one of Walt Disney World's latest and most majestic creations. It is a magnificent tribute, both architecturally and thematically, to the great lodge houses built by the U.S. Park Service around the turn of this century. The Wilderness Lodge has been created with great care, and the mood it achieves is impressive.

The Wilderness Lodge

Near the resort's front entrance, a topiary buffalo and calf graze. The Lodge's bellpersons wear the costumes of Park Service Rangers, from knotted kerchiefs to hiking boots. Once inside the great doors, you will know that you have made the right selection. The cavernous lobby soars eight stories above you and surrounds you with balconies of log railings. Two colossal totems face off across the huge expanse, and a shaft of sunlight enters through a circular window high among the timbers. There is a faint and delicious scent of smoke in the air.

The lobby of the Wilderness Lodge will take your breath away. Its grandeur and its detailing are stunning. The decor is American Indian, and the lobby is a showcase of native craftwork. Behind the front desk is an exhibit of authentic Indian cradleboards, while around the lobby are glass showcases of feathered headpieces, the intricate handiwork of native American artisans. In a far corner is a fireplace that befits the grand scale of the Lodge. The stonework of its massive chimney rises over 80 feet to the beamed ceiling above. A multitude of hued layers simulate the bedrock of the Grand Canyon. The forged iron hearth is artwork, and its hinges are carefully tooled to resemble quivers, each one full of iron arrows.

As grand as it may be, the Lodge is a place for people, too. Comfortable sitting areas, cozy corners, and fireplaces invite you to linger a while. This is a place of creature comforts, with sofas, ottomans, and hearthside rockers. It's a place for holding hands and for sitting quietly together by the fire. Spectacular and huge, the Lodge manages to be intimate and inviting. It may take you days or it may take you only a few moments, but you will discover that the charm and the rustic ambience of the Wilderness Lodge are unrivaled at Walt Disney World.

From a distance, the Lodge resembles a frontier fort. The hewn log walls and green roofs of its great central building turn gracefully into two long wings. The swimming pool is formed by a man-made hot spring that bubbles up in the lobby and flows out into the Lodge's rocky courtyard. As the stream builds to a torrent, it becomes a waterfall, splashing noisily over huge artificial granite boulders and tumbling into the pool.

The resort overlooks Bay Lake and Discovery Island. Every evening, the Electric Water Pageant passes by; with its music and lights, it is the perfect end to each magical day. The Disney imagineers have even provided a steaming geyser that erupts hourly.

The pool at the Lodge is themed and beautiful. During the summer months, there is one hot tub and one cold tub. During the cooler seasons, the cold tub is heated. The lakefront forms a small, sandy swimming beach, and its marina rents a variety of boats and bicycles. Walking, jogging, and cycling paths will take you around the lake to Fort Wilderness or to River Country.

Rooms at the Wilderness Lodge

The standard rooms at the Lodge have a high-timber, western sensibility. Though a bit smaller than those of the other premium resorts, the rooms are comfortable and well appointed. Each is woodsy and charming. The furniture is simple and natural and includes two queen beds and a colorful "quilted" spread. There is a large pine armoire with ample drawer space and a large television set. A small table and several chairs provide the ideal place for intimate dining. The bathroom is fairly standard, with a twin vanity and the usual tub-shower.

Each room at the Wilderness Lodge has its own balcony, and there are a variety of views. Standard-view rooms overlook small parking areas, while woods-view rooms open onto the dense forest surrounding the resort. Our woods-view room was on the side of the resort that faces the Magic Kingdom. At night, we were able to see the fireworks above the treetops.

Courtyard rooms provide views of the courtyard and pool, while lake-view rooms enjoy magnificent vistas of Bay Lake. Most of the standard rooms come with the usual dual queen-size beds, and two other offerings are available in limited numbers. There are about 40 rooms with single king beds. These have been designed for the physically challenged, and they are handsome rooms. Some rooms also offer a single queen bed and a bunk bed. These seem to capture the western feeling of the Lodge and are ideal for families.

Following are the 1996 room rates for the Wilderness Lodge.

1996 Room Rates for Wilderness Lodge

Accommodation	Regular Season	Value Season	Holiday Season
Standard view	$174	$159	$180
Woods view	$190	$175	$195
Courtyard/ lake view	$215	$200	$225
Honeymoon room	$225	$215	$235

Suites at the Wilderness Lodge

A small assortment of suites is available at the Lodge. On the top balcony of the lobby are four charming Honeymoon "suites." While not really a suite, each has a king-size bed and a large bathroom with Jacuzzi tub. These rooms are special, intimate, and private. They are the only ones on this floor, high atop the vast lobby, and you will enjoy the feeling of being away from and above the rest of the world. Priced reasonably, a Honeymoon suite is a real bargain at $225 nightly.

The Junior suite costs about $290 per night and is even less during value season. This suite has a standard bedroom with two queen beds or one king and a small sitting room and wet bar. A standard adjoining room may be added to this suite. During value season, this two-room combination may be available for less than $400 per night with a Magic Kingdom Club discount.

The remaining two suites are the Yellowstone and the Yosemite. The Yellowstone is this resort's premier suite. Michael Eisner, Disney's CEO, stayed here during the resort's opening gala. We think it's the best-themed suite at Walt Disney World. Located on the top floor of the Lodge, this suite of rooms consists of a large foyer, a living room, dining area, master bedroom, and a lavishly large marble bath. From the solid-wood double-front doors to the oversized Jacuzzi tub, the Yellowstone provides every conceivable luxury and detail of Lodge theming. Elkhorn chandelier, artwork, leather sofa, and a library of antique books are just a few of the special touches. The king bed in the master bedroom is a canopy-style four-poster, over which hangs a unique sculpture of natural woods. The Yellowstone costs around $650 per night. Trust us when we tell you it is worth it.

The Yosemite is the Vice-Presidential suite. Somewhat smaller, it enjoys much of the wonderful decoration and theming of the Yellowstone, minus the large dining area. This suite of rooms costs around $520 nightly.

Transportation and Convenience

Convenience is not, we are sorry to tell you, one of the strong suits here at the Wilderness Lodge. Still, transportation is acceptable, although we still hear an occasional complaint.

- To the Magic Kingdom, Fort Wilderness, River Country, Discovery Island: by boat, arrivals and departures from the lakeside dock; the

Magic Kingdom can also be reached by bus via the Ticket and Transportation Center (TTC) and monorail
- To Epcot, Disney–MGM Studios, Blizzard Beach: direct bus
- To Typhoon Lagoon, Pleasure Island, Village Marketplace: 8 A.M. to 4 P.M., by bus to TTC and transfer; after 4 P.M., direct bus

Dining at the Wilderness Lodge

The Lodge has three western-themed restaurants; two have table service, and one has fast food. The Artist Point ♥♥ is the Wilderness Lodge's premier eating place. Dinner specialties are the freshest of meats, seafood, and game from the Pacific Northwest. The Artist Point also features a character breakfast.

The all-purpose restaurant is the Whispering Canyon Cafe. It's a fun place to eat and the food is very good. Each of the day's hearty meals is served family-style and all you care to eat. For reviews and more information about these restaurants, see Chapter 6.

The Lodge has a themed counter-service eatery called the Roaring Fork. Open 24 hours, this self-serve restaurant offers a selection of breakfasts, sandwiches, salads, and desserts. There's even a buffalo burger. During the breakfast hours, a continental-style breakfast bar is offered in the lobby. It's called the Coffee Express and it features a selection of beverages, muffins, and bagels from 6:30 A.M. to 10:30 A.M.

The Lodge also has 24-hour room service with a menu that includes barbecued ribs, pizza, grilled fish, and prime rib. Foods come from either the Artist Point or Whispering Canyon. Wines, beers, and mixed drinks are also available. Room service also features the Romance Dinner for Two. For an evening to remember, this full-course dinner includes a keepsake floral arrangement, choice of entrees, wine or champagne, a personalized cake, specialty coffees, and two hours of child care at the Cub's Den.

Lounges at the Wilderness Lodge

The picturesque Territory Lounge is located adjacent to the Artist Point and serves a selection of microbrewery beers, specialty drinks, and wines from 11 A.M. to 1 A.M. A variety of appetizer foods and sandwiches are also available here, and we think that this beautiful lounge is a real alternative to the resort's restaurants. Give it a try for lunch. The Trout Pass Pool Bar enjoys a nice view of the lodge and of the lake and beach.

Shops at the Wilderness Lodge

There's only one shop at the Lodge, but it's a good one. Just outside the front door of the Lodge Mercantile sits one of the comic sites of the Lodge: a totem pole of Disney characters. Inside, you will discover one of the nicest on-property places to browse. Besides some handsome Lodge logo merchandise, you'll find an impressive array of western craft items as well as quality fashions and the usual assortment of sundries.

Recreational Activities at the Wilderness Lodge

- Swimming pool with small water slide
- One hot and one cold spa
- White sand beach and marina with assorted boat rentals
- Bicycle rentals
- Video arcade
- Fishing excursion
- The Cub's Den children's activity center

OUR IMPRESSIONS OF THE WILDERNESS LODGE

- A beautifully themed resort. The fantasy element here is so powerful that a visit will be a real adventure. As elusive as romance is, we'd have to say that the Lodge has it.
- The assortment of restaurants could be better. The Artist Point is too expensive to eat in every night, and Whispering Canyon basically serves the same three meals every day. If you are here for a week, you'll get tired of them quickly. What the Lodge needs is a restaurant like the Yacht Club Galley, which has a large and diverse menu.
- The Lodge is an outstanding value. It falls in cost somewhere between the premium resorts and the more modestly priced ones, yet it offers extraordinary theming, well-decorated rooms, and most of the services found at the more expensive places.
- The four Honeymoon suites could be the best on-property room bargain.
- The pool is a bit small for a hotel with nearly 800 rooms. Even during the winter months, two hot tubs are simply not enough.
- A car would come in handy here, especially for going to dinner at other resorts.

RECOMMENDATIONS FOR RESERVATIONS

- If you want to have your room located in the main lobby building, ask for it when you make your reservation. A room that is on one of the lobby's balconies is considered a woods-view room.
- Courtyard-view rooms will likely be noisy.
- Some of the lower-floor lake-view rooms have stunning balconies of "granite."

ROMANCE AT THE WILDERNESS LODGE

- Resort theming: ♥♥♥
- The Honeymoon "suite": ♥♥♥
- Having your morning cup of coffee in front of the fireplace on the third-floor landing above the main door: ♥♥
- The Artist Point restaurant: ♥♥
- The Territory Lounge: ♥
- Taking a stroll or a bike ride over to Fort Wilderness: ♥
- Searching for the sixteen hidden Mickeys in the lobby: ♥
- The Romance Dinner for Two (arrange with room service): ♥♥♥♥

Shades of Green

This resort, once known as the Disney Inn, is now reserved for the use of active and retired military personnel, employees of the Department of Defense, and members of the National Guard and military reserves. On long-term lease to the U.S. government, Shades of Green provides an affordable Disney vacation for the men and women of the U.S. armed services and their families.

This lovely resort is nestled between two of Disney's championship golf courses, the Magnolia and the Palm. It features a woodsy and quiet ambience. Rates are based on rank and range from very reasonable to downright deserving. Special passes are available to guests at a discount, and Shades of Green restaurants offer meals at reduced prices. Every effort at Shades is made to make the Disney experience an affordable one for our people in uniform.

The long entry drive at Shades of Green seems more like one to an exclusive country club than to a Disney resort. The grounds are beautifully landscaped, and the resort is handsome and well maintained. Theming isn't an element here, but the atmosphere is unmistakably

Shades of Green

Disney. While guests at Shades of Green do enjoy Surprise Mornings, they do not get Disney resort ID cards.

The staff members at Shades of Green are not Disney employees. We found them to be genuinely dedicated to delivering the best service possible. Employees have all been trained by Disney so that the magic Disney hospitality is definitely present.

Special arrangements can easily be made for small weddings at the resort's own garden gazebo. Family reunions and modest parties are also easily arranged by the resort's eager staff. Arrangements can be as grand or as modest as you can afford, and the many rules and regulations regarding such events at Disney resorts are not a consideration here. Staff members make a real effort to get to know their guests, and we suspect that repeat customers are the rule rather than the exception.

No taxpayer funds are used to support this resort. Shades of Green and all other Armed Forces Recreation Centers are self-supporting.

Rooms at Shades of Green

The resort consists of one large building with two three-story wings. Guest rooms face either the pool courtyard or the golf course. There is no such thing as a bad view here, and the rooms, at 450 square feet, are among the largest standard rooms in Disney World. Furnishings are light oak, and bedspreads are a floral pattern. Of the 290 rooms, 287 have two queen beds. Two of the remaining three rooms have one queen-size bed, and the last is a large suite. Each room has a daybed/sofa, small table and chairs, and balcony or patio. A large, remote-controlled color television occupies a colonial armoire, and the bathroom has twin vanities and a separate shower. Shades of Green is every bit a luxurious Disney resort.

The one suite at Shades of Green has a living room, master bedroom, and a large bath. There is a four-poster king bed in the bedroom and a foldout queen-size sofa bed and two Murphy beds in the living room. This suite can accommodate up to seven persons and has two full bathrooms, one with a small Jacuzzi and bidet.

Suite furniture is of light pine with a ceiling that features varnished, decorative beams. Baskets of crisp linens and objects of art make this lovely suite quite elegant. At $180 per night (regardless of rank), this is an excellent opportunity for honeymooners. It is spacious, luxurious, and romantic. The large patio overlooks the golf course.

Shades of Green is such a bargain that demand is beginning to exceed room supply. We have heard reports that overbooking has caused some Shades of Green guests to be relocated to other Disney resorts, such as the All-Star Resorts, which although they are bargains at $55 per night, are no match for the accommodations at Shades of Green. Other guests have been located at other resorts, mostly the moderately priced resorts such as the Caribbean Beach or Dixie Landings. These resorts are much nicer than the All-Star Resorts. Due to increasing demands for rooms at Shades of Green, still other guests are being put up at the Hotel Plaza resorts.

Shades reservation personnel have assured us that those guests who are going to stay at a resort other than Shades will be told so at the time of reservation. Since this resort is so nice, we suggest that you make your reservations as early as possible to avoid staying someplace less luxurious.

Room rates at Shades of Green are based on rank and civil service rate:

- Category 1, $55 per night: PVT-SGT, E1-E5
- Category 2, $79 per night: SSG-CSM, 2LT-CPT, E6-E9, 01-03, WO1-CW3
- Category 3, $89 per night: MAJ-COL, 04-06, CW4-CW5
- Category 4, $95 per night: BG-GEN, SES, 07-010
- DOD Civilians: GS1-GS10, $79, GS11-GS15 $89 per night
- NAF Civilians:
  ALL NA, NL, NS, AS, PS, NF1-NF4, ALL WG'S $79 per night
  NF5 $89 per night
  NG6 $95 per night

For information regarding rates and rooms at Shades of Green, call (800) GO ARMY-1. Reservations can be made by calling Shades of Green reservationists at (407) 824-3600.

Transportation and Convenience

Transportation to all Disney destinations is by Shades of Green buses. These are not Walt Disney World buses. They run on a schedule that is available at the front desk. Service is on par with that of Disney, and having a printed schedule should take the guesswork out of travel.

Dining at Shades of Green

There are two restaurants at Shades of Green. The Garden Gallery has a delightful garden decor with large potted trees. It features American cuisine in a table-service setting. Breakfast here is an unusual buffet, a sort of help-yourself meal with a la carte pricing. Dinners and lunches include sandwiches, steaks, seafood, and pastas. A nightly buffet features a different cuisine each evening.

The poolside sports bar and eatery is called Evergreen's and has the usual selection of snacks and specialty drinks as well as a good selection of sandwiches. The hamburger is one of the best at Disney. Decor here is interesting, with a collection of antique sports equipment and a tennis court, complete with players, fixed to the ceiling. It's popular with golfers. Both restaurants are open to the public for lunch, and the Garden Gallery offers discounted dinner prices for Shades guests. For reviews and more information about these restaurants, see Chapter 6.

Special Ticketing to Disney Attractions

Along with the usual selection of Disney tickets and passes (all discounted), Shades of Green also offers its own Length of Stay Pass called the Stars and Stripes Pass. It's good for your whole visit and will admit you to all of the Disney attractions. A three-day pass is $102 for an adult, and each successive day adds another $20. Compared to the Length of Stay Pass, this is a considerable savings.

Services Available at Shades of Green

- Room service from 7 A.M. to 11 P.M.
- Coin-operated laundry facilities
- Small refrigerators ($4 per day)
- Video camera rentals $6 for 24 hours

Recreational Activities at Shades of Green

- Two large standard swimming pools
- Two tennis courts
- One kiddie pool
- A children's playground
- A small health club
- Video arcade

Shops at Shades of Green

One small Army-Air Force Exchange Store features a selection of Disney merchandise at discount prices. Also available are a generous selection of sundries, magazines, and books. Military and DOD identification cards are required to purchase goods at this shop.

OUR IMPRESSIONS OF SHADES OF GREEN

- There is no hot tub here at Shades, but the management has assured us that plans are underway to have one built. Just how long the government wheels of progress will grind before this happens is anyone's guess.

ROMANCE AT SHADES OF GREEN

- Resort theming: ♥
- The suite: ♥♥♥

The Epcot Resorts

The Yacht and the Beach Clubs

Next door to Epcot and along the shores of Crescent Lake lie two of Disney's most enchanting creations. Both are visions of nineteenth-century luxury where guests are immersed in a setting that is perfectly exciting, lavishly relaxing, and splendidly romantic. The gray and blue clapboard buildings of the Yacht and the Beach Clubs perfectly evoke a bygone era of grace and hospitality. These picturesque resorts share a quaint, turn-of-the-century New England seaside theme. One reflects a more formal nautical charm, while the other radiates the casual ambience of the beach.

Lakeside, a rope-slung boardwalk, beached shipwreck, lighthouse, and a white sand beach with colorful cabanas complete the seaside illusion. The Disney magic is everywhere, from the antique "woody" station wagon at the front door of the Beach Club to the detailed ship models in the Yacht's elegant lobby. The overall effect is classy and unforgettable. Both the Yacht and the Beach are first-rate resorts from top to bottom. Their intimate and relaxed atmospheres will embrace you both, enhancing the chemistry for your romantic escape.

Stormalong Bay, the shared water playground, is an extraordinary and magical place. It seems more like a river than a pool as it meanders

The Yacht and the Beach Clubs

from the Beach to the Yacht. Along the way are bubbling springs, whirlpool eddies, waterfalls, and hot tubs nestled in surrounding rocks. It even features a sand beach for children. At the Beach Club end of Stormalong Bay is a wild and winding slide that begins in the crow's nest of the shipwreck and ends in the pool with a sudden splash. After a morning of Disney excitement, you will be ready to spend a blissful afternoon here, swimming and sunning. Each resort also has a quiet pool with a hot tub.

Along with Stormalong Bay, the resorts also share a common area that includes Periwig's Salon and Barber, a video arcade, and the Ship Shape Health Club with its old-fashioned indoor spa. Along the waterfront, the Yacht Club features a marina of rental watercraft, while the Beach Club enjoys a lazy stretch of white sand. These areas are separated by a long wooden pier. The charming lighthouse at the end of the pier is one of the signature sights of these idyllic resorts.

The landscaping at the Yacht and Beach Clubs is a showcase of Disney's penchant for details. Colorful gardens and manicured shrubbery will prove an inspiration to home gardeners. Long stretches of trimmed lawns lead gracefully to the lake. On one of them is the lovely gazebo used by Disney Fairy Tale Weddings. Amidst beguiling gardens of roses and the carved, wooden cupids, happy couples tie the knot, Disney-style.

The Beach Club

The relaxed and romantic atmosphere at the Beach has lured us back time and again. We like to think of this place as our home away from home. We confess that staying elsewhere has been done with some reluctance. The casual atmosphere here is elegant yet informal. For us, the Beach Club is simply inviting.

The Beach's lobby is a canvas of pastels, pink marble, and fine woodwork. Large windows facing the lake make the lobby airy and bright. Comfortable wicker furnishings are everywhere on plush carpets of floral designs, and wooden bird cages and large potted palms add just the right touches of warmth.

Around the resort are porches with rockers, beaches with cabanas, and lovely gardens with benches. Enjoying the Disney attractions for a few hours at a time will not be hard. After a morning in the parks, you'll be ready to return.

Rooms at the Beach Club   The "seaside" rooms here are sunny and bright. Ensconced amidst the light pastels and luxurious furnishings, you will not for a minute forget that you are enjoying a romantic vacation at the beach. The verdigris-finished bedsteads and seahorse lamps seem weathered by their "years" at the seashore. Pink and white carnival-striped drapes perfectly mime the beach cabanas of yesteryear. This is a place of creature comforts; it is your own intimate and private retreat. You have landed in the lap of luxury and, if you are like us, you will not be anxious to depart.

Beach Club rooms are indeed inviting. With a choice of either a single king or double queen beds, each room features a large vanity area with twin sinks. The attractive armoire is of light wood. Inside it you will find not only the usual television but also a stocked minibutler. Each room has a small table and several chairs—just the place for breakfast or intimate dining. Many rooms include a daybed/sofa. Balconies are either full-size, with patio furniture, or standing room only. Ground-floor resort rooms all have patios.

There is the usual Disney complement of views. Standard-view rooms look out onto well-landscaped gardens, beyond which are the resort's parking lots. Ground-floor, standard-view rooms have charming little patios that open onto beautiful gardens. Water-view rooms at the Beach overlook Stormalong Bay or the quiet pool area. Other rooms command views of the various gardens on the lakeside of the building, and some rooms provide excellent views of Epcot and IllumiNations, the laser light show.

Following are the 1996 room rates for the Beach Club.

1996 Room Rates for the Beach Club

Accommodation	Regular Season	Value Season	Holiday Season
Standard view	$240	$225	$250
Garden view	$270	$250	$280
Water view	$305	$285	$315

Suites at the Beach Club   From the luxurious to the lavish, the Beach Club offers a variety of suites. The Newport is this resort's Presidential suite. It features a king bedroom with a large vanity, bath, and large Jacuzzi tub. The formal living room is arranged around a fireplace and includes a spacious dining area, wet bar, and room enough for a small party. Located on a corner of the fifth floor, the Newport has a narrow balcony that runs the entire width of the living room and bedroom. The view of Stormalong Bay and of the lagoon is commanding. So is the price: $1,300 nightly.

The Nantucket is the Beach's Vice-Presidential suite. With a beautiful king bedroom and a smaller and less formal living room, it seems better suited for a honeymoon or anniversary. Located on the second floor, the Nantucket overlooks a pleasant garden area. It is charming and is conveniently located near the lobby. Price is $700 nightly.

The Beach also offers several Junior suites. At $410 nightly, there are two varieties, each with a large king bedroom. Junior A features a sitting area that is part of the bedroom, and Junior B offers a separate sitting area with French doors and a daybed. Junior B is a nice choice for a family with one child.

The Yacht Club

The lobby of the Yacht Club showcases its nautical theme. A large antique globe sits in the center of the elegant splendor. You will wonder where the Disney folks get things like this. There are intricate ship models in glass cases that invite more than just a casual glance. Ornate brass chandeliers, polished hardwood floors, and decorative ropework recalls the finery of New England's old yachting establishments. Tufted leather sofas and chairs will tempt you with the promise of luxurious comfort. Muted reds, whites, and blues herald the colors of the grand old yacht clubs of Cape Cod, Marblehead, and Bar Harbor.

This lobby area is more formal but is no less inviting than that of the casual Beach Club. There is a certain classiness to this place and, as one of our mothers said when we arrived, "Now, this is the style I'm accustomed to!"

Rooms at the Yacht Club   Like the rooms at the Beach, guest rooms at the Yacht Club are light and airy. The furnishings have a bit more formal charm, though. Bedsteads and armoires are of white antiqued wood; the lamps are of polished brass. The nautical decor is made complete with fabrics of pale reds, whites, and blues. Like her sister ship, the Yacht Club will embrace you with the luxurious comforts found only at first-class hotels: large, soft towels, signature toiletries, and a host of other details.

Each room at the Yacht Club has a vanity area with twin sinks. There are chairs and a small table, and some rooms even have daybeds. Every room has a large balcony with several chairs and a small table where you can sit and enjoy an early morning breakfast, read the newspaper, or simply sit and watch Disney World awaken.

Most rooms at the Yacht Club are configured with two queen beds, but like the Beach, it has a number of king bedrooms. Here at the Yacht, the assortment of views is the same as that at the Beach, except that no rooms here provide a view of Epcot.

Concierge Service at the Yacht Club   While both the Yacht and the Beach offer a variety of suites, only the Yacht Club features concierge service. All of the rooms and suites on the concierge level's fifth floor enjoy this wonderful service.

Concierge guests enjoy the upgraded room amenities, which include terry bathrobes and special toiletries, and they also enjoy use of the luxurious lounge overlooking the lagoon. The continental breakfast each morning features pastries, croissants, cereals, and muffins. Midday snacks are of chips and salsa, fruit, and cookies and milk. Late afternoons mean wine and cheese and a vegetable tray and, in the evening, cordials and desserts are offered.

Suites at the Yacht Club   Our favorite Yacht Club suite is the Commodore. It is charming and romantic—the perfect accommodations for a honeymoon, anniversary, or a romantic getaway. The Commodore is large and lavishly furnished. With a comfortable sitting room, a large bedroom with a king-size sleigh bed, and concierge service, a stay here will make your time dreamy and idyllic.

The Commodore's bathroom is spacious and luxurious, more of a room than a bath. Complete with television, vanity areas, walk-in shower, and Jacuzzi tub, it is world-class. If you can afford the $660 per night price tag, we are sure that it will not disappoint you.

The Turret suites occupy the first three floors of the resort's beautiful tower-like structure. Each includes an octagonal sitting room in the turret, a large bedroom, and a spacious living room. The Turret room is sunny and bright, offering a thrilling panorama of Stormalong Bay and Crescent Lake. At over $500 per night, these accommodations are unique and lavish.

If you're looking for something really spectacular, there is the Presidential, which is the fourth floor of the turret suites. Highlights include a large dining area, Jacuzzi tub, and two full balconies. The basic suite is around $800, with an additional double-queen bedroom adding nearly another $400.

The Yacht's premier suite is the Captain's Deck. It is one of only a handful here on Disney property that offer such luxury. We have taken to calling it "Arnold's Room" after one of its celebrity guests. The Captain's Deck includes furnishings more lavish than even those found in the other Yacht Club suites. Furniture is dark and varnished. There is enough room here for a large family or a small meeting. In the dining room, the table will easily seat a dozen, and the wet bar is designed to be a serving area for a large room-service event.

The dark wood theme is carried throughout, with a large armoire and four-poster king bed in the master bedroom. The bath has an over-sized shower and tub. This suite of rooms also has a forty-foot wide patio, which opens onto its own secluded garden and pond. An additional five rooms can be connected through adjoining doors. We know that Arnold must have liked this place: when he left, he surely said, "I'll be back." At nearly $1,500 per night, we have no doubt that he can afford it.

Following are the room rates for the Yacht Club.

1996 Room Rates for the Yacht Club

Accommodation	Regular Season	Value Season	Holiday Season
Standard view	$240	$225	$250
Garden view	$270	$250	$280
Lagoon view	$305	$285	$315
Lagoon view with Concierge	$405	$385	$420
Garden view with Concierge	$390	$370	$405

Transportation and Convenience at the Yacht and the Beach

Both the Yacht and the Beach are only minutes from almost any Disney destination. Whether by boat, foot, or by bus, transportation to anywhere is about as easy as it gets.

Reaching Disney–MGM Studios or Epcot from either resort is by Friendship motor vessel. Arrivals and departures are from the lighthouse dock on the beach side of the resorts. The trip to Epcot takes only a few minutes by boat and even less time by foot. All other Disney destinations, except Discovery Island and River Country, are reached by direct buses. Each resort has a bus stop near its front entrances.

- To Disney–MGM Studios: short boat trip from resort dock
- To Epcot: short walk or boat ride to International Gateway
- To Magic Kingdom, Village Marketplace, Typhoon Lagoon, Pleasure Island, Blizzard Beach: direct bus
- To Discovery Island, River Country: bus to Magic Kingdom and boat to either

Dining at the Yacht and the Beach

One of the many advantages here is the outstanding dining. Because these are "Siamese" resorts, guests at either the Yacht or the Beach will find that strolling over to dine at the other resort will be both pleasant and convenient. Each resort boasts its own array of themed restaurants and lounges.

At the Beach, you will find two dining places: the Cape May Cafe and Ariel's. Both offer table service. The Cape May has a delightful beach decor and serves breakfast and dinner, both buffet-style. Breakfast is a character affair, and dinner is a New England clambake. Ariel's serves dinner only and specializes in seafood.

At the Yacht are the Yacht Club Galley and the Yachtsman Steakhouse. The Galley serves a large and varied menu for breakfast, lunch, or dinner, including a wonderful breakfast buffet. The Yachtsman is open only for dinner with its specialty of fine cuts of prime beef. Other entrees include rack of lamb, grilled seafood, and poultry.

In and around the pool area are two other restaurants: Beaches and Cream Soda Shop and Hurricane Hanna's. Beaches is one of our favorite things about these resorts. This delightful fifties-style soda fountain offers a mean double-chocolate ice cream soda, and it has no equal in or around Walt Disney World. Hamburgers and Disney's finest hot dogs are also featured here. Hanna's is the Y & B's poolside bar and eatery, serving an assortment of counter-style drinks and sandwiches. Either of these places is ideal for a light meal while you relax around Stormalong Bay.

The Yacht Club Galley is the source of in-room dining at both resorts. We have made good use of it on our numerous visits and have always found both the food and the service outstanding.

For more details and our reviews of the table-service restaurants, see Chapter 6.

Lounges at the Yacht and the Beach

Each resort has two lounges. One is adjacent to the lobby and the other is near its signature restaurant. In a quiet corner in the lobby of the

Beach, you will find the Rip Tide Lounge. Complimentary coffee and a tea are offered during breakfast hours. Martha's Vineyard Lounge is the Beach's other lounge and is located adjacent to Ariel's. It offers an outstanding choice of spirits as well as an award-winning selection of wines. Martha's is a charming and quiet hideaway. Its soft lighting, wicker furnishings, and rose hues create an atmosphere that is intimate and romantic. In the evenings, wine tastings and a tempting selection of appetizers from Ariel's make Martha's a place not to be missed. We've even enjoyed a light dinner here.

At the Yacht, you'll find the Ale & Compass in the lobby. Varnished brightwork and polished brass are the decor here. Plush sofas and chairs invite you to sit awhile and sample the outstanding selection of imported ales and beers. Complimentary tea and coffee are offered each morning. It is a comfortable place to sit and to make plans for your day's adventure.

The Crew's Cup Lounge is next door to the Yachtsman Steakhouse. Offering a complete selection of beers, wines, and mixed drinks, the Crew's Cup features a clubhouse ambience. Comfortable booths, sofas, and plenty of varnished wood and polished brass make it charming and inviting. There's even a rowing shell overhead. With a varied offering of appetizers, finger foods, and sandwiches from the Yachtsman, this is a place to consider for lunch or a light evening meal.

Shops at the Yacht and the Beach

Each resort features its own shop. The Atlantic Wear and Wardrobe Emporium can be found at the Beach Club, and Fairings and Fittings is over at the Yacht. Both shops offer a large selection of sundries, character merchandise, and gifts. Each features its own line of logo resort wear and a unique line of men's and women's apparel. There's some very nice stuff at these shops, making them two of our favorite shopping places. Check out the sale racks.

Recreational Activities at the Yacht and the Beach

- Stormalong Bay pool complex ♥♥
- Five hot tubs/spas ♥♥♥
- Two quiet pools ♥
- Sand beach on the lake (no swimming) with cabanas
- Lafferty Place video arcade

- Complimentary tennis courts (at the Beach Club)
- Jogging and walking paths (map available at the front desk)
- Ship Shape Health Club, state-of-the-art fitness center with sauna and spa
- Bayside Marina with a variety of rental boats
- Volleyball (ball at health club)
- Bocci ball and croquet court (at the Beach Club)

OUR IMPRESSIONS OF THE YACHT AND THE BEACH

- These are lovely, charming, and romantic resorts.
- With such convenience to Epcot and Disney–MGM and the excellent transportation, a stay at either resort will have you only minutes from anywhere.
- Dining is outstanding. To these choices add the convenience of the restaurants at Epcot, the Swan, Dolphin, and the BoardWalk, and you'll have to narrow your choices down from nearly 30 restaurants, all within walking distance.
- Our penchant for hot tubs is most certainly satisfied here. There are two lovely hot tubs near Stormalong Bay, one more at each of the quiet pools, and one in the health club.

RECOMMENDATIONS FOR RESERVATIONS

- Standard-view rooms on the ground floor of the Yacht and the Beach enjoy quiet garden areas. Parking lots are not very visible from them. This is not true for upper-floor standard-view rooms. Ground-floor standard rooms at the Beach are smoking rooms.
- The fifth floor at the Beach used to be concierge service. The rooms are a bit different and feature a few added amenities and upgraded fabrics.
- If you want real convenience to Epcot, ask for a room near the Beach's quiet pool.
- If you wish to be in one of the upper-floor rooms facing Epcot, ask for it when you reserve and again when you check in.
- Real versus tiny balconies at the Beach Club are hit or miss. On your reservation and at check-in, be sure to request a room with a real balcony.
- Some of the rooms can be a walk from the main elevators. If this is not to your liking, mention it at check-in.

- Some standard-view concierge rooms at the Yacht overlook the front entrance of the resort. This is not our idea of romantic. Opt instead for a lagoon view.

ℛOMANCE AT THE YACHT AND THE BEACH

- Overall resort theming: ♥♥♥♥
- Room ambience: ♥♥♥
- Yacht Club concierge service: ♥♥♥♥
- The Commodore suite, with concierge service: ♥♥♥♥
- Stormalong Bay pool area: ♥♥
- Room-service breakfast in bed: ♥♥♥♥
- A "Wine Flight" at Martha's Vineyard: ♥♥♥
- Hot tubs at day's end or late night: ♥♥♥
- Taking a stroll over to France for espresso and dessert in Au Petit Cafe before IllumiNations:♥♥
- Taking a swim in Stormalong, then going to Beaches and Cream for a double-chocolate ice cream soda: ♥
- The *Breathless* IllumiNations Cruise for Two (see Chapter 7 for more information): ♥♥♥♥
- Watching IllumiNations from the beach: ♥♥♥

Disney's Caribbean Beach Resort

When we first arrived at the Caribbean Beach and were greeted by a valet dressed like a Nassau policeman, we knew that we were about to really go somewhere. Having spent many months on tropical islands, we were able to appreciate the details of this costume. From the starched, white jacket and brass whistle to the braided epaulets and knee socks, here, we knew, was a bit of the authentic Caribbean. Once out of our car, the fragrances of jasmine and blossoming foliage embraced us.

Like all fantasies, this Disney creation will take a bit of willing participation. You will need to bring along a bit of imagination. Not too much though, because this fantasy is real enough. From check-in right to the door of your own little piece of this relaxing paradise, you will both be entering yet another of Walt Disney World's perfectly rendered themed resorts.

When you arrive, follow the signs for Guest Check-In, and you will arrive at the front door of the Customs House. The Customs House

Disney's Caribbean Beach Resort

re-creates the lobby charm of an old-world island hotel. Trust us when we tell you that these places are few and far between even in the real Caribbean. Disney's knack for this kind of re-creation is uncanny. Ceiling fans, potted palms, and shuttered windows are but a few of the details typical not only of the Customs House but of the entire resort.

The Caribbean Beach Resort has been created as five small "island" villages with names that recall the exotic ports of call of the Caribe: Martinique, Aruba, Barbados, Jamaica, and Trinidad. Each offers its own white sand beach, pool, playground, and shaded courtyard. Everywhere is the lush and exotic foliage of the tropics: hibiscus, mango, jasmine, and palms. The scents of the islands are in the air.

The buildings of each village are distinctive in both color and design, to give each area a feeling of uniqueness. Two-story and stucco, these "tin-roofed" structures are rich with a taste of the tropical islands. The variety of brightly colored buildings and whimsical gingerbreads reminds us of some favorite down-island destinations.

The island villages surround Barefoot Bay, a 50-acre lake. Old Port Royale Center Towne, a Disneyesque version of a bustling West Indies village, is the resort's central hub. Colorful, gay and lively, this little "town" is home for the Caribbean's shops, restaurant, food court, water playground, and marina. Enjoy a soak in the hot tub or a dip in the pool, hop on a bike, rent a boat, or lounge around the Banana Cabana pool bar to the strains of Jimmy Buffet. It is a fun place to be.

In the middle of the lake is Parrot Cay, an island connected by foot bridges to the villages on one side of the lake and Old Port Royale Center Towne on the other. Narrow paths, live parrots, gazebos, a kiddie playground, and picnic area are all set against a lush backdrop of dense bamboo and a tropical garden. It is just the place for a quiet breakfast or a romantic evening stroll.

The colors, the foliage, and the ambience will relax you. Take your time to savor this place and your time here. The Caribbean Beach does exactly what the best of resorts anywhere do and what Disney resorts do better than anyone: it takes you above the everyday and transports you to that unforgettable place called "vacation."

Rooms at the Caribbean Beach

Our king bedroom was located in the island village of Aruba. Resort rooms with king-size beds are located on the corners of the buildings. This gave the sitting area two windows, one on either wall, rather than the usual single window. With the curtains open and the sheer drapes drawn, the room was bright and airy.

While color schemes vary from one island village to another, the room furnishings are similar. Our room had pale sage walls, bordered at the ceiling by a strip of flowered wallpaper. Its deeper greens and hints of pinks matched the flowered bedspread. The posts of the wooden bedstead featured carved wooden pineapples, the symbols of hospitality.

A large armoire with television was opposite our bed. Next to it was placed the minibutler, stocked with soft drinks, beers, wines, and lots of snacks. One bonus was a coffeemaker, complete with a daily filter pouch of coffee. For us, having our first cup of coffee while still in our room (or bed) was heavenly.

The vanity area featured double sinks and a large mirror. Plenty of room for both of us to get ready for an evening out. The bathroom, a bit on the small side, had the usual shower-tub combination.

Overall, the room was pleasant and comfortable, and we enjoyed our time there. Everything seemed rather new and extremely well maintained, even though this resort is not one of Disney's newest. This, you will find, is the trademark of all Disney resorts.

There are two basic room configurations at the Caribbean Beach: rooms with king-size beds and rooms with twin double beds. All of the king bedrooms here at the Caribbean have connecting doors to adjoining rooms with two doubles. If you are visiting Walt Disney World with your children, this may be an enticing choice.

A small variety of views are available at the Caribbean Beach. Our room had a courtyard view. It was quiet, even though the resort was fully booked. The view onto the courtyard was beautiful and enhanced our visit. Standard-view rooms look onto crowded parking lots. We would not recommend one of these if you are intent on immersing yourselves in the ambience of this resort. Pool or lake views overlook some kind of water. Some of the pool-view rooms merely look onto the walls around the pool—not an attractive option.

Following are the 1996 room rates for the Caribbean Beach.

1996 Room Rates for the Caribbean Beach

Accommodation	Regular Season	Value Season	Holiday Season
Standard view	$99	$95	$104
Pool or lake view,			
king bed	$129	$124	$134
Courtyard	$124	$119	$129

Transportation and Convenience

Service from this resort is quite good, with buses running at least every 20 minutes throughout the day and every 10 minutes during peak hours.

• To all Disney destinations: by bus

Dining at the Caribbean Beach

If there is a drawback to this resort, it is the limited dining options. At Old Port Royale Center Towne is a single table-service restaurant and a food court. The Captain's Tavern is open only for dinner, from 5 P.M. to 10 P.M. It is a small but quaint table-service restaurant and is moderately priced. For reviews and information about this and other restaurants, see Chapter 6.

The Old Port Royale food court is called Market Street, and it is a rather cute little avenue of food shops. Decorated with palms, colorful kites, and other Caribbean artifacts, these exotic storefronts come complete with balconies and "roofs." The effect is delightful. Counter-service shops have names such as Cinnamon Bay Bakery, Montego's Deli, and Bridgetown Broiler.

The seating here is more comfortable and private than most food courts, and with the choice of eating outside on a pleasant porch, we think that this place rates well for a Disney fast-food outlet. Open from 7 A.M. to midnight, Market Street serves a large variety of foods for each of the day's meals.

While the Caribbean Beach does not offer room service, it does offer the same delivery service available at most limited-amenities Disney resorts.

The Caribbean Beach Souvenir Thermal Mug   Many of the Disney resorts offer a souvenir mug, either available right in your room or at the food court. This quality mug, which comes with a travel lid, has an interesting feature at the Caribbean. Buy one, and you get unlimited free refills at the beverage bar. The mug costs around $7 and, with most beverage prices around $1, it will not take long for it to pay for itself. We carried ours along with us on outings around the resort. Be advised that beverages included in this deal are soft drinks, coffee and tea, and whatever variety of fruit drinks are available at the beverage island.

The Banana Cabana is the Caribbean's single lounge and is located next to the main pool. It serves the usual specialty drinks, beers and wines, and a few snacks.

Shops at the Caribbean Beach

Several shops are located in Old Port Royale Center Towne. The Straw Market offers a selection of Caribbean Beach logo merchandise and a variety of tropical and "piratical" souvenirs and toys. Also found here is a very nice collection of tropical sportswear, as well as a small selection of fruits and snacks and Jamaican Blue Mountain coffees.

Adjacent to the Straw Market is the Calypso Trading Post, where you will be able to purchase the usual variety of Disney character merchandise, postcards and stamps, books and newspapers, and a variety of snacks, souvenirs, and sundries such as sunblock and nonprescription medications.

Recreational Activities at the Caribbean Beach

Recreational activities are one of the Caribbean's strong suits. In addition to a themed main pool area are six more private pools. The central pool at Old Port Royale boasts a themed swimming area that includes a spa, water slide, and kiddie pool. The surroundings are an "old" Spanish fort, complete with turrets, cannons, and waterfalls. A short slide runs from the ramparts to the water. The pool is exactly the kind of thing that we love so much about Disney resorts: it resembles a movie set more than a hotel pool. The hot tub is, unfortunately, rather small. Although the Caribbean offers sparkling white sand beaches, no lake swimming is allowed. With chaise lounges, cabanas, and some nice hammocks, the beaches are attractive places to catch some sunlight or moonbeams.

If you plan to spend time at the Caribbean, a Length of Stay recreational package is available. For around $60, you get unlimited use of recreation, including bikes and boats. Considering that most motor boats are $20 for half an hour's use, this package can be a great deal if you make use of it.

OUR IMPRESSIONS OF THE CARIBBEAN BEACH

- Guest Services is located far away in the Customs House, and dining options are minimal. This is more of a problem at breakfast time, when the food court is the only option.
- A car would be of some advantage here, especially for traveling to other resort areas to dine.

RECOMMENDATIONS FOR RESERVATIONS

- Barbados and Trinidad South are a bit far from the central resort area and should probably be avoided (or resort guests in these areas should be given complimentary bicycles). We prefer either Jamaica or Aruba. Both are a short walk from the central areas, and the walk takes you across Parrot Cay. We found this stroll pleasant and, in the evenings, even a bit romantic.

ROMANCE AT THE CARIBBEAN BEACH

- Resort theming: ♥♥
- Courtyard-view room: ♥♥
- King bed resort room: ♥♥
- Early picnic breakfast on Parrot Cay: ♥♥
- Late-night swim at a quiet pool: ♥♥
- Beach hammock by starlight: ♥♥♥♥
- Evening stroll around the resort: ♥♥

The Swan and the Dolphin

Here's a story we have heard about these two places. The Walt Disney Company had worked out a deal with the Sheraton and Westin Hotels to permit them to operate a dual hotel complex on Disney World property. John Tishman, representing both the owners and his construction company, had overseen the selection of the architectural plans. Before construction began, Michael Eisner came aboard as Disney CEO. Shown the plans, he was unimpressed.

"Come meet my architect," he was reported to have told Tishman. Eisner's architect was the world-renowned Michael Graves. What ensued was a competition to see whose design would win the most accolades. This contest resulted in the construction of what has been termed a masterpiece of "entertainment architecture." Whatever you may think about them, the Swan and the Dolphin are unlike any hotels that you have ever seen. While located in the very heart of Walt Disney World, neither is run by Team Disney. The Swan is a Westin resort, and the Dolphin is managed by Sheraton.

These two resorts sit perfectly aligned, set together like sisters and nestled neatly between Epcot and the Disney–MGM Studios. Separate,

The Swan and the Dolphin

yet part of a greater whole, these two share something special. The coral and aquas of their exteriors and the perfect convergence of shapes tell us that there is a juncture happening. These fantastic structures were designed from the ground up to occupy each other's space, to be seen together and from each other. The theme of these resorts is fantasy and fun. Everything from the fifty-foot swans perched atop one resort to the nine-story cascading waterfall at the other serves to evoke a feeling of whimsy and delight. A visit here after dark will work its magic spell.

Each resort has its own Olympic "lap" pool with hot tub. Both resorts share a water playground that ranks second only to the Yacht and the Beach Clubs' Stormalong Bay. The Grotto is a long and narrow lake/pool. Waterfalls, secluded hot tubs, and a water volleyball court are several of its highlights.

Virtually no expense has been spared in the landscape design of these resorts. Date palms, magnolias, and other well-tended foliage abound. Driveways, walkways, and paths are all integral pieces in the big and beautiful picture.

Because neither the Swan nor the Dolphin is owned or managed by the Walt Disney Company, there are a few things that you will not get here. Most noticeable will be the Length of Stay Pass. Each resort maintains a Guest Services desk that offers the usual selection of tickets and passes. Your Swan or Dolphin resort card will be limited to charging at your resort only. Aside from these, you will enjoy all of the benefits of staying at a Disney resort: Surprise Mornings, preferred tee times, same-day dinner reservations, and guaranteed park admission, to mention only a few.

Transportation and Convenience

The Swan and the Dolphin enjoy the same wonderful transportation that serves the Yacht and the Beach Clubs. This group of resorts is the most convenient of all Disney resort areas.

Both the nearby Epcot and Disney–MGM are reached by boat from a dock on the walkway between the resorts. All other Disney destinations are via direct buses, leaving from the bus stops near each front entrance.

The Swan

The Swan was the first Disney resort that we visited without our kids. We hadn't been to Disney World in more than ten years when we arrived at the Swan. We'd never seen Epcot, and Disney–MGM Studios had just opened. We had no idea what to expect and were ready for just about anything. What we got was a few days of intimate and relaxing fun. We had a wonderful time strolling around and discovering the parks and we had an even more memorable time at this classy resort. We enjoyed hot tubs, swimming, and fine dining, all accented with occasional touches of Disney magic. We were hooked.

On this first trip, we slowed our car as we approached the Swan. We marveled at the elaborately complex landscaping and ornate cast-iron street lamps. Above and around us loomed a building the likes of which we had never seen. The huge, twin swans sitting on its roof were not even its most unusual details. The resort's paint job seemed more like a giant mural: huge, aqua waves broke on hues of coral. The balconies included ironwork so intricate that it appeared to have been carved.

So intriguing was this place that we felt more like exploring than registering. The tropical theme of the grounds and building were carried gracefully into the interiors. A fountain of swans and a flock of parrot chandeliers were but a few of the many delightful decorations. The furnishings featured carved swans, and even the sand in the ashtrays was imprinted with the seal of the swans. Hallways, windows, and porticos were all in symmetry. This confluence, we were to discover, was one of the essentials of Michael Graves' design.

Rooms at the Swan   Our first room at the Swan had two queen beds. It would take a few more visits before we would discover king-size sleeping accommodations. The room's bright array of tropical colors was cheerful and gay. Woodwork was lightly colored and trimmed in pastel aquas and pinks. Our balcony looked out onto a small lake and, across it, to an as yet unfinished Dolphin. A quick look around our room revealed a large armoire with a color television, a massage showerhead, and a basket of luxurious toiletries. In the closet were bathrobes with embroidered swans. The level of luxury, we knew at once, was something that we were going to get very used to.

In subsequent visits, we discovered that this room was one of two basic views: the standard resort room and the Epcot Center view. Epcot rooms all look out onto the World Showcase of Epcot—a view that is slightly more obstructed now by the creation of Disney's BoardWalk. From the upper floors, guests can still get an impressive view of IllumiNations, the nightly laser light show.

Many of the resort rooms look out onto the Dolphin, which is a very attractive and impressive sight. Many more have views of Disney–MGM Studios, and others look out over the swimming areas. There really aren't any bad views here, simply better ones. Rooms are available with either a king-size bed or two queens. Not all rooms, however, have balconies. Value season at the Swan is considerably longer than it is at Disney resorts and includes summer.

Following are the 1996 room rates for the Swan.

1996 Room Rates for the Swan

Accommodation	Regular Season	Value Season
Standard resort room	$310	$260
Epcot Center view	$350	$300
Royal Beach Club (concierge)	$380	$330

Concierge Service and Suites at the Swan   Concierge service at the Swan is known as the Royal Beach Club and is located on the exclusive east end of the twelfth floor. A continental breakfast is served each morning, and beverages and fruit are offered at midday. Hors d'oeuvres and cocktails begin before dinner, and cordials and coffee are served in the evening. In all, you receive a day's worth of delights. The Swan's dedicated concierge staff is available to assist with all of your reservations and special needs. There is even a complimentary shoe shine service. All you have to do is ask.

There are five different suite designs at the Swan. Each has something unique to offer. The Junior suite is the most affordable. Each comes with a lavishly furnished bedroom, a king bed, desk, and sofa and chairs. The ample living room and dining area feature a round table and four cane-back chairs. Cloth robes, private bar, and live plants are a few of the indulgences.

The color scheme of these suites is that of the resort: aqua and rose. Fabrics are soft and plush. Each occupies the end unit of the Swan's wings. This corner position provides for many windows and an outstanding panorama. At $350 during value season and $400 during the regular season, the Junior suite has a lot going for it. A stay here will be indulgently romantic.

From this modest start, the suites become considerably more expensive. Beginning with the Grand suite at nearly $1,000 per night, followed by the Governor's suite at nearly $1,300, and reaching all the way to one of the two incredible Presidentials at around $1,500 nightly, these suites are well suited to those able to afford them. The two Presidential suites each feature a theme. One is the Oasis room, the other is the Southwestern room. With over 1,000 square feet, these multiroom suites each feature a marble entryway, grand piano, fully stocked bar, king-size bed, Jacuzzi tub, and full kitchen stocked with assorted beverages. Furnishings are lavishly extravagant. It is hard, even for us, to imagine traveling in this style.

Dining at the Swan   As we have mentioned, dining options at this resort are exceptional. With memorable eating places at the neighboring BoardWalk and the Yacht and the Beach Clubs as well as those at the nearby countries of Epcot, the choices begin to look limitless. And they are. For convenient, varied, and outstanding dining, this is the corner of Walt Disney World to be in.

The Swan offers its guests three interesting table-service eateries. The all-purpose restaurant is the Garden Grove, which serves every meal in a pleasant garden gazebo. At dinner, it becomes the Grill at the Garden Grove, featuring seafood and steak dinners. Disney character breakfasts are served here on Wednesdays and Saturdays and character dinners are served on Mondays, Thursdays, and Fridays.

Palio offers fine Italian dining in a romantic atmosphere. Featuring strolling musicians and outstanding food, Palio is one of our favorite dining spots at Disney. The Splash Grill and Deli is the Swan's convenience-food location. Located near the lap pool, this small restaurant features a variety of lunches, dinners, and snacks. Even more convenient is the Swan's 24-hour room service. Its large menu can furnish snacks, meals, beverages, or the makings for intimate in-room dining. For reviews and information about these and other restaurants, see Chapter 6.

Lounges at the Swan   Kimonos is a beautiful and stylishly created retreat that features an Oriental flair. Relax and watch the sushi chefs perform their graceful art. Kimonos can be a romantic place to have a drink and some very interesting appetizers.

Cappuccino's is the lounge that accompanies Palio. Fine wines and cognacs are the specialties of the house. This is the place to go for gourmet coffee and the World's best pastries and desserts. The dessert counter at Cappuccino's is so good that it should be designated a deadly weapon.

The Lobby Court Lounge, besides offering a selection of wines and spirits, also offers the best cup of coffee in Disney World, made from the beans of Seattle roaster Torrefazione Italia. Open in the morning and again in the evening, the Lobby Court Lounge also features a decadent assortment of pastries and chocolate desserts, more than enough to tempt the stalwart. This is a delightful place to sit in the evening and listen to the lounge's player piano.

Shops at the Swan   Disney's Cabana is the Swan's souvenir and Disney character merchandise store. It also offers a large selection of casual men's and women's sportswear.

Services Available at the Swan

- Complimentary valet parking
- Full bell service
- Valet and laundry service
- Beauty salon
- Concierge desk
- Nightly turndown service
- Pay-per-view movies

Recreational Activities at the Swan

- Lap pool with spa, and the Grotto (a three-acre water playground)
- Kiddie pool
- White sand beach with watercraft rentals
- Swan Health Club
- Jogging and walking path
- Tennis club and basketball court
- Camp Swan and Camp Dolphin children's activity centers
- Video game room

$\mathcal{R}$ECOMMENDATIONS FOR RESERVATIONS

- Since this resort is managed by Westin Hotels, reservations are handled not only by Disney Central Reservations but also by Westin and the Swan. For reservations, call Swan reservations at (800) 248-7926; Westin reservations at (800) 228-3000; or Disney Central Reservations at (407) 934-7639. For brochures and information, write:

The Walt Disney World Swan
1500 Epcot Resorts Blvd.
Lake Buena Vista, FL 32830-2653

- Westin Hotels runs a variety of specials and package deals throughout the year, and we heartily recommend that you ask about these when you call. Summer specials are frequent.

ℛOMANCE AT THE SWAN

- Resort theming: ♥♥♥
- Room amenities: ♥♥♥
- Fine dining: ♥♥♥
- Breakfast on your balcony: ♥♥♥
- Dinner at Palio, listening to the music of a strolling violinist: ♥♥♥
- Hot tubs: ♥♥♥
- Evening walks to BoardWalk, Epcot countries, and the Yacht and the Beach Clubs: ♥♥
- Watching IllumiNations from your balcony: ♥♥♥

The Dolphin

Water is the theme of this resort, and it is everywhere. From rows of fountains at the front gate to trickles that flow down the stone walls of the foyer, the pleasant sound of rushing water is music for Dolphin guests. One of the sights here is the waterfall on the Swan side of the resort. Overlooking Crescent Lake, this giant fountain cascades along nine stories of huge, shell-shaped levels and into a 60-foot-wide clamshell.

The scale of everything here is grand. The most prominent part of the resort's main building is the 27-story pyramid that has become a fixture of the Disney skyline. Nearby sit the two 56-foot dolphin statues that celebrate this resort's aquatic theme. Next to the Statue of Liberty, they are the tallest free-standing sculptures in the U.S. From their perch high atop the resort, they stand watch upon a colossal creation of tulip-shaped floral fountains that adorn the tower wings. At night, this array seems too large to be real.

Keeping to the color theme of the two resorts, the building's coral hues are swathed in painted, turquoise banana leaves. Reaching from ground level to the tenth floor, this outrageous mural took six months to complete. It creates a fantasy aura that is part of the Dolphin's mystique.

The lobby too is whimsical and entertaining. Brightly colored fabric hangs from its ten-story ceiling to create a cavernous tent. Flowering vines climb trellises that encircle the lobby floor, and, arranged symmetrically around the central fountain are clusters of sofas and chairs. You see artwork everywhere: murals, paintings, and sculptures; the works of

Picasso, Matisse, and Rousseau. Even the elevator seems bright and tropical.

Rooms at the Dolphin   The rooms are bright and cheerful. A large and well-appointed vanity and a cozy sitting area will make you feel at home. From the floral drapes to the coral and turquoise bedspread, your romantic Disney vacation will take on the fun and tropical theme of the Dolphin. One look out the window and you know that you are in the middle of all of the magic that Disney has to offer.

The variety of resort rooms at the Dolphin come with a choice of either one king bed or two doubles. That is two doubles, not two queens. The Enchanted Forest view is the standard resort view. Enchanted Forest views look out onto the front of the hotel. Other views may be of the pool, Crescent Lake, Epcot, or Disney–MGM. As with hotels everywhere, the more spectacular the view, the more spectacular the price.

Our favorite room at the Dolphin is called the King View Premier. Located on the ends of the wings of the main building, these charming rooms look out in two directions with an unmatched view of the lake, the Swan, Epcot, and Disney's BoardWalk. Each has a king-size bed and twin balconies. A coffeemaker will make mornings a pleasure. At $365 during the brief peak season, this room enjoys many specials during the remainder of the year.

Value season at the Dolphin does not mimic Disney's. It is much longer and runs from early January to mid-February and again from mid-April to the end of the third week in December.

Following are the room rates at the Dolphin.

1996 Room Rates for the Dolphin

Accommodation	Regular Season	Value Season
Enchanted Forest (standard)	$280	$245
Resort view (Epcot, MGM, pool):		
with balcony	$365	$305
without balcony	$345	$290
Lake view (no balcony)	$325	$275
Premier King view	$365	$305
Dolphin Towers (concierge)	$395	$365

Concierge Service and Suites at the Dolphin   The 77 spacious and lavishly decorated guest suites of concierge service are located in the

Dolphin Tower. Private check-in will begin your journey here, and along the way you will learn the meaning of "pampered." As Tower guests, you will receive champagne and a complimentary gift upon arrival. You'll be treated to a host of luxurious toiletries, Dolphin bathrobes, hair dryer, special stationery, and coffeemaker.

The plush Tower Lounge is available exclusively for the use of Tower guests. This area features a large entertainment center, magazines and newspapers, and a small library. A continental breakfast will be the perfect way to start each day. If you desire, fresh coffee and orange juice can be delivered to your room. Hors d'oeuvres and cocktails service are offered before dinner. After dinner and before your romantic evening out, don't forget to stop by and have a dessert while you watch the fireworks.

Complimentary use of both the Dolphin's health and fitness center and the tennis courts are also part of your romantic Dolphin Tower visit. A light pressing service is also available upon request. And, of course, the concierge staff eagerly awaits your every request.

The Dolphin boasts that it offers more suites than any other resort at Walt Disney World. While this may be true, many of them are better suited for business purposes. The two suites worth mentioning are the Junior suite and the Presidential.

The Junior suites are in various places throughout the resort. Each consists of a parlor connected to a regular resort room with either a single king bed or two doubles. The parlor offers a sitting area with a pull-out sofa bed and several comfortable chairs.

While you might not feel the need for an extra room, you might find it a good place for the kids if they are with you. During the brief peak season, a Junior suite will cost around $550 per night. Most of the year, the same suite is $475.

There are four Presidential suites at the Dolphin. Each has been extravagantly decorated with its own exotic personality. At nearly 3,000 square feet, these suites are larger than many private homes. Named Los Presidentes, the Pharaoh's suite, the Emperor's suite, and Caesar's suite, each is the final word in luxury. Service even includes a round-the-clock butler. These three-bedroom suites offer a large entertainment center, gold-plated bathroom fixtures, ten telephones, four VCRs, and a fully stocked kitchen. Some of the famous persons who have occupied these rooms are Dustin Hoffman, Macauley Culkin, Eddie Murphy, Dolly Parton, and Michael Jackson.

If this sounds like something that you would both enjoy, then a five-night, six-day package is available. Virtually everything that you might ever think of is included, along with some things you probably wouldn't have imagined. The cost of the package is a mere $24,000. For around $1,500 per night, you can get this room without all of the accompanying hoopla.

Dining at the Dolphin   As guests at the Dolphin, you will enjoy a large variety of restaurants. Six table-service restaurants include everything from the poolside Cabana Bar & Grill to the elegant and unforgettable Sum Chows. The Coral Cafe is the Dolphin's all-purpose restaurant, featuring varied menus for each of the day's meals. The Dolphin Fountain is located on the ground floor of the resort and is a fifties-style soda shop with a menu of American fountain classics. Juan and Only's, Harry's Safari Bar and Grill, and Sum Chows offer only dinner, and each presents a unique and special cuisine. For reviews and information about these and other restaurants, see Chapter 6.

The Dolphin offers the option for fast food too. Tubby Checkers Buffeteria is a cute little cafeteria that offers a pretty standard selection of convenience foods. Snacks, breakfasts, lunches, and dinners are the offerings, and there is even a small convenience store that offers a variety of sundries.

Room service at the Dolphin should not be overlooked as a dining option. The menu is large. We love having our dinner served to us on a white tablecloth right in the privacy of our own room. We suggest that you give it a try. Also available for delivery are Chinese food and pizza. To order breakfast the night before, turn your television set to Channel 88 and follow on-screen directions. A Japanese-style breakfast is also available.

Room service also features something particularly well suited for a romantic evening. The Dolphin offers some memorable alternatives to the usual nightly turndown with chocolates. Return to your room to find "Carnevale," an Italian-style festive turndown with almond biscotti and two small bottles of Sambuca liqueur. Or you might select "Chocolate Lovers" and discover handmade truffles and two nips of Grand Marnier. The ten choices range from the comic to the sublime. The offerings are part of the room service menu. Surprise someone.

Lounges at the Dolphin   When it comes to nightlife, only Pleasure Island and the BoardWalk have more to offer than the Dolphin. The Copa Banana is the Dolphin's nightclub. Dance the night away to the rhythm of the islands and enjoy a fruitful selection of tropical drinks. Harry's Safari Bar and Juan's Bar and Jail are two other exotic lounges to visit. Both offer a large selection of wines, beers, and cocktails. Have a yard of ale at Harry's or sip a rare tequila at Juan's while you listen to live flamenco guitar. Both are fun and colorful places and well worth your time.

You shouldn't have any trouble finding the Lobby Lounge. Drop by this quiet bistro for a glass of wine or aperitif while you enjoy the music of a live pianist. And at poolside, you can enjoy beer, wine, or tropical cocktails at the Cabana Bar & Grill.

Shops at the Dolphin   There are four shops in the lobby of the Dolphin. From gourmet chocolates to jewelry and fine apparel, these shops should provide some interesting browsing and even something special to celebrate your visit here.

Services Available at the Dolphin

- Complimentary valet parking
- Full bell service
- Beauty salon
- Multilingual concierge
- In-room massage
- Valet and laundry service

Recreational Activities at the Dolphin

- Heated pool, and the Grotto (a three-acre water playground)
- Kiddie pool
- White sand beach with watercraft rentals
- Body by Jake Health Club
- Jogging and walking path
- Tennis club and basketball court
- Camp Dolphin and Camp Swan children's activity centers
- Video game room

RECOMMENDATIONS FOR RESERVATIONS

- For brochures and other printed information, write:

The Walt Disney World Dolphin
1500 Epcot Resorts Blvd.
Lake Buena Vista, FL 32830-2653

- For reservations, call Sheraton Central Reservations at (800) 325-3535; Dolphin Reservations at (800) 227-1500; Disney Central Reservations at (407) 936-7639.
- The Sheraton offers many discounts and vacation packages throughout the year.
- Being a member of the Sheraton Club will give you such perks as late check-out and free room upgrade. It may be worth joining. Call the Sheraton reservation number for details.

ROMANCE AT THE DOLPHIN

- Resort theming: ♥♥♥
- Room amenities: ♥♥
- Dolphin Tower concierge service: ♥♥♥♥
- Premier King View room: ♥♥♥♥
- Fine dining: ♥♥♥
- Breakfast in bed: ♥♥♥♥
- Dinner at Sum Chows: ♥♥♥
- Hot tubs: ♥♥♥
- Evening walks to BoardWalk, Epcot countries, the Yacht and the Beach Clubs: ♥♥
- IllumiNations from your balcony: ♥♥♥

Disney's BoardWalk

In the summer of 1996, nearly a year after this guide goes to press, Disney's latest creation, the BoardWalk, will open its doors. This puts us in an interesting situation, reminding us of a book we once read in which a travel writer was an "armchair expert": he never left home to visit the places that he wrote about. This is just not our style. We like to do more than just visit the places that we write about, we like to scour them in search of that something extra to tell our readers.

At the time of this writing, the BoardWalk is little more than a construction site. After visiting the site, speaking at length with the BoardWalk's general manager, looking at renderings and room mock-ups, and reading everything we could get our hands on, we will make our best "armchair" effort to tell you about this new and exciting area.

Located on the shores of Crescent Lake, directly opposite the turn-of-the-century Yacht and the Beach Clubs, is Disney's BoardWalk. It is

BoardWalk

the perfect creation to cohabit this corner of Walt Disney World. The BoardWalk is a 1930s Atlantic seaside village. Its shops, inns, and restaurants dot the picturesque waterfront. Along its Atlantic City–style promenade, the buildings seem to be part of a town. If there is an architectural theme here, it is one that has changed over time, lending the waterfront a colorful mix of Victorian artistry. Each building has its own unique personality, creating a sense of history. All of the hustle and bustle of this era's seaside life comes magically alive here and it is brought to life with style and elegance.

While the focus of the BoardWalk is its waterfront, there is something more going on. This place is not just a resort. It is something new for Disney. The BoardWalk is the first Disney area to feature a mix of entertainment, retail outlets, and resort accommodations. No other Disney area comes close to matching the excitement that the BoardWalk delivers.

Besides two outstanding resorts, the BoardWalk offers a number of shops, a 1930s dance hall, an ESPN sports club, a brew pub, a bakery, and a "dueling-pianos" nightclub. Throw in three excellent eateries and a themed water recreation area, and what you have is truly original. With both Epcot and Disney–MGM a short walk away, the BoardWalk gives the phrase "in the middle of things" a whole new meaning.

Don't come to the BoardWalk expecting the usual Disney resorts. There isn't anything usual about the two resorts at Disney's BoardWalk. The BoardWalk Inn is Disney's smallest and most intimate resort. With only 378 rooms, this bed-and-breakfast-style hotel is just the right size to make good on its promise of personalized service for pampered patrons.

The Inn shares a large Victorian lobby with its sister resort, the BoardWalk Villas. With 532 rooms, the Villas feature a seaside cottage atmosphere and offers an assortment of luxurious lodgings. The Boardwalk Villas are a Disney Vacation Club property, and accommodations are for the use of both Club owners and Disney resort guests.

Those who elect to stay in either resort will rediscover the hospitality of this era. The barrel-vaulted ceiling of the lobby shared by the two resorts and its Victorian charm are impressive indeed. Overstuffed sofas, giant potted palms, and a host of ornate and decorative details welcome guests to this perfectly rendered bit of yesteryear.

The grounds of the BoardWalk are beautiful, relaxing, and hospitable. Mowed lawns, beguiling gardens, and manicured shrubbery carefully accentuate the interesting blends of architecture. "Casual elegance" is the operative phrase here, and the outdoor areas are both inviting and comfortable. Courtyards, rose gardens, a croquet lawn, and the BoardWalk Green are all places made for people.

While each of these resorts has its own quiet pool, they share a fantasy water playground known as Luna Park. Named for the turn-of-the-century Coney Island amusement park, this 6,000 square-foot pool features a 200-foot roller coaster water slide called the Keester Coaster.

Rooms of the BoardWalk Inn

Standard rooms at the BoardWalk Inn feature an eclectic collection of furnishings to create the sensibilities of an intimate and deluxe bed and breakfast. Most rooms feature two queen-size beds, and 24 standard rooms feature king-size beds. Standard room rates at the BoardWalk Inn match those of the Yacht and the Beach Clubs.

Concierge service is located on the Inn's fourth floor. With a mere 40 rooms, it is the smallest concierge area in Walt Disney World. Guests are promised highly personalized service. A full offering of tempting treats is to be found daily in the plush concierge lounge, and a full-time staff awaits.

The Presidential and Vice-Presidential suites are located on the top floor, overlooking both the lake and Epcot. The level of luxury here is unsurpassed, with nightly rates to match. At 2,200 square feet and $1,500 per night, the Inn's Presidential suite is large, lavish, and memorable.

The most interesting accommodations here are the Garden suites. Each of these fourteen suites features an entrance through its own private rose garden. Another indulgence is the oversized Jacuzzi tub, which is the perfect place for you to soak together after a day of Disney excitement. A Garden suite is the quintessential place for your honeymoon or romantic getaway.

Rooms of the BoardWalk Villas

The seaside cottage accommodations of the Villas come in a variety of shapes and sizes. The bright decor perfectly fits the BoardWalk's nostalgia. Accommodations are similar to those found at the Disney Vacation Club, except that they are located in five-story buildings rather than townhouses. There are one-bedroom studios and an assortment of one-, two-, and three-bedroom villas. The studios offer a single large bedroom with two queen beds and a wet bar. The villas have full kitchens, a private master bedroom, a large living room area with pull-out bed, and a Jacuzzi for two. Villas typically include private laundry areas, fully equipped kitchens, and VCRs. The studios and villas have either balconies or patios.

Transportation and Convenience

Guests at Disney's BoardWalk are sure to find it the ultimate in convenience. As we mentioned earlier, the Epcot resorts enjoy the best location of all the Disney resorts.

- To Epcot, Disney–MGM Studios: by short walk or boat ride
- To Discovery Island, River Country: bus to Magic Kingdom and boat to either
- To all other Disney destinations: by direct bus

Dining and Entertainment at the BoardWalk

Even without including the nearby Epcot, Disney–MGM Studios, the Yacht and the Beach Clubs, and the Swan and the Dolphin, we will tell you that there is a lot to do right here at the BoardWalk.

- The Atlantic Ballroom is a 1930s style big-band dance hall. The ten-piece Atlantic Ballroom Orchestra plays the very best of dance music from the thirties to today.
- The ESPN Sports Club is the ultimate in sports bars. This interactive multimedia sports complex is also a full-service restaurant.
- Crazy Fingers Dueling Pianos Bar features a full-service bar and the nightly entertainment of two very zany piano players.
- The Big River Grill and Brewing Works is the first microbrewery on Disney property. The pub's numerous brews are made right here from whole grains.
- Spoodle's will be a family-style eatery with a deli atmosphere and features pizzas, salads, and seafood.
- Seashore Sweets Soda Fountain is where you'll find ice cream treats in the setting of a traditional soda fountain.
- The BoardWalk Bakery is the supplier of breads and pastries for the restaurants at the BoardWalk. You'll find it right on the waterfront, and you'll be able to look through the window and watch the bakers work. Should temptation overcome you, the pastries, cookies, and sweets are all available.

- There will also be one more full-service restaurant. No plans have been finalized at the time of this writing.

Shops at the BoardWalk

Numerous shops are planned for the BoardWalk promenade. Although no firm plans have been announced, we expect the usual assortment of men's and women's apparel shops, perhaps a jewelry store, and, of course, someplace to purchase Disney merchandise. There will also be some sort of general store. The promenade will feature a colorful variety of sidewalk vendors offering food and other interesting items.

Recreational Activities at the BoardWalk

- Large, themed swimming area called Luna Park and two quiet pools
- Three hot tubs
- Muscles and Bustles Health Club
- Little Toots children's activity center
- Two tennis courts and lawn croquet

The Village Resorts

Port Orleans and Dixie Landings

It's not the mighty Mississippi, but it's a river and it's known as the Sassagoula. It wends its way from Lake Buena Vista through the Disney Village Resort area. If you hop a boat at the Village Marketplace and head upstream past the grand old paddle wheeler Empress Lilly and past the Disney Institute, you might just imagine yourself on the Ol' Mississippi. Upriver, you'll make harbor at Disney's Port Orleans resort. This quaint and colorful little city, with its narrow, cobbled streets, gas lights, and relaxed French Quarter ambience, will make you feel as though you've gone back in time to walk the streets of old New Orleans.

Further up the Sassagoula, you'll enter Magnolia Bend, part of Disney's Dixie Landings resort. The banks of the river here are lined with stately magnolias and graceful willows. Here and there, an occasional footbridge crosses the waterway, leading off to the grand "old mansions" of the resort.

Port Orleans

Dixie Landings

A bit farther upstream, the boat will bring you to Alligator Bayou. Now you've entered the back river country and another part of Dixie Landings. Here, the resort more reflects the rural charm of the bayou. The rustic resort buildings are nestled amidst a dense forest of slash pines. Shaded footpaths crisscross in all directions past small ponds and along tiny streams. At night, the crickets "sing" in the bushes, compliments of the Disney imagineers.

This is what you'll find along Disney's Sassagoula River: three delightfully different areas that together are the Port Orleans and Dixie Landings resorts. While they combine for over 3,000 rooms, the feeling here is anything but that of hustle and bustle. Along the banks of the Sassagoula, you will enjoy a sense of privacy and harmony.

We have grouped Port Orleans and Dixie Landings together not because they are so alike but because, together, they make up this Disney picture of "life on the river." What they have in common is that they are both moderately priced and beautifully themed resorts.

Port Orleans

This lovely resort evokes the ambience of the old French Quarter. The delight begins the moment you pass through the iron gates and into the tree-lined drive. The Disney artists have been hard at work. The main building is the Mint, and it is a masterpiece of ornate wrought-iron work topped with a canopy of glass. Check-in is more fantasy than a chore. The vaulted ceilings and iron railings here more resemble a bank than a hotel lobby, and friendly service is the coin of this realm. The hotel staff is attired in perfect period costume. Not a detail has been missed. The imagineers have been busy, and the promise of Mardi Gras is everywhere.

The Port Orleans grounds are splendidly landscaped. A stroll here at night will be relaxing and romantic. The narrow, cobbled streets have names such as Rue d'Blues and Rue d'Baga. The small parks and lovely stone fountains are enchanting. Narrow sidewalks, gaslights, and iron hitching posts combine to create a real sense of small neighborhoods in this small "old city" on the river.

Port Orleans's row houses have distinct personalities, too. Each has its own unique yard, surrounded by an iron fence just a bit different than its neighbor's. The quaint charm is convincing. Nothing has been overlooked, and we suggest that you overlook nothing. Spend some time strolling about in the evening. Find a nice bench in a cozy garden and sit awhile.

The swimming pool here is Doubloon Lagoon. A huge dragon slithers its way around and through this fantasy playground, forming a water slide with its long and slippery tongue. It is colorful and exciting. Here and there you will come across colorful statues of "crocodile musicians," each with a musical instrument. Don't miss the crocodile shower at poolside for a memorable photo opportunity.

The resort's hot tub is located in an enchanting garden near enough to the pool to invite a quick dip but far enough away to keep it fairly quiet. The garden's cast-iron benches and ivy-covered trellises make this a beautiful spot after dark.

Rooms at Port Orleans   The rooms here are fairly typical of the moderately priced Disney resorts. Although a bit smaller than Disney's luxury resort rooms (314 square feet), we found ours to be both spacious and comfortable. Each features a small vanity area, complete with two pedestal sinks and mirrors. Beneath the drapes are genuine wooden Venetian blinds. The antiqued wood furniture, ceiling fan, and formal armoire enhance a sense of the old French Quarter. Our room was just elegant enough to be romantic. One look out the window and onto the French Quarter streets below, and we knew that we were someplace special.

Most of the rooms at Port Orleans have two double beds, but there are also 58 king bedrooms. These rooms are a bit more expensive, but we always find a double bed to be rather small. King bedrooms here at Port Orleans are all corner rooms, making for a slightly larger sitting area.

Following are 1996 room rates for Port Orleans.

1996 Room Rates for Port Orleans

Accommodation	Regular Season	Value Season	Holiday Season
Standard view	$99	$95	$104
Pool/river view	$129	$124	$134
Courtyard	$124	$119	$134
King	$129	$124	$134

Transportation and Convenience   Port Orleans is fairly convenient to the rest of the World. There is one large bus stop in front of the resort. Buses run every 20 minutes and even more frequently during the busier hours.

A boat service runs to Pleasure Island and the Village Marketplace. The small launches are fun and will take you through parts of Walt

Disney World that you would never have a chance to see otherwise. Don't miss this trip.

- To Village Marketplace, Pleasure Island: by boat or bus
- To Magic Kingdom, Epcot, Disney–MGM Studios, Village Marketplace, Typhoon Lagoon, Pleasure Island, Blizzard Beach: by bus

Dining at Port Orleans   There is one table-service restaurant at Port Orleans, Bonfamille's Cafe, and a Mardi Gras–themed food court called the Sassagoula Floatworks and Food Factory. Bonfamille's is a delightful garden courtyard restaurant that serves both breakfast and dinner. The cuisines here are American and Creole. For more information and our review of Bonfamille's, see Chapter 6.

The Sassagoula Floatworks is a warehouse full of Mardi Gras props. Giant masks and colorful floats are suspended from the ceiling. Food-wise, the choices are many with a definite New Orleans flair. The variety of "shops" offer everything from scrambled eggs and muffins to burgers and Creole chicken with red beans. There's even fresh pasta and pizza. Don't miss the traditional French Quarter treat, beignets, at the bakeshop.

While Floatworks seats 300, the resort has over one thousand rooms. Of course, this means that if you eat at the more traditional times, you're likely to find it crowded. If the two of you are like us, you may not like to spend mealtimes in such an atmosphere. An alternative is to take your trays into one of the pleasant outside sitting areas or out by the pool.

Another meal alternative is Sassagoula Pizza Express, which delivers pizza, salads, beverages, and desserts from 4 P.M. to midnight.

Lounges at Port Orleans   Scat Cat's is a delightful little lounge adjoining the lobby. It has a full bar and, in the evening, frequently features live entertainment. Hors d'oeuvres are available from the kitchen of Bonfamille's. Mardi Grogs is the poolside bar, serving a variety of non-alcoholic and specialty cocktails during pool hours. Also on the menu are snacks and deli sandwiches.

Shops at Port Orleans   Jackson Square Gifts and Desires offers the usual selection of Disney character merchandise as well as a line of clothes and accessories with the Port Orleans logo. This shop also has a variety of general store items as well as offering authentic Creole condiments and New Orleans chicory coffees.

Recreational Activities at Port Orleans

- Doubloon Lagoon, a themed swimming pool with water slide
- Hot tub (spa)
- Boat and bike rentals
- Walking or jogging paths
- Video arcade

OUR IMPRESSIONS OF PORT ORLEANS

- Of the moderately priced resorts, we think that Port Orleans is the most romantic. After dark, it is simply enchanting.
- The boat service to Pleasure Island and the Village Marketplace is delightful. It turned our routine trip into an adventure. It is especially pleasant around sunset.
- If you are heading over to Dixie Landings, whether to look around or to have a meal, you'll find that it is a short walk away via a delightful footpath that runs along the river.

RECOMMENDATIONS FOR RESERVATIONS

- If you can, avoid the standard parking lot view. The beautiful part of this resort is inside the courtyard.
- Pool-view rooms are convenient for swimming, but you may find that you have sacrificed peace and quiet.

ROMANCE AT PORT ORLEANS RESORT

- Overall theme: ♥♥♥
- Room with king bed: ♥♥
- Doubloon Lagoon: ♥♥
- Bonfamille's Cafe: ♥♥
- Taking food from food court to the outside area: ♥
- Taking a nice, long hot tub at day's end: ♥♥♥
- Taking an evening stroll to Dixie Landings: ♥♥♥
- Taking a late-night swim: ♥♥
- Enjoying a sunset cruise to Pleasure Island and the Village Marketplace: ♥♥
- Renting a boat or bicycles and exploring: ♥♥

Dixie Landings

With a bit of the old Disney magic, Dixie Landings manages to be two very different resorts in one. The Magnolia Bend area of Dixie Landings reminds you of the plantations of the Old South. Stately courtyards, charming fountains, and formal gardens re-create the sweeping grandeur of the antebellum South. Resort rooms here are in large mansion-like buildings with winding stairways and imposing columns. The weeping willows and sloping lawns of Magnolia Bend give way to dense thickets of pine and Florida maple at Alligator Bayou. Here, the "weathered" resort buildings are quaint and small. Their tin roofs peek through the treetops. Footpaths seem narrow and winding and the charm is more rustic and homey.

While Dixie Landings has over 2,000 rooms, the resort is so spread out that it does not feel so large. Still, a visit to the central building, the Sassagoula Steamboat Company, will serve to remind you that this is indeed a big place. During the busier times of day, there is a lot of traffic here.

The Steamboat Company re-creates a small port on the river with docks, warehouses, and a water-driven cotton mill. The Disney penchant for detail is everywhere. Even the bathrooms in the lobby have old-fashioned cisterns and wooden toilet seats. Talk about theming.

Check-in will be the beginning of your Dixie adventure. The reservationists wear the costumes of clerks, and they will help you "book passage" on your trip upriver. The front desk resembles a steamship office more than a hotel. Piles of old steamer trunks and exotic ports of call create a pleasant sense of fun.

The Sassagoula Steamboat Company is home to the Dixie Landings restaurants, lounge, general store, and food court. Also located here is Guest Services. The guest buildings of both Alligator Bayou and Magnolia Bend surround Ol' Man Island, a three-acre water recreation area with pool, playground, spa, and a stocked fishing hole.

Ol' Man Island has one large pool with a short water slide. There are also five quiet pools located around the resort. These are convenient to most rooms and are a bit more intimate. There is only one hot tub here at the Landings, and we feel that it is not enough. It is located right in the middle of things at Ol' Man Island, minimizing peace, quiet, and privacy.

Rooms at Magnolia Bend   Magnolia Bend is made up of four "parishes." With such names as Parterre Place and the Acadian House, each is really a large resort building housing more than 250 guest rooms. The feel here is a bit big for our tastes, especially in the standard rooms that look out onto the parking areas. Rooms on the river side of the complex are infinitely more relaxing and private.

The rooms at both Magnolia Bend and Alligator Bayou are the same general size and shape. With 314 square feet of space, each is adequate and comfortable. While the rooms at both the Bend and the Bayou are the same dimensions, they are worlds apart in decor. The ambience at Magnolia Bend is definitely more formal. French Provincial furniture, brocade upholstery, and an antiqued, mirrored armoire are suited perfectly to the antebellum grand manor. Each room has a ceiling fan, a small sitting bench, table and chairs, and a spacious and well-lit vanity area. There are two pedestal sinks and each has its own mirror, giving you both a place to get ready for your evening out. Rooms feature either two double beds or one king.

Rooms at Alligator Bayou   Alligator Bayou offers much more of a down-home feeling. Instead of four large mansions, the same number of guest rooms are spread out among 16 rustic and weathered buildings, each housing about sixty rooms. The look here is "backwater cracker" but the ambience translates into something more intimate. The Bayou's buildings are tucked away in a small forest. Each feels a bit hidden and the sensation of being in a large resort is lost.

The Bayou rooms manage an aura of homespun comfort and warmth. The log bedstead frames, patchwork "quilts," and other details give the rooms a feeling of fantasy and fun. In-room theming is at its best here in Alligator Bayou. Rooms with twin doubles also feature a trundle bed. This is the only moderately priced resort that has accommodations for more than four persons.

Following are 1996 room rates for Dixie Landings.

1996 Room Rates for Dixie Landings

Accommodation	Regular Season	Value Season	Holiday Season
Standard view	$99	$95	$104
Pool/river view	$129	$124	$134
Garden view	$124	$119	$129
King bedroom	$129	$124	$134

Transportation and Convenience   Transportation at Dixie Landings is the same as at Port Orleans. Dixie Landings, though, has four bus stops situated around the perimeter of the resort. The same wonderful boat service runs to the Village Marketplace, and travel to all other Disney areas is by bus. Service here is quite good, although the buses get crowded during the peak morning and afternoon travel hours.

- To Village Marketplace, Pleasure Island: by boat or bus
- To all other Disney destinations: by direct bus

Dining at Dixie Landings   The restaurants at Dixie Landings are all located in the resort's large central area. While the guest accommodations are organized around this area, it can be a trek from some of them. While we found that this made for a pleasant morning stroll, you might want to locate yourselves according to your own needs.

At the Landings, you will find one table-service restaurant, Boatwright's Dining Hall, and a colorful food court with five counter-service food outlets. Boatwright's serves hearty breakfasts and dinners, and the food is surprisingly good. For reviews and information about this and other restaurants, see Chapter 6.

The Dixie Landings food court is called the Colonel's Cotton Mill, and it offers a good selection of fast foods for the day's meals. It even manages to provide an interesting ambience. Breakfast offerings run the gamut from a muffin or bagel to French toast or eggs, while the other meals get a hearty treatment of burgers, sandwiches, pizza, and Cajun specialties.

If you need to escape the noisy food court atmosphere, go out by the pool and sit at one of the tables there. They are well-shaded and comfortable. In the early morning hours, you are likely to encounter only the occasional swimmer or landscape workman. The Cotton Mill is open from 6 A.M. to midnight, with hours varying for some of the shops. Like its "sister resort," Port Orleans, Dixie offers pizza delivery.

Lounges at Dixie Landings   There are two lounges at Dixie. In the central building is the Cotton Co-Op. Its long mahogany bar looks like something out of a movie. Besides the usual beverage offerings, the Co-Op also features a small variety of finger foods prepared at Boatwright's. There is also a live entertainer in the evenings. Muddy Rivers is the poolside bar.

Shopping at Dixie Landings   Fulton's General Store is located in the main resort building and will be your source for Dixie Landings logo merchandise as well as a fairly good selection of other character stuff. It has a country store feel with a large penny candy counter. Lots of cute knickknacks, little dolls, humorous signs, and jams and jellies. It has the usual sundries as well as an interesting selection of wines and liquors.

RECREATIONAL ACTIVITIES AT DIXIE LANDINGS

- Five quiet pools throughout the resort complex
- Ol' Man Island, a 3 1/2-acre themed water recreation area
- One hot tub
- Marina with boat and bicycle rentals
- Guided fishing excursions on the river

RECOMMENDATIONS FOR RESERVATIONS

- For the sake of convenience, you may wish to request a particular building when you reserve your room. Oak Manor would be our choice at Magnolia Bend, and in Alligator Bayou, buildings 14–17 or 27 are our suggestions. All are nearest the central building and Ol' Man Island.

ROMANCE AT DIXIE LANDINGS

- Overall theming: ♥♥
- Rooms with king-size beds: ♥♥
- Late night swim in a quiet pool: ♥♥
- An evening stroll to Port Orleans: ♥♥♥
- Sunset boat ride to Marketplace and Pleasure Island: ♥♥
- Renting a boat or bicycles and exploring: ♥♥
- Taking the boat to Port Orleans and eating at Bonfamille's: ♥♥♥

The Vacation Club

Team Disney is constantly expanding into new territory. The Vacation Club is Disney's venture into the realm of time-sharing properties. Since the Vacation Club is also available as nightly rentals and, since it has so much to offer, we thought we'd give it a try. We must admit to being a bit skeptical. It seemed large and not particularly close to anything, and it looked like condos. Whatever reservations that we'd had, however, were quickly put to rest when we arrived at our one-bedroom villa.

The Club's Key West theme is executed as only Disney can do it. The Florida Keys should look this nice. The pastel villas, with their "tin" roofs and gingerbread gables, are scattered in clusters throughout the area known as Conch Flats.

Landscaping at the Vacation Club is lush and tropical. The villas are surrounded by dense stands of foliage and flowering trees, providing a feeling of privacy that you will find hard to equal elsewhere in Walt Disney World. Plants are larger than life. If you are from a northern clime, you will marvel at the variety of greeneries, most of which you've probably only seen as potted house plants. Like much of Walt Disney World, this place is one big garden. Palms, crepe myrtle, blossoming hibiscus, and spider lilies abound. Quaint and narrow Key West streets wander gently among the Florida cracker-style villas. Southern porches, iron streetlamps, and old-fashioned bus stops add the finishing touches to the little taste of Key West created by the Disney imagineers.

Driving, we followed Old Turtle Pond Road to our villa. Parking was a few steps from the front door. Once inside, our curiosity turned to sheer delight. Our villa was not only surprisingly large but surprisingly beautiful. The ambience was definitely Key West style, open and airy, bright, and casually comfortable. Greeted by a mix of pastels, a splash of florals, and an expanse of open spaces, we hurried from room to room to survey our new abode. Ceiling fans, numerous large windows, and a king-size bed were just the beginnings. The villa had a huge living room/kitchen where we found a comfortable chair, love seat, and sofa with queen-size, foldaway bed. Handsome watercolors of Key West scenery, silk "tropical plants," and a carved wooden conch combined to give the villa a lived-in, at-home feeling.

The kitchen was integral with the living area, just the way we like it. Furnished with the best of appliances, it surpassed our expectations. It was handsomely tiled and was not only functional but beautiful. The kitchen featured a large refrigerator, microwave, dishwasher, stove, toaster, coffeemaker, and enough basic culinary gear to cook up whatever we might have cared to. There was even a blender and an electric hand-mixer. In the drawers and cupboards were mixing bowls, quality utensils, and dinner service for eight. With the cloth placemats, terry napkins, and napkin rings provided, we could easily have entertained. There were even wine glasses. The kitchen and the living room were separated by a tile-topped island that held a large-screen television and VCR.

There was also a lovely patio overlooking water. Featured here were another ceiling fan, a table, and chairs. Surrounded by dense growths of tropical plants, it had the feel of privacy. The master bedroom for our villa was comfortable and beautifully appointed. The king-size bedstead was made of decorative, enameled iron. The floral "quilt," was a wedding-ring pattern, and the armoire was an antiqued white. Here we found yet another television set. In one corner of the bedroom, we found a wicker chair and ottoman; in another corner, we discovered a glass door that opened onto the tiled patio. This was beginning to look like paradise. And then we entered the bathroom. We knew that we'd arrived. The Jacuzzi was easily large enough for two. Next to it, louvered shutter doors opened onto the sleeping area. A charming pedestal sink and beautiful tile work tied everything together neatly. As big as the tub was, the bathroom itself was even larger. Adjoining it was yet another room, with toilet, large walk-in shower, and another sink and vanity area. There was even a laundry room, complete with full-size washer and dryer, a small supply of laundry detergent, and iron and ironing board.

What made this place so nice was not merely its list of furnishings. Distinguishing this casual elegance from the usual was the caliber of furnishings. Everything from the beautiful prints to the varnished-wood Venetian blinds spoke of quality. It was a completely and beautifully furnished little apartment, a place where almost anyone would be glad to live. A few hours after we'd arrived, we were happily calling it "home."

Accommodations at the Vacation Club

There are two basic types of accommodations at the Vacation Club: the Deluxe room and the Vacation Villa. Vacation Villas can have one, two, or three bedrooms. The Deluxe Room comes with one configuration, offering two queen beds, an outside patio, and a small "kitchen" with microwave oven, wet bar, and mini-refrigerator. To make a two-bedroom villa, an adjoining Deluxe Room could be added to the single-bedroom villa. The combination would then provide accommodations for eight.

The three-bedroom Grand Villa is a two-level townhouse, something quite different altogether. Accommodations are for twelve. The master bedroom still has the king bed and Jacuzzi tub, but upstairs are two queen-size beds in one room and two double beds in the other. The fine furnishings of the Grand Villa and its cathedral ceiling create an impressive effect.

Following are 1996 room rates for the Vacation Club.

1996 Room Rates for Vacation Club

Accommodation	Regular Season	Value Season	Holiday Season
Deluxe Room	$215	$195	$225
One-bedroom Villa	$290	$265	$300
Two-bedroom Villa	$385	$365	$395
Grand Villa	$780	$780	$795

Transportation and Convenience

We are pleased to tell you that getting places from Conch Flats is fast and easy. To make things even better, the buses follow a schedule, which you receive in your check-in packet.

• To all Disney Destinations: by bus

Dining at the Vacation Club

There is one table-service restaurant, Olivia's, and two counter-service snack shops, Good's Food-To-Go and the Turtle Shack. Both Good's and Olivia's are located in the resort's central area, adjacent to the main swimming area. The Turtle Shack is in one of the outlying pool areas. Both fast-food outlets offer a selection of sandwiches and snacks.

Olivia's is one of our favorite "off-the-beaten-path" dining spots. We rarely visit Disney without enjoying a meal at this delightfully casual Key West–style eatery. Olivia's features a Disney character breakfast on Sundays and Wednesdays. It serves breakfast, lunch, and dinner, offering a large and intriguing menu of Key West cuisine. The Vacation Club also features room service from Olivia's. For a review of Olivia's and other restaurants, see Chapter 6.

Shops at the Vacation Club

The Conch Flat General Store will be your source for just about everything at the Vacation Club. There is even a substantial grocery section. Every room comes equipped with a grocery check-off list that you can drop off at the General Store. They'll do the shopping and deliver the goods for a mere buck. Now we're talking vacation.

Recreational Activities at the Vacation Club

- One themed central pool area with sauna and hot tub
- Three quiet pool areas, one with a hot tub
- 1.5-mile biking, jogging, walking, biking path
- Children's playground and kiddie pool
- Marina with rental watercraft
- Bicycle rentals
- Tennis, basketball, and volleyball
- Fitness center
- Video game room
- Complimentary video tape library
- In-room massage, by appointment

ℛESERVATION RECOMMENDATIONS

- Forget the Deluxe Rooms, which are nice but nothing compared to the luxury and space of the villas.
- The one-bedroom Villa is an ideal place for a family, especially during value season when the prices come down.

ℛOMANCE AT THE VACATION CLUB

- Resort theming: ♥♥
- Villa amenities: ♥♥♥♥
- Jacuzzi: ♥♥♥♥
- Taking a bike ride or walking on the path to the Village Marketplace, and taking a look at the Treehouse Villas, too: ♥♥
- Taking a boat to the Village Marketplace: ♥♥

The Studio Resorts

All-Star Resorts

The All-Star Resorts, one of the World's newest, is also Disney's foray into the budget market. Rooms here are the most inexpensive on-property and, as you would expect, the All-Star Resorts is one of Disney World's busiest destinations.

The resort is divided into two large areas, All-Star Sports and All-Star Music. Each carries its lively and colorful themes all the way from

All-Star Resorts

landscaping and architecture to the details of room furnishings. The All-Star Resorts is Disney's largest resort, with nearly 4,000 rooms.

The road to the All-Star Resorts takes you right past Blizzard Beach, Disney's newest water park. A peek at this fantastic playground will definitely get you in the mood for the bright and comic-strip-like All-Stars. This resort is larger-than-life and we mean a lot larger than life.

The resort buildings here are dwarfed by the sculptures that decorate them. The All-Star Resorts will dazzle you with five-story footballs, soaring surfboards, towering trumpets, mammoth maracas, and dozens of other uniquely large objects. Not for a minute will you forget that you are on vacation and that the theme is fantasy.

Both Music and Sports are further divided into smaller areas, each comprised of two buildings with a more specific theme. Our room was at Jazz Inn. Jazz has a definite New Orleans feel to its fountains, cast-iron benches, and walkways. The railings around the upper-floor walkways are musical scales, appropriately decorated with colorful notes and clefs. Piped-in music around the grounds has a jazz flavor, and the tops of the buildings are edged in silhouettes of musicians.

Other areas in All-Star Music are Calypso, Country Fair, Rock Inn, and Broadway Hotel. Each is imagineered with its own theme from top to bottom. Calypso, for example, is decorated with brightly colored palm leaves, four-story-tall conga drums, and spectacular, rainbow-like marimbas. The music here is the lively beat of the tropics. Taking a walk around this resort is a musical adventure.

Over at the All-Star Sports, things are much the same. Which is to say that they are quite different. The theme there is sports, and the areas have names such as Center Court, Hoops Hotel, and Touchdown.

While the actual buildings are the same, the theming has created a whole different atmosphere. The courtyard area at Touchdown is arranged like a football stadium, complete with gigantic helmets, a playing field, goal posts, and towering "floodlights." Over at Surf's Up, the landscaping will take you to the seashore. Here, the grounds around the pool resemble grass-covered sand dunes. Mounds of pampas grass and thickets of palms complete the picture.

Music and Sports each have a central area with front desk, Guest Services, a food court, shop, video arcade, and lounge. The central areas are called Melody Hall at Music and Stadium Hall at Sports.

If you elect to stay at the All-Star Resorts, whether Music or Sports, we suggest that you take a stroll around both properties. There are a lot of wonderful little touches that have been created to delight you. And they will.

Rooms at All-Star Resorts

There are two basic types of rooms, standard with two double beds and rooms with a single king bed. The king room is also the handicapped room. All-Star rooms are on the small side, 260 square feet, which is to say that they are about the same size as most budget motels. The room furnishings are decidedly more Disney than off-property rooms but, by Disney standards, they are pretty modest.

Our king bedroom at Jazz Inn lacked many of the amenities of even the Disney moderately priced resorts. The room decor was festive and modern. The "quilted" bedspread and bathroom wallpaper both featured patterns of jazz musicians, and the drapes were decorated with musical scales. The room furniture is similar throughout the All-Star. Modern and cartoon-like, it seemed entertaining. The theming in the rooms was simple. Creature comforts were minimal. One thing that we did like about our room was the environmental system, which we found very quiet.

Each room at the All-Star has a rather small vanity. Our king bedroom had only a shower. Wonderfully designed for the use of those physically challenged, it was very spacious with a handy seat right under the water. The double room has the more conventional shower-tub. King bedrooms each come with a small refrigerator.

Following are 1996 room rates for the All-Star Resorts.

1996 Room Rates for the All-Star Resorts

Accommodation	Price
Standard view	$69 (no seasonal prices)
Courtyard view	$79 (no seasonal prices)

Transportation and Convenience

With so many rooms here, we were concerned that transportation would be slow. We are delighted to report that service to all Disney destinations is quite good. Both Music and Sports each have their own bus fleets, and we found service to be frequent and convenient.

- To all Disney destinations: by bus

Dining at the All-Star Resorts

Both the End Zone Food Court at Sports and the Intermission Food Court at Music offer a complete array of food for breakfast, lunch, and dinner. All of the food served here is cooked on the premises, and much to our surprise, it was considerably better than many other Disney food court offerings. The hamburger was actually very good, and the tabouleh roll-up was outstanding.

The dining areas here, like most food courts, are noisy and at peak hours are crowded. Try taking your trays the few steps out to the pool area and eat at a table, under an umbrella.

There are several other interesting options for eating at All-Star. One is ordering out. There is a pizza delivery at All-Star, and while this pizza is nothing to write home about, it is decent. The menu also includes beers, wines, salads, and subs. There are also food trucks that drive around during the day, hawking breakfast stuff in the morning and sandwich goodies later.

Lounges at the All-Star Resorts

Each central area has a lounge that serves beers, wines, and specialty drinks, both alcoholic and nonalcoholic. The Singing Spirits Pool Bar is the lounge at Melody Hall, and at Sports, it's the Team Spirits Pool Bar. As their names imply, each is adjacent to the main pool.

Shops at the All-Star Resorts

Sport Goofy Gifts and Sundries is at All-Star Sports, and Maestro Mickey's is at Music. Each offers a selection of its own logo merchandise, and both have the usual Disney character products, sportswear, gifts, souvenirs, sundries, and even a small selection of liquor. Also available are a small offering of magazines, books, and newspapers. And if you are planning to snack in your room, each shop has a modest selection of chips, beverages, and groceries items.

Recreational Activities at All-Star Resorts

Music and Sports each have two pools—one large main pool and one smaller, less centrally located pool. At All-Star Music, the large pool is shaped like a huge guitar. An island in the center features a frolicking gang of sculptured Disney characters who occasionally spray near-by swimmers with jets of water. It is a delightful sight gag. The quiet swimming area at Music is the Piano Pool and is—you guessed it—shaped like a huge piano. At Sports, the main pool is called Surfboard Bay and is located amidst the beachside landscaping of Surf's Up. It has a California beach theme. A bit farther away is the quieter swimming area, the Grand Slam Pool. Each main swimming area also has a nice kiddie pool.

OUR IMPRESSIONS OF THE ALL-STAR RESORTS

- For the cost-conscious, this place is an affordable way to stay on-property. It is a charming and themed Disney resort, albeit a bit spartan.
- Many of the rooms are a hike from the parking lots. The luggage assistance system is awkward and runs on its own schedule, not yours. A stay here will teach you the real meaning of LUGgage. Plan on carrying your own bags to your room unless you simply cannot. If so, speak with the front desk upon check-in.

RECOMMENDATIONS FOR RESERVATIONS

- At Music, the Calypso area is closest to Melody Hall and is adjacent to the main pool. It is also the noisiest area. Country Fair is the most secluded but it is a hike from the parking area. Rock Inn, Broadway Hotel, and Jazz Inn seemed to be the most convenient, are relatively quiet (for this resort), and are near the quieter pool. We would recommend that you request one of these areas if you are staying at All-Star Music.
- At Sports, the busier area is Surf's Up. All other areas seemed quiet by comparison. Touchdown and Home Run Hotel would be our recommendations. Both are convenient to the quieter pool area and to parking.

ROMANCE AT THE ALL-STAR RESORTS

- Separate room for the kids: ♥♥

Fort Wilderness Campground Resort

Fort Wilderness Campsites and Homes

If you have never been to Fort Wilderness, you'll find that there's a lot more going on out there than a campground. More than any other Walt

Fort Wilderness Campground Resort

Disney resort area, Fort Wilderness is a world unto itself. With 750 beautifully wooded acres, Fort Wilderness would have little trouble drawing guests even without the nearby Disney attractions. What this amazing place has to offer includes a sandy beach, two swimming pools, a host of watercraft, sports activities, a petting farm, a water park, a popular dinner show, a themed restaurant, and a couple of shops. And besides offering a real variety of quality campsites and motor home hookups, Fort Wilderness even has its very own lodgings, the Wilderness Homes. To say that Fort Wilderness is a campground would be like calling the Magic Kingdom an amusement park. Fort Wilderness is a campground, but it is much, much more.

Fort Wilderness has a distinctly western flavor. Weathered log buildings, rough hewn timbers, split-rail fences, and meadows filled with wildflowers are set amidst a shady forest of slash pine, cypress, and live oak. Fort Wilderness does not feel much like Florida.

There are two basic types of accommodations at Fort Wilderness: campsites and the Wilderness Homes. Each offers something quite different. A Wilderness Home is a Disney resort lodging. The campsites, of course, furnish a place to either pitch your tent or to hook up your motor home or trailer.

Fort Wilderness Campsites

Fort Wilderness is Disney, and that means everything will be something special. The campsites, whether for tents, motor homes, or travel trailers, are all fairly large and relatively private. Each comes with either a full or partial hookup. Full hookups include water, sewer, electric, and cable television. Partials supply only electric and water. All offer ample space, a small barbecue grill, and a picnic table, and all provide 110 and 220 electricity.

Wherever your campsite is, you won't be far from an air-conditioned Comfort Station. Each of these features private showers and restrooms, an ice machine, and a coin-operated laundry. They are all clean and well maintained.

There are a small number of campsites where guests are allowed to have pets. Availability is limited, and these sites are all partial hookups. Cost is $3 per night for each pet. If you want to bring your pet on a Disney adventure, be sure to reserve one of these when you make your reservation.

Fort Wilderness Homes

The Fort Wilderness Homes are something altogether different. Each is really a small, air-conditioned 12-by 50-foot mobile home. Each has a full kitchen with utensils, pots and pans, a microwave oven, and a dishwasher. Every home includes a color television with cable, a ceiling fan, and a bathroom. A living area has a pull-down, double Murphy bed, and the homes are offered with a choice of one of two different bedroom designs. One style features a double bed and a set of bunk beds; the other has one double bed. Each Wilderness Home has a raised, outside deck, a picnic table, and an outdoor grill.

While certainly not equal to the luxury found at the Vacation Club, the Wilderness Homes have their charm. Furnishings are quaint and homey. Chairs and table are woodsy and rustic. The overall feeling is surprisingly pleasant. Each is large: 504 square feet.

If you are visiting Disney with your children, a Wilderness Home can provide the privacy for your romantic Disney holiday. Being able to prepare many of your own meals will save you some serious money as well. Maid service is included with the Wilderness Homes and, amazingly, it includes dishwashing. So cook up a storm and leave the cleaning to Disney.

Location, Location, Location

As the old adage goes, there are three important elements to real estate. The same is true for Fort Wilderness. The central area is around Pioneer Hall. It is here that you will find the resort's restaurants, Guest Services, the Settlement Depot, the beach, River Country, and most of the other recreational activities. We suggest that you locate yourselves as close to it as possible.

Fort Wilderness is large. The roads here wind lazily through the resort's 750 forested acres. The campsites and homes are all located on small "loop" roads that connect to the larger streets. There are nearly thirty such loops. Some are closer to things than others. Some offer a bit more seclusion. Others offer convenience to the pools or to the beach or bus stops. Each loop is numbered, with the series beginning at Loop 100 and ending with Loop 2800.

Loops 100 through 500 are the Preferred Campsites, and you will pay about $6 more per night to stay in one. They are all full hookups. It is well worth the extra expense, and we suggest that you request one when you make your reservation. We also suggest that you make your reservation as far in advance as possible. These puppies go fast.

If you are planning a stay in one of the Wilderness Homes, you'll be a bit farther away. These homes occupy loops 2100 through 2800. The partial hookup campsites are also a little farther out, occupying loops 1500 to 2000.

Following are 1996 accommodation rates at Fort Wilderness.

1996 Accommodation Rates for Fort Wilderness

Accommodation	Regular Season	Value Season	Holiday Season
Wilderness Home	$215	$185	$220
Preferred Campsite	$58	$49	$59
Campsite, full hookup	$52	$43	$54
Partial hookup	$44	$35	$45

Occupancy rates are based on two adults per accommodation with children under 17 years of age at no extra charge. A maximum of six persons are allowed in each Wilderness Home and 10 persons maximum at any one campsite. Extra adults at the homes are $5 each per night and $2 each per night at the campsites.

Transportation and Convenience

Transportation to the Magic Kingdom and Discovery Island is by boat and quite convenient. All other destinations are by bus to the Ticket and Transportation Center, followed by a bus transfer or, to Epcot, a monorail trip. If there is a problem with Fort Wilderness, this is it. Such trips are time-consuming, especially during the busy seasons.

There are two bus services at Fort Wilderness: one that carries guests around the resort, and another that takes guests to the TTC. Buses come and go about every 20 minutes. For complete bus directions, see your resort information and check-in newspaper, *The Gazette*.

Since Disney asks that you not drive your car around in Fort Wilderness except to arrive and depart, you'll want to give some thought to getting around this large resort. Rental electric carts are available either for your length of stay or by the day. At $23 per day or $35 for a 24-hour period, these carts are expensive, but if you are in one of the more distant areas, one will come in handy. There are also rental bicycles, available either by the hour or for $15 per day. With miles of peaceful, wooded paths, a couple of bikes would be nice. During our time at Fort Wilderness, we noticed many people riding around on their own bicycles. So, if you are driving and can bring your bikes along, do it. Don't forget a couple of good locks.

- To all Fort Wilderness areas: by internal bus
- To Magic Kingdom, Discovery Island: boat launch from Bay Lake dock
- To all other Disney destinations: bus to Ticket and Transportation Center, then transfer to other buses; monorail from TTC to Epcot

Restaurants and Eating at Fort Wilderness

Many guests staying at Fort Wilderness fix their own meals. Whether you are visiting in your motor home or staying in a Wilderness Home, a real advantage of Fort Wilderness is the ability to cook for yourselves and save a lot of money.

We suggest then, on your way through one of the surrounding communities, that you stop for groceries. There are two Trading Posts here at Fort Wilderness, and while they offer a decent selection of basic foodstuffs, they do so at Disney prices. If you are looking for a real supermarket, Gooding's at the Crossroads Plaza near the Marketplace is convenient.

There are several restaurants at Fort Wilderness. Pioneer Hall is home for the Hoop-Dee-Doo Revue, a dinner show, and Crockett's Tavern, a cozy and rustic eatery featuring a small menu of steaks, ribs, and chicken, each served with a frontier flair. Trail's End Buffeteria is Fort Wilderness' all-purpose eatery and features cafeteria-style breakfasts, lunches, and dinners. After 9 P.M., Trail's End becomes a pizzeria.

Recreational Activities at Fort Wilderness

- Two heated swimming pools and white sand beach
- Marina with rental craft
- River Country water park
- Two lighted tennis courts
- Jogging and walking paths
- Video arcade
- Swamp Trail nature walk
- Petting farm

- Horseback riding and nightly hayrides and campfire program
- Volleyball, tetherball, basketball
- Fishing excursions

OUR IMPRESSIONS OF FORT WILDERNESS

- No doubt, this is a super campground. The facilities are first-rate—sparkling and clean. Everything seems new. There is so much to do here that you hardly have to go anywhere for fun.

ROMANCE AT FORT WILDERNESS

- Taking an evening stroll around the resort: ♥♥
- Having a pleasant dinner at Crockett's Tavern: ♥
- Taking a late afternoon dip in the lake on a hot summer day: ♥
- Having your privacy when you bring your family to a Wilderness Home: ♥♥
- Watching the Electric Water Pageant from the beach: ♥♥

The Disney Institute and the Village at the Institute

The Disney Institute

The Disney Institute is not a training program for Disney cast members. Opening in early 1996, the Institute provides something completely unique for Disney guests. This "resort" features discovery vacations for couples, singles, and families with children over 10 years of age. The Institute offers individually designed learning activities that can be selected from more than 80 different programs. Topics range from animation and film production to sports and the culinary arts.

If you visit the Institute, don't come expecting to sit in classrooms listening to lectures. We're talking hands-on stuff here. Each program area is designed to get you involved in the creative processes. Select a program on rock climbing and you'll be out on the Institute's 25-foot rock wall, learning the ropes. A course in television production will have you in the Institute's very own production studio, working on programming. Ready for your golf experience? You'd better bring along your clubs, you'll need them out on one of Disney's five PGA courses.

The Disney Institute and the Village at the Institute

All of the programs have been designed to get you doing what you came here to learn about. The basic philosophy of the Disney Institute is that the programs must be fun and they must be hands-on. Custom-make a schedule that suits you both perfectly. Be as active as you wish and relax as much as you'd like. You're on vacation and, here at the Institute, it's going to be a fascinating one.

The Institute's programs are organized into nine areas of interest, each offering dozens of individual programs. The nine areas are Entertainment Arts, Sports and Fitness, Lifestyles, Story Arts, Culinary Arts, Design Arts, Environment, and Performance Arts. There is also a complete offering of youth programs in each area. From Power Baby-sitting to Wilderness Adventures, the Disney Institute has something for every member of the family.

The Guest Artists

The Institute features an Artist-in-Residence program that will have you interacting with a mix of artists from virtually every field of interest offered. Here's just a small sampling of the guest artists that have agreed to participate:

- The Alvin Ailey Repertory Ensemble
- Tim Burton (film director)
- Walter Cronkite
- The New England Culinary Institute
- Michael Graves (architect)
- Penn & Teller (performers)

Is this beginning to sound interesting? We think so. The Disney Institute has been a pet project of Disney CEO Michael Eisner's since he first came aboard. This is Walt Disney World's first resort that has been created especially for adults and families with older children. It offers first-class accommodations and a limitless range of stimulating pursuits.

The buildings of the Disney Institute evoke a sense of small-town America. Barns, mills, porches, and a town square all work to enhance the rural charm and essence of the Institute. The lakeside Institute facilities include 28 studios, an outdoor amphitheater, a state-of-the-art television production studio, cinema, closed-circuit radio station, and a youth center.

Accommodations at the Disney Institute

As guests at the Institute, you will stay nearby in beautiful and luxurious lodgings. In order to provide them, the Institute has taken over two adjacent areas of the Village Resort, the Club Suites and the Vacation Villas. The remainder of the Village Resort is now known as the Village at the Institute and will be available both to Disney guests and to residents of the Disney Institute.

The Club Suites and Vacation Villas have both been totally refurbished to provide all guests with the finest of accommodations. These are now known respectively as the Bungalows and the Townhouses. These lodgings are located a few minute's walk from the Institute. This area of Walt Disney World, with its lakes and tree-lined streets, is beautiful and relaxing.

The one bedroom bungalows are L-shaped, with a comfortable sitting area and patio or balcony. Each has a "kitchen" area with a small refrigerator, sink, coffeemaker, and microwave oven. The separate bedroom features two queen-size beds and a small bath, with a shower-tub combination.

The Townhouses are available as either one- or two-bedroom units. The one-bedroom townhouse can sleep four, with a king-size bed in the bedroom and a pull-down sico bed in the living area. The two-bedroom unit accommodates up to six guests. Both feature living rooms with cathedral ceilings and luxurious furnishings. Both the one- and two-bedroom Townhouses have fully equipped kitchens.

Four swimming pools and hot tubs are located throughout the area, and a central building offers coin-operated laundry facilities.

Rates at the Institute

Because of the unique program offered, the Disney Institute has a three-night minimum stay. A small selection of packages are featured, with three, four, or seven nights. Additional days can easily be arranged. Due to the nature of the programs, guests are encouraged, but not required, to begin their Disney Institute vacations on either Mondays or Fridays. We are told that if you are not able to do this, then arrival on another day will be arranged.

There are two basic package types. Both include the Institute's programs and accommodations. One provides three meals per day, the other does not provide meals.

Package One: the All-Inclusive Package This package includes accommodations, programs, all meals and gratuities, beverages (non-alcoholic), and a One Day/One Park Disney Theme Park pass. The following prices are per couple.

Package One, The Institute's All-Inclusive Package

Accommodation	Three Nights	Four Nights	Seven Nights
Bungalow	$1,522	$1,856	$3,248
One-bedroom Townhouse	$1,746	$2,154	$3,770
Two-bedroom Townhouse	$1,832	$2,270	$3,972
Additional adult	$518	$604	$1,058
Additional youth	$457	$522	$914

Package Two This package includes accommodations, programs, and a One Day/One Park Disney Theme Park Pass. The following prices are per couple.

The Institute's Package Two

Accommodation	Three Nights	Four Nights	Seven Nights
Bungalow	$1,224	$1,466	$2,564
One-bedroom Townhouse	$1,452	$1,762	$3,084
Two-bedroom Townhouse	$1,538	$1,878	$3,288
Additional adult	$371	$409	$1430
Additional youth	$310	$327	$572

Dining at the Institute

There will be one restaurant at the Disney Institute, Seasons, and it will feature four differing areas, each with its own theme, cuisine, and menu. Summer is expected to be completed first, with the other seasons to follow soon.

OUR IMPRESSIONS OF THE INSTITUTE

- Since the Institute will not open until after publication of this guide, we are unable to report our first-hand findings. The programs sound interesting and the hands-on promise makes everything sound very attractive.
- While this may not strike you as romantic, we think that, mixed with a bit of nightlife, some fine dining, and a few mornings or evenings in

the parks, this may be a memorable time for two lovers. We're ready to give it a try.

- When looking at the package prices, remember that both packages include more than merely accommodations. Albeit expensive, the all-inclusive package is on par with what you would expect to spend on other Disney packages. It simply offers something very different.

The Village at the Institute

The Village is unlike any of Disney's other resorts. It offers a variety of accommodations, all set in the quiet and secluded surroundings of Lake Buena Vista and the Lake Buena Vista golf course. There are three basic types of lodging, and each is able to accommodate more than the usual four persons. If you plan to visit Walt Disney World with your family, then one of these lodgings may be just the place for you.

The Treehouse Villas

The Treehouse Villas are some the most interesting accommodations at Walt Disney World. Built deep in the woods along one of the many canals that crisscross the Lake Buena Vista area, these octagonally shaped lodgings are called "treehouses" because they are on stilts. With simple, rustic exteriors, they are modern and luxurious inside. The Treehouse area seems more like a national park than a Disney resort. It is peaceful and secluded. There are even a handful of peacocks that roam the grounds.

The upstairs portion of each Treehouse has two bedrooms. One has a single queen bed, and the other has two doubles. There is a small kitchen and living room, and the living area is surrounded by a large, elevated deck. This is the perfect place to relax or dine under the canopy of trees.

The downstairs area features another bedroom with a single double bed. There is also a laundry room with washer and dryer. Each "home" has its own driveway and yard. Other Treehouse Villas are barely visible through the dense woods.

The Treehouse Villas all share one common recreation area where guests may enjoy a small pool and lounging deck. A short way across a footbridge are several miles of walking, jogging, or biking paths that lead either to the Village Marketplace or to the Vacation Club. Take a morning stroll along the lush golf course or bike up to Olivia's at the Vacation Club for lunch.

The Treehouse Villas are subject to amazing discounts during the off season. Rates under $200 per night are common but must be reserved far in advance.

The Fairway Villas and Grand Vista Homes

The Fairway Villas offer even more luxurious accommodations for a large family. These modern, cedar-sided townhouses are located right along the fairways of the golf course. Each has two bedrooms and a large living room with a cathedral ceiling. With a single queen in one bedroom, two doubles in the other, and a pull-down, double sico bed in the living room, there's sleeping space here for eight.

With the nearby Gourmet Galley and a full kitchen, guests here can enjoy the convenience and savings of preparing their own meals. Dining at any of the World's fine eateries is but a bus hop away.

The Grand Vista Homes are unlike anything else at Walt Disney World. These were originally designed as model homes for a Disney development that never developed. There are only four of these lavish places: three two-bedroom homes and one three-bedroom home. The two-bedroom homes can accommodate six, while the three-bedroom home sleeps eight. Each comes with a golf cart and bicycles, and the refrigerators of each kitchen are stocked upon arrival with chips, dips, drinks, and milk. Nightly turndown service and daily newspaper delivery are standard. All of the accommodations at the Village enjoy full, daily maid service, which includes dishwashing. There are no restaurants in the resort area but, with full kitchens, the idea here is to cook at "home" and dine out occasionally. Several pools are scattered throughout the Village, making a swim fairly convenient.

Following are 1996 Village room rates.

1996 Rates for the Village

Accommodation	Regular Season	Value Season	Holiday Season
Treehouse Villa	$375	$355	$390
Two-bedroom Fairway Villa	$400	$375	$415
Two-bedroom Grand Vista Home	$975	(No seasonal prices)	
Three-bedroom Grand Vista Home	$1,150	(No seasonal prices)	

Townhouses and Bungalows of the Institute

As availability allows, both the Bungalows and the Townhouses of the Institute will also be available to general resort guests. The following prices are for accommodations only and do not include any Institute activities.

1996 Rates for the Bungalows and Townhouses

Accommodation	Regular Season	Value Season	Holiday Season
One-bedroom Bungalow	$215	$195	$220
One-bedroom Townhouse	$305	$285	$315
Two-bedroom Townhouse	$340	$320	$355

Transportation and Convenience

The Village at the Institute is not centrally located. Despite this, it is an easy matter to reach any Disney destination. It is, however, time-consuming. Buses run every 20 minutes but make a great many stops. For travel within the Village, rental golf carts are available (a Grand Vista Home comes with one) for $20 per day, $30 for a 24-hour day, or $20 per day for three days or more.

- To all Disney destinations: by bus, every 20 minutes

Dining at the Village

There are no restaurants at the Disney Village at the Institute. Because of its proximity to the Village Marketplace, however, guests are able to dine conveniently at any of the numerous restaurants at the Marketplace. A host of fine-dining alternatives can also be found at nearby Pleasure Island. While none of these restaurants are within easy walking distance, bus service makes them all fairly convenient. A car will come in handy at the Village and will make your options nearly limitless.

Shops at the Village

With both the Village Marketplace and Pleasure Island so nearby, shopping is outstanding for guests of this resort.

Recreational Activities at the Village

- Two swimming pools
- Rental bikes

ℛOMANCE AT THE VILLAGE

- Resort ambience: ♥
- Treehouse Villas: ♥♥
- Riding a bike or taking a stroll: ♥♥

The Hotel Plaza Resorts

Hotel Plaza is a group of seven on-property hotels located near the Disney Village Marketplace. None are owned or managed by Disney, but they provide an interesting alternative to staying in one of the Disney resorts. While these can be an economical alternative to the other on-property resorts, a stay in one of them will not provide the same benefits as a visit to one of the Disney resorts. Hotel Plaza resorts do not have Surprise Mornings, Length of Stay Passes, Resort Cards, or full use of Disney transportation. These are privately owned and independent hotels.

On the plus side, these resorts are infinitely more convenient than anything off-property and they are all quite nice. Some are truly luxurious. Accommodations range from good to lavish.

Hotel Plaza has its own bus system, which ferries guests to most Disney destinations. It is important to note, though, that these buses do not drop off guests at the same bus areas used by Disney buses. While this amounts to a matter of a few dozen yards at both Epcot and MGM, it is more noticeable at the Magic Kingdom, where the purple and green Hotel Plaza buses leave guests at the Ticket and Transportation Center. On a busy morning, the trip from the TTC to the Magic Kingdom can take twenty minutes. Also, we have heard Hotel Plaza guests complain that bus service is slow and crowded. Hotel Plaza buses run every 25 minutes, a little less frequently than those of Disney.

Guests have convenient access to a selection of restaurants, lounges, and nightclubs at the resorts along Hotel Plaza Boulevard. Each of the hotels on the Boulevard has a Disney store that offers a selection of Disney character merchandise and the usual assortment of tickets and passes. Both Pleasure Island and the Disney Village Marketplace are within walking distance, as is the Crossroads Shopping Plaza.

Generally speaking, these hotels are attractive. While they really do not enjoy the theming found at such places as Dixie Landings, their rooms are well decorated, comfortable, and well maintained. Pools and grounds range from good to beautiful, but none begins to approach the likes of Stormalong Bay at the Yacht and the Beach Clubs or even Doubloon Lagoon at Port Orleans.

If you desire a Disney resort experience, want to be within arm's reach of the parks, or yearn to enjoy the magic of a themed resort room, then Hotel Plaza may not be for you. Pretty uniformly, these are regular hotels.

Price remains the most attractive element in the Hotel Plaza formula. These hotels often feature discounts, many of which are excellent. Even during Disney's regular season, competition on Hotel Plaza Boulevard can get downright cutthroat. All the better for you. Magic Kingdom Club members get discounts at all of the Hotel Plaza Hotels. Most of these hotels are featured in one or more of the packages offered by Delta Airlines and the Walt Disney Travel Company.

The Grosvenor Resort

Pronounced "Grove-nor," this 19-story hotel is one of the nearest to the Village Marketplace. Its 629 rooms are all well appointed and brightly decorated. Each room at the Grosvenor has a wet bar, coffeemaker, and VCR. Situated on 13 beautifully landscaped acres, this is a rather nice hotel. The British Colonial–style lobby is bright and airy. Of all the hotels along the Boulevard, the "very British" Grosvenor makes the best effort to give itself a theme.

Standard rooms begin at $150 during value season to $160 during the regular season, with a maximum of five persons per room. Specials and packages are seasonal, vary greatly, and will no doubt provide rooms for considerably less than these prices. AAA discounts apply. There are a few suites here at the Grosvenor; prices begin at $450 per night. For reservations, call Disney CRO, or the Grosvenor at (800) 624-4109.

Restaurants and Lounges at the Grosvenor

Restaurants and lounges at the Grosvenor all enjoy the British theming that is evident in the lobby. Here, guests can drop by Crumpet's Cafe for a quick snack or bite to eat 24 hours a day. Pastries, muffins, hot and cold sandwiches, beverages, and espresso are a few of the cafe's offerings.

Cricket's Lounge is also located in the lobby. This full-service bar offers espresso and cappuccino as well as a large-screen television.

Baskerville's is the Grosvenor's full-service restaurant and has a Sherlock Holmes theme. Baskerville's features a Disney character breakfast buffet on Tuesdays, Thursdays, and Saturdays. On Sunday, the restaurant offers a special brunch buffet with a more ambitious menu. Every day, there is a large offering of a la carte items. The dinner specialty at Baskerville's is the prime rib buffet, with chicken and seafood. On weekends, you can enjoy the Sherlock Holmes Dinner Theater.

Baskerville's lounge is Moriarty's, named after the famous detective's infamous adversary. Neither restaurant nor lounge has an atmosphere that we would call memorable.

Barnacle's is the Grosvenor's poolside snack bar and lounge. Its menu includes drinks and a small selection of burgers, hot dogs, and sandwiches. Sunday afternoons feature live entertainment.

Services Available at the Grosvenor

The Grosvenor offers services found at most hotels, such as bell service, valet parking, 24-hour room service, valet service, on-property car rentals, and automated teller machines.

Recreational Activities at the Grosvenor

- Two heated swimming pools with kiddie pool
- Fitness center, whirlpool, hydrotherapy spa
- Tennis, basketball, shuffleboard, volleyball
- Video game room
- Video movie rental

Buena Vista Palace

This, the largest of the Hotel Plaza resorts, is also one of the closest to the Village Marketplace. The lobby is rich with crystal chandeliers, broad expanses of glass, and plush furnishings. With more than 1,000 guest rooms, this 27-story multitower resort offers 139 suites and its Crown concierge service. Four rooms come with Jacuzzis, and every guest room has a minibar and a private balcony or patio and is lavishly furnished. Standard guest rooms feature either two queen beds or one king.

The Buena Vista's Palace Suites complex is located adjacent to the resort's recreational area. It is connected to the main building by landscaped walkways and houses 100 one- and two-bedroom suites. Standard here are minibars, coffeemakers, and hair dryers. A queen sleeper-sofa is in each living area, and a single king or two queen beds can be found in each bedroom. A microwave oven and small refrigerator are available upon request.

The Palace also offers twenty Evergreen Rooms. Hailed as "ecologically friendly," these accommodations are smoke- and odor-free. The very latest in technology has been applied to water filtration, and these rooms include nonallergenic pillows and blankets as well as undyed bathroom tissues and linens.

Nightly room rates at the Palace run from $145 to $254. There is no charge for children under the age of 18. AAA discounts are applicable, and special packages and seasonal bargains are usually available. We suggest that you call the Palace's toll-free reservation number, (800) 327-2990, or Disney Central Reservations to get the most current offerings.

Restaurants and Lounges at the Buena Vista Palace

The Palace offers an outstanding assortment of dining places. Starting at the top (the twenty-seventh floor, that is), you will find Arthur's 27, an award-winning gourmet restaurant that features international cuisine. The Outback Restaurant (no connection to the Outback Steakhouse chain) specializes in prime beef and seafood. The atmosphere is "down under" and includes waterfalls and palms. Overlooking the lake is the Watercress Cafe. Open 6 A.M. to midnight every day, this is the Palace's all-around eatery. Breakfasts here are Disney character buffets. The Courtyard Cafe offers counter-service food in a pleasant courtyard setting. There is even a poolside snack bar and 24-hour room service.

For afternoon happy hour or a late nightcap, the Palace features four lounges, one of which is high atop this 27-story building. Complimentary champagne is served there daily at sunset. The Laughing Kookaburra Good Times Bar, a happening nightspot, features live entertainment and 99 brands of beer.

Services Available at the Palace

The Palace offers full bell service, valet parking, a hair salon, children's activity center, laundry service, on-premises car rental, and concierge desk.

Recreational Activities at the Palace

- Two swimming pools and kiddie pool
- European-style health spa and sauna
- Three lighted tennis courts and a volleyball court
- Complete health club and three-mile jogging and walking trail
- Children's activities

The Hilton at Walt Disney World Village

The very name of this hotel has come to be synonymous with fine accommodations. The Hilton is a Four Diamond, 800-room resort, located directly across the street from the Disney Village Marketplace. Of all the Hotel Plaza resorts, it is the closest to the Marketplace. The Hilton's list of amenities is nearly endless. Spacious and well-appointed rooms, 27 elegant suites, and seven restaurants and lounges make the Hilton one of Hotel Plaza's most outstanding travel destinations. Recently refurbished, the Hilton boasts a tropical theme, which is carried beautifully from the lush garden grounds to the tropical ambience of the guest rooms.

With either two double beds or a single king bed, each room features a comfortable sitting area, perfect for romantic in-room dining. Furnishings, though not themed, are first class. Prices run from $315 during the Hilton's off-season to $350 during the busy season.

Tower Level rooms, on the ninth and tenth floors, feature concierge service. Private lounge, plush bathrobes, continental breakfasts, hors d'oeuvres, and a late afternoon honor bar provide part of the personalized service that comes standard in this "hotel within a hotel." There are nearly thirty suites at the Hilton. They are large and luxurious. Each features a large dining table and chairs, full-size desk, refrigerator, coffeemaker, bath scale, and a host of other upgraded amenities.

The Hilton also offers a number of vacation packages that seem quite competitive with those of Disney. The Four-Night Romance Package Deluxe includes accommodations, airport transportation, a Four-Day Park Hopper Pass, welcome champagne, and one breakfast in bed. Prices begin at under $1,200 per couple. A golf package is also available.

For reservations and information, call the Hilton at the Village Marketplace at (800) 782-4414, Hilton reservations at (800) HILTONS, or Disney Central Reservations.

Restaurants and Lounges at the Hilton

The Hilton boasts a large number of restaurants even for a hotel of its size. Finn's Grill is its premier eatery, and it specializes in seafood and steaks. County Fair is more of an all-around place to eat. Guests can enjoy a la carte breakfasts, lunches, and dinners in the relaxed atmosphere of an old-fashioned country fair. Foods to go are offered at the County Fair Terrace, while the County Fair Buffeteria features breakfast and dinner buffets.

Other eateries include Rum Largo, the poolside bar and cafe, an old-fashioned soda shop, and a Benihana's Japanese Steakhouse. Disney character breakfasts are also on the menu here at the Hilton.

Services Available at the Hilton

The Hilton offers full bell service, 24-hour room service, curbside check-in, on-premises car rental, concierge desk, men's and women's apparel shops, American Express Travel Desk, special services for Japanese guests, and valet service.

Recreational Activities at the Hilton

- Two heated, outdoor swimming pools
- Tropical outdoor spa
- Complimentary Nautilus health club
- Children's activity center
- Preferred tee times at Disney golf courses
- Golf shop
- Video arcade
- Two lighted tennis courts

The Hotel Royal Plaza

At the time of this writing, the Royal Plaza is undergoing a major renovation and refit that should be completed by the time this book reaches you. While this hotel does not quite equal either the Hilton or the Buena Vista Palace in restaurants, shops, and recreational facilities, we expect that the rooms will be equally spacious and beautifully appointed.

The Royal Plaza is putting on a Bermuda-style look. This will be reflected not simply in room decor and amenities but across the entire spectrum of restaurants, lounges, lobby, and shops. There will even be a poolside lanai that features private courtyards, a la Bermuda. We were shown several of the newly completed floors as well as some renderings of restaurant and pool areas, and everything looked very nice.

With fewer than 400 rooms, this resort is able to offer a more personalized service than many other, larger establishments. Accommodations include the standard bedroom with either twin double beds or a single king. Off-season prices begin at under $100 per night. Superior and Deluxe rooms offer upgraded views. Prices begin at around $110 nightly, off-season. The busy seasons here at the Royal Plaza do not coincide with those of Disney, so we suggest that you call for special deals.

Every room at the Royal Plaza has a private balcony, VCR, color television, Mickey Mouse telephone, and clock radio. The Royal Plaza is also building five concierge service floors, complete with private lounge, upgraded amenities, and the usual concierge benefits. Plans include rooms with Jacuzzi tubs and king beds. Prices are unavailable at this time.

There are ten designer suites here at the Plaza, with rates beginning around $300 nightly. This hotel also features a varied assortment of vacation packages. The Royal Romance Four-Night Package includes superior accommodations, breakfast in bed, one additional restaurant breakfast for two, two Four-Day Park Hopper Passes plus admission to either Pleasure Island or River Country, welcome cocktails, deluxe fruit basket and champagne delivered to your room, and two souvenir polo shirts. All for $740 per couple.

For reservations and inquiries, call the Hotel Royal Plaza at (800) 248-7890 or Disney Central Reservations.

Restaurants and Lounges at the Royal Plaza

Once the renovation is complete, guests here will enjoy an entirely new selection of restaurants and lounges. A promenade with Jamaica-Bermuda theming will host the new shops and eateries. Among them will be the Jamaica Grill, an ale house lounge, and a buffet dining spot.

Services Available at the Royal Plaza

Guest services at the Royal Plaza include valet parking, bell service, car rental, laundry service, and room service until midnight.

Recreational Activities at the Royal Plaza

- Heated pool
- Large spa and sauna
- Four lighted tennis courts
- Table tennis
- VCRs
- Video arcade

The Travelodge Hotel

The Travelodge has a pleasant, tropical theme. Its lobby is colorful and bright. Cages of tropical birds add an exotic background rustling and chirping. The winding staircase, large potted trees and palms, wicker furnishings, and faux marble finish lend the lobby a comfortable and inviting feeling. A pleasant change indeed from many of the other nearby resorts, where lobbies tend toward cold and imposing.

While we found the rooms clean and well appointed, they seemed a bit tired. Standard rooms each have a private balcony with table and chairs and many command impressive views of Lake Buena Vista. Each includes in-room pay movies, hair dryer, minibar, free daily newspaper, coffee and tea maker, and either double queen beds or a single king. Room rates begin around $120 per night, but special offers should make rooms available at less than $100 year round, with even larger savings during the off season.

Four suites are all located on the top floor. At around $200 to $300 per night (depending on the season), one of these suites would be on our list of bargains at Walt Disney World. Each suite includes a large master bedroom with king bed, a large sitting area with pull-out queen, a wet bar, coffeemaker, and large television set. What makes each so attractive is a large sunroom with glass ceiling. Complete with lovely wicker furnishings, this area makes the entire suite, and its panoramic view, quite attractive.

For reservations and information, call the Travelodge Hotel at (800) 578-7878 or Disney Central Reservations.

Restaurants and Lounges at the Travelodge

Trader's is this hotel's table-service restaurant. Its large expanse of glass opens onto trickling fountains and an attractive dining porch. Steaks and seafood are the specialties. With a breakfast buffet and an a la carte dinner menu, Trader's is a moderately priced eatery. Surroundings are pleasant, and the food is good.

Located near the lobby is the Parakeet Cafe, a counter-service restaurant, which features a variety of quick meals, snacks, beers and wines, and liquor. Homemade doughnuts, pizza, and "croissandwiches" are several of the offerings.

There are two lounges here at the Travelodge. The Flamingo Cove is the hotel's lobby bar. Upstairs is Topper's, a lively sports bar. Topper's offers several pool tables, free popcorn, and a commanding view of the neighborhood.

Services Available at the Travelodge

Included during your stay at the Travelodge are bell service, babysitting, room service until midnight, and a Guest Services desk for reservations.

Recreational Activities at the Travelodge

- Heated pool and children's playground
- Video arcade
- Disney Channel in all rooms

DoubleTree Guest Suites Resort

This modern resort rightfully claims to be the only all-suites hotel inside of Walt Disney World. Its lobby is large, and the restaurants are clean and colorful. The pool area is attractive yet unremarkable. Rooms at the DoubleTree are spacious, nicely furnished, and comfortable. Here comes the "but": this place is just like a thousand other nice hotels. It offers little or none of the fun, fantasy, and artfulness that is present in great quantities in virtually all of the Disney resorts.

Each "room" here is actually two, a living/dining area and a bedroom. Bedrooms come with a choice of twin doubles or a single king. The single bathroom is large and features a spacious vanity area with a hair dryer and television set. The living room includes a sofa bed, desk, dining area, refrigerator, microwave, coffeemaker, and television. Rates for the one-bedroom suites run from $125 to over $200, depending on the season (April to mid-December is considered the off-season). The

DoubleTree also offers two-bedrooms suites, with prices beginning around $300 per night and hitting $400 during the winter holiday season. The DoubleTree also offers a variety of seasonal and special packages. For reservations and pricing of both the suites and packages, call the DoubleTree at (800) 222-TREE or Disney Central Reservations.

Restaurants and Lounges at the DoubleTree

Streamer's is the restaurant at DoubleTree. Adjacent to the atrium-style lobby, this eatery offers a large menu. Breakfasts include the usual entrees and a few specials such as the "Last Resort Breakfast." For dinner, choose among burgers, pizza, fajitas, shrimp tortellini, and Cajun swordfish.

DoubleTree also has a poolside snack bar and lounge. For those wishing to do for themselves, there is the Cool Pool Deli and Market. This place offers a very large selection of sandwiches, snack foods, and groceries. Given that each suite comes with a microwave and a refrigerator, this is an opportunity to throttle-back on dining expenses. There is no room service.

Recreational Activities at the DoubleTree

- Tropically landscaped, heated pool with spa
- Separate kiddie pool
- Exercise center, tennis courts, and a jogging and walking trail
- Video arcade
- Children's activities

Marriot Courtyard at Walt Disney World Village

Here is yet another of Hotel Plaza's attractive yet bland offerings. The large lobby features tiered corridors in a surrounding atrium style. The lobby lounge is colorful and bright but features little, if any, real character. The grounds here at the Marriot are well maintained but nearly featureless, compared even to some of the other resorts at Hotel Plaza. The pool area is large and there is even a whirlpool hot tub. This 14-story hotel is clean, well kept, and well appointed.

There are 325 rooms here at the Marriot Courtyard. Two of them are large executive suites. Bedding choices are either twin doubles or a single king or queen. Each room has a coffeemaker, color television with pay movies, and small table and chairs. Furnishings are standard hotel fare. Bedspreads are floral and drapes are aqua. The guest rooms here are bright and new, though devoid of any interesting features. Rooms here could be in a hotel virtually anywhere.

For reservations and inquiries, call the Marriot Courtyard at the Village Marketplace at (800) 223-9930, Marriot Courtyard reservations at (800) 321-2211, or Disney Central Reservations.

Restaurants at the Marriot

The Courtyard Cafe and Grill is one of several places to eat at the Marriot Courtyard. This restaurant serves both breakfast and dinner. The Village Deli features pizza and frozen yogurt. Pizza is also available at the Courtyard Cafe.

Recreational Activities at the Marriot

- Two swimming pools with whirlpool spa
- Children's pool and playground
- Video arcade and in-room Nintendo
- Exercise room

OUR IMPRESSIONS OF HOTEL PLAZA

- The seven Hotel Plaza hotel/resorts are competently managed. The Boulevard itself is shady and beautifully landscaped. The hotels are all nice. None of them, however, offers the Disney magic that you come here for.
- We have heard many complaints about the slow bus service at Hotel Plaza. Given that each bus serves all seven of the hotels on each trip, we guess that such complaints may not be unfounded.

ROMANCE AT HOTEL PLAZA

- We didn't find much at Hotel Plaza that we found particularly romantic. The fantasy that we so enjoy at the themed Disney resorts is simply not an element here.
- Dinner at Arthur's 27: ♥♥♥♥
- An evening stroll over to Pleasure Island or the Marketplace: ♥

What to Do Once You Get There

$\mathcal{G}$etting Started

Well, here you are—you've made it. After all of your careful planning and eager anticipation, you've finally arrived at Walt Disney World. What next?

One of you grabs the camera, and you both run out to the first park that strikes your fancy. With whatever you have left of the day, you try to get in as much as you can. You run from ride to ride and show to show. You stay out all day, racing from place to place, eating fast food, returning to your room at midnight to collapse exhausted into your bed. Your last thoughts before falling into a deep, comatose sleep are "Will we be able to see everything at Epcot tomorrow?"

We hope that this is not what you do. Let others turn Walt Disney World into a track and field event. We would like to head you in another direction, one that will be a lot more satisfying. Remember that the two of you have come for a special time together and to see the attractions too. Doing both, and staying in the mood, will be a simple matter of balance.

Look through this book for the heart symbols ♥. Intersperse your theme park adventures with enough time together doing what is blissful and intimate. Spend a morning at the Magic Kingdom, then go back to your resort for a few hours in the pool. Ride a bike or rent a boat. Relax, then go back out for an evening of dining and excitement. But remember, come home early for a nice soak in the hot tub and then some time together. Get the picture? All it takes is resisting the notion that you have to see as much of Disney World as possible.

Tools of the Trade

Things change constantly at Walt Disney World. We're talking not so much about the big things but about the small ones. Show times, performers, fireworks shows, parades, and even park hours are all subject to seasonal and even daily variations. The first thing you'll want to do after settling in is to get a handle on what's happening and when. There are several useful tools for this.

"The World Update"

At check-in, you should receive this colorful information sheet. It will give you the latest facts about Surprise Mornings and which rides will be running early. It will tell you about new attractions, special events, rehabs (which attractions are down for maintenance), and the operating hours of all the Disney attractions for the days that you'll be guests. There's lots more, too, and much of it will be helpful in planning your days.

Map Guides

A map guide is available for each of the three theme parks. Whether you're looking for a restaurant, a ride, or a bathroom, you'll find them all on each of these colorful and detailed maps. All three are available either at your resort's Guest Services or at the entrance to each of the three theme parks. There are map guides of the other Disney attractions too. Looking at them all might help you decide what you want to see.

Theme Park Entertainment Guides

In recent months, the entertainment and show-time guides have undergone some changes. There are three of these too, one for each of the parks. Get them all, whatever their current incarnations. They describe what is happening in each theme park on the days that you will be visiting. From giving you the performance times for the Marimba Mariachi band at Mexico to listing the kickoff time of the afternoon parade at the Magic Kingdom, the entertainment guides will be indispensable. All three should be available at your resort's Guest Services. If not, you can pick one up as you enter each park, at the following locations:

- City Hall in the Magic Kingdom
- Crossroads of the World, in the middle of the entrance plaza at Disney–MGM
- Spaceship Earth gift shop at the main entrance to Epcot and the World Traveler shop at the International Gateway

More Good Stuff

There's more going on at Disney than even the guides can cover. Drop by your Guest Services and ask what specials or special events are going on at Pleasure Island, the water parks, and the Village Marketplace.

Getting Around at Walt Disney World

Walt Disney World is a big place. Getting around its nearly 40 square miles will be something that you will want to get good at. It will not be hard. The bus system at Disney runs an astounding 160 buses with nearly 600 drivers to keep them going. It is the third largest bus system in Florida.

We're not going to tell you that busing around Walt Disney World will be romantic. What we will tell you is that there are a lot of other ways to get around and that some of these are most certainly special and, yes, even a bit romantic. Besides the usual buses, there's the monorail, a fleet of boats, carriages, trollies, and double-decker buses. We encourage you to take the road less traveled.

Disney Bus Service

This past year has seen some new strategies in Disney bus service. We are happy to report that there seems to be real improvement. During the Disney rush hours (9 A.M. to 11 A.M. and 5 P.M. to 7 P.M.), buses are running more frequently. With buses promised every 20 minutes, the reality seems more like every 10 minutes. Routes have been altered to make better use of buses. You will find that most buses make a round-about series of stops, and some of them may surprise you. As you board a bus, always ask the driver if it will be stopping at your destination.

Bus service at Walt Disney World is really quite good. Buses can get just about anywhere in ten or fifteen minutes. Plan on five minutes to get to your bus stop and, along with a short wait for the bus, you can count on thirty minutes to actually arrive at your destination.

The Disney Navy

If you both enjoy a pleasant outdoor trip, there is nothing like a boat ride. Dozens of watercraft ply the waters of the World, and as Disney resort guests you'll be free to use all of them. From the dock at the Magic

Kingdom, boats make their arrivals and departures for the Wilderness Lodge, the Grand Floridian and the Polynesian resorts, Discovery Island, Fort Wilderness, and River Country. At Epcot's World Showcase Lagoon, catch a watercraft across the lagoon to either Germany or Morocco. At Epcot's International Gateway, Friendship water taxies carry passengers to the BoardWalk, to the Yacht and the Beach Clubs, and to the Swan and the Dolphin. Hop off at any for a meal or to catch a connecting boat to Disney–MGM.

The Disney Village Marketplace and Pleasure Island are both located on Lake Buena Vista, which connects to a series of waterways. Here, watercraft leave for trips up the Sassagoula to Port Orleans and Dixie Landings as well as to the Vacation Club.

The Monorail

There are three monorail spurs at Walt Disney World running on more than 13 miles of elevated track. Two spurs run around the Seven Seas Lagoon. The express carries day guests to the Magic Kingdom from the Ticket and Transportation Center (TTC). The local, for Disney resort guests only, makes stops at the TTC, the Polynesian, the Grand Floridian, the Contemporary, and the Magic Kingdom. The third monorail line runs from the TTC to Epcot. This monorail line is long and scenic, but expect crowds in the early morning hours when Magic Kingdom resort guests flock to Epcot.

The best seats on the monorail are in the front car with the driver. Ask the monorail attendants if seats are available (only four or five can ride at a time). If not, try waiting for the next train. Better yet, try this on the Epcot spur. This is not a loop run, and whoever is in the front car will be getting out.

Trolleys and Tramways

There is a host of odd transportation throughout The World. These include the Walt Disney Railroad, horseless carriages, horse-drawn trolleys, the Skyway to Tomorrowland, double-decker buses, and lots more. Each of these is waiting to take you on a pleasant fantasy ride.

Travel to Other Resort Areas

Getting to any of the attractions is simple. Traveling to other Disney resort areas is a bit more complicated, though, and you will likely want to do it for a Disney character breakfast, for dining, or for just looking around. If you have a car, then driving may be the simplest thing to do. But busing is not too difficult. During the day, the easiest way to get to another resort will be to go to any park and catch a bus returning to where you want to go. Frequent buses come and go all day long from all resorts. After park closing, this same technique can be used from the bus centers at the Village Marketplace and Pleasure Island. Buses to all Disney resorts arrive and depart from the Marketplace beginning at 10 A.M., and after 11 P.M. buses continue into the wee hours from the Pleasure Island bus area.

CHAPTER 4

$\mathcal{T}$he Attractions

Walt Disney World is home to eight attractions: the three major theme parks (the Magic Kingdom, Epcot, and Disney–MGM Studios), Discovery Island, Typhoon Lagoon, River Country, Blizzard Beach, and Pleasure Island. Each is a complete and independent entertainment area. We'll tell you about Pleasure Island later, in Chapter 5.

If we were to give you one piece of advice about which attractions to include in your visit, it would be: keep an open mind. Consider everything, especially if you have never heard of it. Often, that small and unsung attraction is what we remember long after the thrill of Splash Mountain has faded. If you aren't interested in the fast-moving thrill rides, there are still plenty of things to do. If you do enjoy the more exciting attractions, then fasten your seat belts and get ready for some of the most exciting rides in themedom.

The map guides and entertainment schedules for the three theme parks are important tools for knowing where things are, what's happening, and when. Be sure you have them with you. If not, you can pick them up near the entrance to each of the parks.

Surprise Mornings

Surprise Mornings are an important benefit for Disney resort guests. Surprise Mornings provide early entry into a different theme park each day, a full hour-and-a-half before the public onslaught. The schedule repeats weekly.

- Magic Kingdom: Monday, Thursday, and Saturday
- Epcot: Tuesday and Friday
- Disney–MGM: Sunday and Wednesday

Only certain attractions in each park are open early, and these may vary from month to month. Check your "World Update" information sheet or ask Guest Services.

✐IPS FOR THE THEME PARKS

- The busiest days in each of the three theme parks are that park's Surprise Morning. Most Disney guests arrive early on those days and stay for the remainder of the day. Avoid spending the day at the busiest park. Once the park opens to the public, zip over to one of the other two parks to take advantage of the first few hours of its day.
- Each of the three theme parks has a Tip Board near its entrance that provides up-to-the-minute reports of show times and estimated waits. Use these to avoid wasting your time in lines.
- Signs at many of the rides and shows will tell you how long the wait will be from a certain point. For shows, always ask the cast members that patrol the line if you are waiting for the next show or the one after it.
- Many rides and shows have two aisles for their lines, and most people take the line on the right. Don't go with the flow. The left line is frequently faster.
- Try arriving at one of the parks an hour or two before closing. You may feel like salmons swimming upstream, but you'll be amazed at how much you can accomplish while most people are leaving.
- Small storage lockers are located near the entrances to each of the three theme parks. Small lockers cost $.50 for a day's use and larger ones cost $.75.

The Magic Kingdom

When most people think of Walt Disney World, they think of the Magic Kingdom. In fact, the Magic Kingdom is only a small part of what there is to do and to see at Walt Disney World. Children tend to think of it as the best part of Disney, which often leads adults to think that it is largely for children. Lately, we have found ourselves returning to the Magic Kingdom and enjoying it more and more. While there are many child-oriented attractions here, do not assume that the child in you won't enjoy them.

The Magic Kingdom

The Magic Kingdom is made up of seven different areas: Main Street USA, Adventureland, Frontierland, Liberty Square, Fantasyland, Tomorrowland, and Mickey's Starland.

MAGIC KINGDOM TIPS

- The most important thing to know about this theme park is that it is the busiest part of Walt Disney World.
- Don't try to see it all in one day.
- If you are interested in seeing the big-name attractions, we suggest that you make them your first effort. Start early. Surprise Mornings at the Magic Kingdom are on Monday, Thursday, and Saturday.
- Try the busier attractions during a parade or fireworks show.

Main Street USA

Main Street, a re-creation of a turn-of-the-century American town, is really a collection of shops, small eateries, and a movie house. The Victorian architecture is beautiful. Slate mansard roofs and carved gingerbread evoke the days of the horseless carriage. It is easy to run through this part of the Magic Kingdom on your way to the big-name attractions. While you probably will do so on your first few visits to the Magic Kingdom, you will find it worthwhile to slow down here eventually. Main Street opens at least half an hour before the actual park. Come early and browse, then head for the rides when the park opens.

Walt Disney World Railroad

This is a real steam-powered railway that huffs and puffs its way around the borders of the Magic Kingdom. These authentic old trains were discovered by the Disney people in Mexico, hauling sugar in the Yucatan. The ride takes a bit over 20 minutes and is an entertaining way to get a good overall view of the park. There are three stations, one on Main Street, one in Frontierland, and the other at Mickey's Starland. All aboard!

Harmony Barber Shop

Who would ever need to get a haircut at Disney? Well, Rick did, and we got a very pleasant experience as well as an exceptionally good haircut. It makes for a great photo, as the barbers are in period costumes. If you inquire first, you may find yourself in the barber chair while the Dapper Dans, Disney's barbershop quartet, gather 'round and harmonize.

Main Street Cinema

This theater features six small screens and nonstop animated classics. It's especially nice if you want to catch Mickey's debut in *Steamboat Willie*.

Transportation on Main Street USA

The trolleys, horseless carriages, and fire engine make a one-way trip up or down Main Street. They are interesting but hardly worth a wait in line.

Main Street Eateries

Main Street is bustling with food establishments. Tony's Town Square is a traditional Italian eatery. Around the corner, near the end of Main Street, is the Plaza Restaurant, offering sandwiches, burgers, and salads. There are lots of fast-food offerings along Main Street, too. There's the Main Street Bakeshop, the Plaza Ice Cream Parlor, and Casey's Corner, which serves the all-American hot dog. Just around the corner from it is the Crystal Palace, Main Street's cafeteria-style restaurant. The Crystal Palace serves each of the day's meals with a variety of entrees. Food is acceptable and most meals are inexpensive. The Crystal Palace has a pleasant garden atmosphere.

The Shops of Main Street

There are lots of shops along Main Street and, depending on your tastes, you should find at least something that interests you. Some of our favorites are Disneyana Collectibles, the Main Street Book Store, and Main Street Athletic Club, which features real sports memorabilia.

Adventureland

At the end of Main Street, hang a left and cross a small footbridge into another world. With dense jungle on your left and what appears to be Zanzibar on your right, you will head off into the heart of Adventureland. This has always been a favorite of ours. We enjoy strolling about, looking closely at all of the architectural details.

The Swiss Family Robinson Treehouse

✓ Walk-through exhibit
✓ Lasts about 30 minutes
✓ Line moves slowly

Talk about artificial plants. This attraction is a huge treehouse built in a man-made tree. The tree has 80,000 vinyl leaves on it, and the tree-house contains a variety of cute and interesting "inventions" created by the castaway Robinson family.

INTERESTING, but not enough to make it worth a long wait
Tip: Try this attraction when there is hardly any line. Don't attempt this one with cranky kids if there is a wait.

The Enchanted Tiki Birds: The Tropical Serenade

✓ Sit-down show
✓ Lasts 20 minutes
✓ Line moves fairly quickly

This is Disney's very first audio-animatronic attraction, featured originally at Disneyland. More than two hundred birds, plants, and statues all come to life with lots of music, special effects, and corny Disney humor.

QUITE GOOD, entertaining, and a nice cool place to relax

The Jungle Cruise

✓ Boat ride
✓ Lasts 10 minutes
✓ Line moves slowly

This boat ride through Africa (and India) is one of the Magic Kingdom's signature attractions. It is loaded with gags and audio-animatronic animals. Each boat's pilot gives the ride his or her own special brand of groan-a-minute humor. We did this ride once at night, in a misty rain. It was great.

EXCELLENT, especially at night—don't miss it

Pirates of the Caribbean

✓ Boat ride
✓ Lasts 8 minutes
✓ Line moves quickly

This is a terrific adventure, one of the best that the Magic Kingdom has to offer. It is a boat ride through a Caribbean town that is being plundered by a gang of fun-loving pirates. The special effects and audioanimatronics are some of Disney's finest despite the age of this attraction.

EXCELLENT, not to be missed
Tip: This ride may be too intense for very young children.

The Restaurants of Adventureland

There are a variety of counter-service food and beverage places around Adventureland. The Adventureland Veranda offers some interesting alternatives: teriyaki chicken, noodles, and sandwiches. Then there's the Eggroll Wagon and Aloha Isle, where you can find fresh fruit and juices. Aloha is a good spot to quench your thirst. El Pirata y Perico (the Pirate and the Parrot) offers tacos and hot dogs, while the Sunshine Tree Terrace has beverages and frozen yogurt.

The Shops of Adventureland

Shopping is very good in Adventureland, and we recommend some browsing later in the day. Plaza del Sol Bazaar has an outstanding selection of tropical clothes, while other shops, such as Traders of Timbuktu, Elephant Tales, and Tiki Tropics, offer some interesting items. Drop by Lafitte's Portrait Deck for a souvenir FotoToon. You'll love it.

Frontierland

The Wild West comes alive in this area of the Magic Kingdom. It boasts several outstanding rides and a few good shows.

Splash Mountain
✓ Water-flume ride
✓ Lasts 10 minutes
✓ Line moves quickly

This is one of Disney's newer attractions and it is also one of the busiest. Waits here can run as long two hours. Themed after Disney's movie, *Song of the South*, this ride is essentially a log-flume trip through the world of Brer Rabbit. The music is a pure delight, and the ride tells the tale with more than 100 robotic characters. When you finish this ride, you will be pleasantly spritzed with water and humming "Zippity Doo Dah." We guarantee it. (Or, if you sit in the very front of the log, you may be half-drenched and singing "Blow the Man Down.")

EXCELLENT, not to be missed
Tip: Arrange, at nearby Splashdown Photo, to have your picture taken while you are on this ride. It will be one of your most memorable Disney photos.

Big Thunder Mountain Railroad
✓ Mild roller coaster
✓ Lasts 3 minutes
✓ Line moves quickly

This ride is one of those attractions that you can go on time after time and still see new things. It is a "runaway" mining train careening through an old-time mining camp and is loaded with thrills, fun, sight gags, and great special effects.

EXCELLENT, not to be missed
Tip: Try Big Thunder a second time after dark.

Country Bear Jamboree
✓ Audio-animatronic show
✓ Lasts 15 minutes
✓ Line moves slowly

This cute show features bears that sing, dance, and generally horse around. It is entertaining, and we recommend it.

GOOD, especially for children
Tips: Try this one during an afternoon or evening parade. There is a special Christmas version of this show.

The Shootin' Arcade
✓ Electronic shooting arcade
✓ Costs $.25
✓ Line moves slowly

We visited Disney World when our son was 12 years old. He spent virtually all of his time here sharpening his shooting skills. We checked up on him now and then to be sure that he was all right and even dropped by with an occasional hamburger.

OK, if you like this sort of thing
Tip: Walk by and take a look at the Hawken rifles.

Diamond Horseshoe Jamboree
✓ Combination restaurant and live show

This used to be a ticketed show. No longer. Now, the Diamond Horseshoe Jamboree is more like a saloon. There is live entertainment going on nearly continually, and all you have to do is stroll in and pull up a chair. A small counter-service restaurant is at the bar, featuring a pretty unremarkable selection. If you wish, you can simply sit and watch the shows. The entertainment varies, but some of it is quite good.

Tom Sawyer Island
✓ Walk-through playground
✓ No time limit
✓ Line moves slowly

This attraction, a raft trip to a small island, may not be high on our list of things to see, although it isn't such a bad place to bring an overactive child. It's basically an island-playground, complete with cave, fort, and lots of places to explore.

Mostly for kids
Tip: This could be a good place for tired parents to rest.

Frontierland Grub

Pecos Bill's is this area's big restaurant. It features an enjoyable sidewalk atmosphere that, unfortunately, gets pretty crowded. Barbecue, burgers, and hot dogs are on the menu. Keep an eye on the animals on the wall while you are eating. Aunt Polly's Landing, over on Tom Sawyer's Island, features a pleasant porch but only if you want a peanut butter and jelly sandwich or cold fried chicken. Westward Ho is a food cart that should be named Westward Ho Junk Food. During the busier seasons, you may find the Turkey Leg Wagon over by Pecos Bill's, which features an interesting lunch.

The Shops of Frontierland

The shops of Frontierland have a definite western flair. The Prairie Outpost and Supply and the Frontier Trading Post both have nice collections of Native American and frontier clothing. After that, there's the Trail Creek Hat Shop, the Briar Patch, and Frontier Wood Carving.

Liberty Square

This area, snuggled between Fantasyland and Frontierland, is a small slice of Revolutionary War Americana. Take a look at the Liberty Tree, complete with its 13 lanterns representing the original 13 states. This tree was actually moved here, with great difficulty, from another location at Disney World.

Liberty Square Riverboat
✓ Boat ride
✓ Lasts 15 minutes
✓ Line moves quickly

This magnificent re-creation of a paddle-wheel steamer was built right on Disney property. The ride makes a short loop on Frontierland's River of the Americas and provides a relaxing view of the attractions along it. This boat, by the way, is pulled along on an underwater track and is not a thrill ride.

GOOD, pleasant, can be cool and restful
Tip: Try queuing up just when the boat arrives, as it can hold virtually everyone waiting.

The Hall of Presidents
✓ Audio-animatronic show
✓ Lasts 25 minutes
✓ Line moves quickly

This show is neither exciting nor funny, but it is interesting, especially if you are history buffs.

INTERESTING, with good audio-animatronics

The Haunted Mansion
✓ Low-speed ride
✓ Lasts 9 minutes
✓ Line moves slowly

We won't tell you much about this one except to say that it is more fun than scary. We'll leave the rest for your delight.

EXCELLENT, do not miss

The Restaurants of Liberty Square

The Liberty Tree Tavern is a pleasant, colonial-style restaurant and offers a nice variety of lunches (entrees and sandwiches) and a character dinner buffet. Food is good and prices are moderate.

In addition, there are two other good places to eat here, both of them offering counter service. Sleepy Hollow has a selection of vegetarian foods, from avocado salad to pita sandwiches; we enjoy the offerings here. The Columbia Harbor House has a seafood theme, offering fish, chicken, and salads.

The Shops of Liberty Square

There is a lot to be said for the shops in Liberty Square. The assortment is unusual and the quality is good. This is not your usual array of theme park shops. The Yankee Trader is one of our favorite shops. It specializes in kitchen-related items. Other places of interest are the Silversmith, Old World Antiques, and the Heritage House.

Fantasyland

Cinderella's Castle marks the main entrance to Fantasyland. The only structure at Walt Disney World that is taller is the new Twilight Zone Tower of Terror at Disney–MGM Studios.

Cinderella's Golden Carousel ♥
✓ Merry-go-round
✓ Ride lasts 2 minutes
✓ Line moves slowly

This handmade, beautiful old carousel was built in 1917, when "handmade" really meant something. This ride can actually be romantic, especially at night.

QUITE GOOD, more fun and romantic than you might think
Tips: Almost always open for Surprise Mornings. Ask a cast member to snap a picture of you both.

Skyway to Tomorrowland
✓ Cable car ride
✓ Lasts 5 minutes
✓ Line moves quickly

This is a one-way aerial tram ride to Tomorrowland. It provides an interesting view as well as a relaxing, away-from-the-throngs escape. Handicapped visitors are allowed to leave their wheelchairs at one end and take a round trip.

QUITE GOOD
Tip: Try getting on in Tomorrowland—the line there is usually much shorter.

It's a Small World
✓ Boat ride
✓ Lasts 10 minutes
✓ Line moves quickly

This pleasant and upbeat musical boat ride was created for the 1965 New York World's Fair. The music is catchy and it will get you both in the mood for Fantasyland.

QUITE GOOD

Legend of the Lion King
✓ Live and animated show
✓ Lasts 25 minutes
✓ Line moves to fill theater

This stage show combines live action, animation, and impressive special effects to create a simply wonderful miniversion of the animated film. This one may require a wait; it is worth it.

EXCELLENT, do not miss
Tip: Try this early or any time that you see that the line is not huge.

Peter Pan's Flight, Snow White's Adventure, and Mr. Toad's Wild Ride

✓ Low-speed rides
✓ Each lasts about 2–3 minutes
✓ Lines move slowly

We put these three rides together because they are so much alike. Despite the fact that these are basically kiddie rides, you might find them fun. Snow White has been redesigned due to complaints that it was too frightening for younger children. It may still be too scary for some young children.

OK, especially if you have small children
Tips: The waits can be long. Any of these rides may be intense for very young children.

Dumbo

✓ Midway-type ride
✓ Lasts less than 2 minutes
✓ Line moves very slowly

Six new Dumbo cars have been added to this ride in an effort to shorten the typically long waits.

A MUST for young children
Tips: Catch this one early. It is usually open for Surprise Mornings. Waits may still be long.

The Mad Tea Party

✓ Midway-type ride (spins)
✓ Lasts 2 minutes
✓ Line moves slowly

The speed of rotation of these spinning teacups can be controlled by the riders. Usually, this is a rather mild ride, aimed mostly at younger children.

OK; can be fun, especially if you enjoy feeling dizzy
Tip: Usually open for Surprise Mornings.

The Restaurants of Fantasyland

King Stefan's Banquet Hall is a beautiful restaurant located inside the castle. For atmosphere and ambience, it is hard to beat. The food is not great, though, and you'll need reservations to get in. The other Fantasyland eateries offer fast food. The Pinocchio Village Haus is a large indoor restaurant that features burgers, bratwurst, sandwiches, and even a turkey burger. Lumiere's Kitchen has a great selection of kid's meals, and the Tournament Tent, Round Table, and Troubadour's Tavern are all beverage or snack outlets.

The Shops of Fantasyland

The King's Gallery, inside Cinderella's Castle, has an interesting assortment of trinkets created by old-world artisans. Pricey, but nice to look at. Mickey's Christmas Carol offers a selection of Disney Christmas ornaments. There is also a candy store and several novelty shops.

Tomorrowland

Tomorrowland used to resemble a 1950s shopping mall: lots of concrete and neon and very little of "tomorrow." We are happy to tell you that a total redesign has been completed and, with the help of creative geniuses such as George Lucas, this area has become imaginative and exciting. The theme is more like a Jules Verne science-fiction vision: a strange blend of the old and the new. Whatever you want to call it, it looks really neat. The tired old rides have been replaced with several outstanding attractions.

Alien Encounter
✓ Special-effects show (not a ride)
✓ Lasts 20 minutes
✓ Line moves quickly

This attraction got off to a bad start when Michael Eisner, the Disney CEO, rode it during a test run. "Not scary enough," he declared, and it was back to the drawing boards for Alien. We have ridden it before and after and were impressed both times. The plot, a botched attempt at teletransportation, is good. The show is an awesome display of new technology.

QUITE GOOD, **kind of creepy**
Tips: The lines here are usually long. If you do not like being in total darkness, skip it. Too intense for young children.

The Transportarium
✓ Film and audio-animatronic show
✓ Lasts 15 minutes
✓ Line moves quickly

This show, which includes a CircleVision 360 (360-degree) film narrated by a Robin Williams robot, is exciting, clever, wild, and zany in a way that only Robin Williams could have made it.

EXCELLENT, **not to be missed**
Tips: This attraction is held in a large theater, which, if the lines aren't outrageous, will allow everyone in to see it. Ask the cast members at the door how long the wait will be.

Space Mountain
✓ High-speed roller coaster ride
✓ Lasts 3 minutes
✓ Line moves quickly

This is one of the World's most popular attractions. It is a roller coaster inside of a planetarium. It is fast and fairly rough. The waits in line here can be interminable.

EXCELLENT, **if you like this type of ride**
Tips: If you go for a Surprise Morning and this ride is not open, ask for the opening time and be there to get in line. It often opens later but before the park opens to the public.

Tomorrowland Transit Authority
✓ Gentle tram ride
✓ Lasts 10 minutes
✓ Line moves very quickly

This is the old WED-Way People Mover, renamed. It is a magnetically propelled car (called linear induction), the kind Japan is investing heavily in as a train system.

INTERESTING, but not memorable
Tip: If you want to see the inside of Space Mountain without riding it, this is the way to do it.

The Astro Orbiter
✓ Midway-type ride
✓ Lasts about 2 minutes
✓ Line moves very slowly

This is a recycled version of the old StarJets ride. It will give you a good view of Tomorrowland. Definitely mild.

OK, more interesting to look at

The Carousel of Progress
✓ Show with revolving stage
✓ Lasts 20 minutes
✓ Line moves quickly

This audio-animatronic show demonstrates how technology has impacted the home over the last three decades.

QUITE GOOD
Tip: Try this show when the other attractions are busy.

Grand Prix Raceway
✓ Miniature raceway
✓ Lasts about 5 minutes
✓ Line moves slowly

This is nothing more than a raceway with small, motorized go-karts. The pace is slow, and a runner-track restricts steering. This ride is very popular with children, especially those whose parents don't let them drive the family car.

OK, a kiddie ride

Dreamflight
✓ Special-effects ride (very mild)
✓ Lasts 6 minutes
✓ Line moves very quickly

This ride travels slowly through the history of aviation. Not only interesting, it has one segment that is even exciting.

GOOD, not Splash Mountain, but worth it
Tip: Try it when the other rides begin getting too crowded.

Skyway to Fantasyland
✓ Cable car
✓ Lasts 5 minutes
✓ Line moves quickly

This is the one-way aerial tram ride back to Fantasyland.

Food in Tomorrowland

We hope that the future has better food to offer than this area. Cosmic Ray's is the Magic Kingdom's largest fast-food restaurant. It is the perfect place to stand in line for barely acceptable food and then eat it in a noisy, crowded dining area. For snacks and drinks, try the Lunching Pad over by the Astro-Orbiter. The Plaza Pavilion Restaurant is another counter-service place that has pizza, pastas, and even a few interesting sandwiches. Auntie Gravity's is a breath of fresh air with its frozen yogurt and natural foods.

Mickey's Starland

This small land is tucked away behind Fantasyland and is aimed at young children. However, if you are interested in having your picture taken with a Disney character, this is the place to go. In fact, there are more than just a few good photo opportunities here. First and foremost is Mickey. You will find him here in his dressing room, available for pictures. Someone is even available to take a snapshot of the two of you arm-in-arm with the Mouse himself. As silly as this may sound now, you will cherish this picture later. We promise.

Mickey's House and Mickey's Starland Review
✓ Live show
✓ Lasts 15 minutes
✓ Line moves quickly

This live show is very popular with young children. Afterwards, meet the characters backstage for countless photo opportunities, complete with scenery.

OK, fun for kids

Grandma Duck's Farm
✓ Live animals
✓ No time limit
✓ Line moves quickly

It may be worth dropping by here to see "Minnie Moo," the famous cow endowed with a more famous spotting pattern.

OK, for small children

MAGIC KINGDOM ATTRACTIONS NOT TO MISS

- Big Thunder Mountain
- The Haunted Mansion
- The Jungle Cruise
- Legend of the Lion King
- Pirates of the Caribbean
- SpectroMagic Light Parade ♥♥♥ (see Chapter 5)
- Splash Mountain and Splash Mountain photo ♥
- The Transportarium

Epcot

We love the fantasy of the Magic Kingdom: the rides, the shows, and the delightful and fanciful realities created there. MGM is a celebration of the cinema, and we do love the movies. But there is something more at Epcot. Educating while entertaining is something that Disney does better than anyone, and every area and every exhibit in Epcot is rich with information and fun. This is an exciting place for curious minds.

Epcot is nearly twice the size of the Magic Kingdom. It is divided into two areas: Future World and the World Showcase. Future World displays the triumphs of science and technology. Its themes are health,

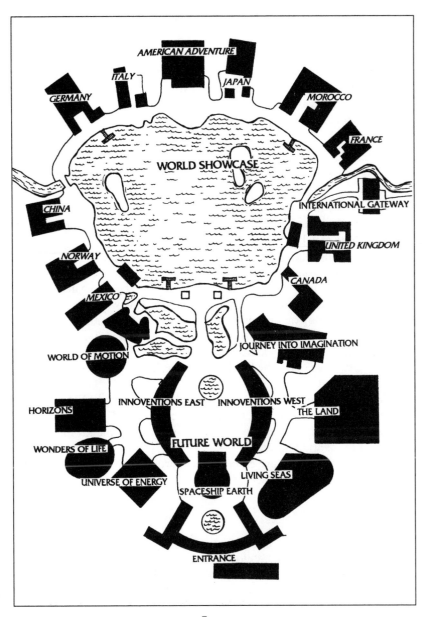

Epcot

energy, agriculture, the oceans, transportation, imagination, and communications. Each theme is featured in a different pavilion, and each pavilion has its unique attractions and exhibits. The eleven countries of the World Showcase encircle a sparkling, freshwater lagoon. Together they comprise a small world's fair.

*Ɛ*PCOT TIPS

- Each area of Epcot has different operating hours. Future World opens early and stays open until 7 or 8 P.M. The World Showcase opens at 11 A.M. and then closes after IllumiNations, at either 9 or 10 P.M., depending on the season. On the busiest days of the year, both areas may be open until 10 P.M.
- Surprise Mornings at Epcot are on Tuesday and Friday.
- Don't forget your entertainment and show-times guide. You will need it here. You can pick one up at one of the shops just inside either the main entrance or the International Gateway.
- The World Showcase is least crowded right after it opens.
- Future World is busiest in the morning after about 9:30 A.M. and into midafternoon. By late afternoon, the crowds begin to thin out as guests move on to the World Showcase. The hour or two before Future World closes is a good time to visit.
- Try splitting up your Epcot tour. Spend one morning at Future World, then do something fun at your resort. Another day, spend the morning around the pool and get to Epcot in time for the opening of the World Showcase.
- Don't miss the great live entertainment around the World Showcase. For more information, see Chapter 5.

Future World

This part of Epcot is a celebration of human triumphs. It is also the busiest part of Epcot. There's lots to do, much more than can be done in one day. If you want to see everything here, count on at least a few days.

Spaceship Earth
✓ Slow ride
✓ Lasts about 15 minutes
✓ Line moves quickly

This ride is inside the huge geosphere and will take you through the history of communication.

EXCELLENT, one of Epcot's best attractions—don't miss it
Tips: This ride is usually open for Surprise Mornings. After the park opens to the public, this is the first place where the entering crowds stop, and it very quickly becomes too busy. Save it for later if there is a long line.

Earth Station and the WorldKey Information Service

Located at the base of the geosphere and as you exit from Spaceship Earth, Earth Station is the place to go for information and dining reservations. The WorldKey terminal is a video display that will connect you to actual living people who will make your reservations. Be forewarned: they can see you.

Innoventions

Innoventions is one of the newer attractions at Future World. It is a showcase for the latest technologies. From automated home appliances to Personal Digital Assistants, you will find the most fascinating pieces of innovative electronics.

Detractors feel that it is little more than an advertisement for the high-tech companies that display their wares. Be that as it may, this place is neat. Innoventions offers hands-on displays, live demonstrations, and the latest in interactive media. Not just for computer nerds, this place is cool.

The Disney imagineers promise to keep Innoventions changing with the times and, from what we are able to see, they are making good on that pledge.

Tip: Innoventions gets very crowded. Either get there as soon as the park opens or try it late in the day.

The Fountain of Nations Water Ballet   This delightful fountain, located at Innoventions Plaza, is a classic example of Disney imagination. The formula is simple: take one large fountain and add the genius of Disney. The result is simply wonderful. The columns of water are controlled by a computer and are timed perfectly to accompanying music. It is a symphony of motion. If you think that this is neat in the daylight, try dropping by after dark. Don't miss the other lighting effects around

the plaza. For fountain "performance" times, consult the Epcot entertainment guide.

The Wonders of Life Pavilion

This pavilion is our favorite. It gets very busy, and we suggest that you
come right after opening. Inside are shows, films, and dozens of hands-
on displays. All of it is good.

Body Wars
✓ Simulated thrill ride
✓ Lasts 5 minutes
✓ Line moves quickly

Like Star Tours at Disney–MGM, this ride doesn't really go anywhere;
it merely creates the illusion. The show is a journey into the human
body aboard a miniaturized "inner-space ship." It's realistic and exciting. The motion of this ride is jerky.

EXCELLENT
Tip: Lines can get long, but they move quickly.

The Making of Me
✓ Film
✓ Lasts 15 minutes
✓ Line moves very slowly

This cute film ♥♥ features Martin Short, and it is both humorous and
touching. If it starts in a few minutes, get in line.

EXCELLENT
Tips: The theater is small and the lines can get long. Make an effort to see it
early, or wait until late in the day.

Cranium Command
✓ Show
✓ Lasts 20 minutes
✓ Line moves to fill theater

Another of our favorites, this show features audio-animatronics, animation, and special effects. Throw away your preconceptions about this attraction and see it. It is what Disney does best.

EXCELLENT, not to be missed
Tips: In all but the busiest of times, the wait for this show should not be much of a factor. Don't miss the preshow.

Goofy About Health
✓ Show
✓ Lasts 15 minutes

This low-key multiscreen show features Goofy getting wise about fitness and health.

OK, for children

Hands-on Activities
✓ Various displays and exhibits
✓ No set time limits
✓ Lines move slowly

The Wonders of Life Pavilion is full of exhibits that involve your participation. Have your golf swing analyzed, or hop onto a video exercycle and see the sights. There are lots of things to do that are fun and informative. Don't miss the Sensory Funhouse.

GOOD to VERY GOOD, don't pass by this area

The Universe of Energy Pavilion

This pavilion is also a ride.

Universe of Energy
✓ Slow ride
✓ Lasts about 30 minutes
✓ Line moves slowly

Huge "cars" take you through a combination of cinema and audio-animatronics retracing the history of energy. This ride is known primarily for its robotic dinosaurs.

BORING, but well-done effects and audio-animatronics
Tips: This ride holds nearly 600 people at a time. The only movement of the line is when one show gets out and the next goes in. The wait here looks much worse than it is (we wish we could say the same thing for the ride).

The Horizons Pavilion

This pavilion is currently closed. It is rumored to reopen in early 1996, as the World of Motion begins its reconstruction.

Horizons
✓ Slow ride
✓ Lasts 15 minutes
✓ Line moves quickly

This ride takes you through a series of sets that re-create past and current visions of the future. The sets and effects are quite good, and the ride is interesting.

GOOD

The World of Motion Pavilion

This pavilion will undergo a total reconstruction as of early 1996. A joint Disney–General Motors project, it will be a behind-the-scenes look at auto testing and will involve guests in a thrilling, high-speed auto test run. The pavilion is scheduled to reopen in 1997.

The Living Seas Pavilion

The centerpiece of this pavilion is its saltwater aquarium. Some 200 feet across, it is one of the largest fish tanks in the world. It's brimming with reef fish of every sort. The layout of the Living Seas is such that you're nearly surrounded by glass walls, water, and scores of tropical fish. Next to a reef dive, it doesn't get much better than this. The pavilion is divided into three areas, each with its own exhibits and theme.

The Caribbean Coral Reef Ride
✓ Slow ride
✓ Lasts 3 minutes
✓ Line moves slowly

This ride is only mildly interesting. It takes you "down" to the aquarium in a "hydrolator" and for a brief ride through an underwater tunnel.

OK

Sea Base Alpha   This part of the Living Seas is the real meat and potatoes of this pavilion. It is a prototype research facility and is chock-full of intriguing displays.

Sea Base Concourse   This part of the research facility is an interesting but quick walk-through.

The Land Pavilion

This is the largest of the pavilions in Future World, and its focus is agriculture. While this may not be on your top ten list of interests, this pavilion has a lot to offer both in entertainment and in food. Besides the ride, film, and show, it is home to the Sunshine Season Food Fair, which is the largest collection of eateries in Epcot.

Living with the Land
✓ Boat ride
✓ Lasts 10 minutes
✓ Line moves very quickly

This cool and pleasant boat ride takes you through the history of agriculture and into its future. It is scenic and fascinating. The sets and special effects are memorable.

EXCELLENT, not to be missed

Food Rocks
✓ Audio-animatronic show
✓ Lasts 10 minutes
✓ Line moves to fill theater

This show features a kitchen full of rockin' and rollin' fruits and vegetables. The music here is classic rock, with lyrics praising good nutrition.

GOOD and cute
Tip: Waits here never seem too long.

The Circle of Life

✓ Film
✓ Lasts 20 minutes
✓ Line moves to fill theater

This film replaces the tired and unexciting *Symbiosis*. The theme of this film is ecology, and the stars are Simba, Timon, and Pumbaa from *The Lion King*. The message is inspiring and upbeat.

GOOD

Tip: This theater seats more than 400. Check for times at the entrance and ask if you will make it into the next show.

The Greenhouse Tour

✓ Walking tour
✓ Lasts 45 minutes
✓ By reservation only, $5 per person

This fascinating tour goes through the greenhouses of the Land, where you will see the latest in agriculture techniques. The tours are conducted by real agriculturists.

QUITE GOOD

Tips: Make your reservations inside the pavilion, at the small kiosk near the entrance to Food Rocks. This is a popular tour.

Journey Into Imagination Pavilion

This wonderful pavilion is definitely one not to miss. There are lots of fun things to do here. After you have spent some time inside, don't miss the whimsical fountains outside.

Journey Into Imagination

✓ Slow ride
✓ Lasts 13 minutes
✓ Line moves quickly

This ride seems to lack the excitement typical of most Disney attractions. Cute, happy, and warmhearted, yes, but captivating and interesting, no.

OK

Honey, I Shrunk the Audience
✓ 3-D film
✓ Lasts 25 minutes
✓ Line moves to fill theater

Remember Professor Wayne Szalinski from Disney's feature film, *Honey, I Shrunk the Kids?* Well, he's back. This "movie experience" could easily be one of the most fun things here at Walt Disney World. We'll keep the details a surprise.

EXCELLENT, what you came here for—don't miss it!
Tips: Usually open for Surprise Mornings. Try this early or try it late. Whatever you do, be sure to catch this. Waits here can be long.

The Image Works   This area is a fascinating playground of hands-on devices that utilize touch, sound, and light in ways too unusual to even describe. There are no lines and, when it is crowded, you will have to wait to use some of the "games." Children, unfortunately, tend to monopolize them.

The Restaurants of Future World

There are only two table-service restaurants in Future World. The Coral Reef ♥♥ is located in the Living Seas Pavilion, and it combines a memorable atmosphere with very good food. The Garden Grill at the Land Pavilion is set on a turning carousel. For our reviews and more details about them, see Chapter 6.

The Sunshine Season Food Fair in the Land Pavilion is a carnival of eateries. It features five or six "shops" and a large selection of foods: sandwiches, soups, barbecue, ice cream, and lots more. Go early, as it gets crowded and noisy. Other interesting eateries are Pure and Simple at the Wonders of Life Pavilion and Pasta Piazza and the Electric Umbrella at Innoventions. Drop by Fountain View Espresso and Bakery in the Innoventions Plaza for some rich pastries and good espresso. The Odyssey Restaurant is currently closed, and no plans have been announced.

The Shops of Future World

There are quite a few shops in Future World, although many of them seem to specialize in souvenir items. For more interesting stuff, check out Sea Base Alpha at the Living Seas Pavilion, the Green Thumb

Emporium at the Land, Field Trips at Innoventions West, and Well and Goods at the Wonders of Life.

FUTURE WORLD ATTRACTIONS NOT TO MISS

- Body Wars
- *Cranium Command*
- *Honey, I Shrunk the Audience*
- The Innoventions Plaza fountain
- The Living Seas aquarium
- Living with the Land
- *The Making of Me*
- Spaceship Earth

The World Showcase

The World Showcase is a pleasant stroll around a large freshwater lagoon. Each of the eleven areas in this grand walk is a "country," and each has been carefully created to present an architectural, cultural, and culinary taste of that land. Each nation has some sort of exhibit or show, and two even feature rides. All of the pavilions have shops with arts, crafts, and other products that represent each of the countries. Some of the pavilions feature outstanding films.

Don't expect to find the real Norway or the real Japan here. This is Walt Disney World, and these countries are merely interesting concoctions imagineered to provide a taste of Italy or the flavor of Morocco. But neither should you dismiss the World Showcase as totally fanciful. Exceptional care has been given to the landscaping and architecture of each country. From the well-tended version of Vancouver Island's Bouchart Gardens to the real olive trees of Italy, a serious effort has been made to present a horticultural sampling of each nation represented. The gardens and landscaping around the lagoon are a gardener's dream. With such attention paid to buildings and streets, it is easy to get the sense of a Japanese garden or a Bavarian village. To complete the travel experience, each pavilion offers a sampling of foods, and many of the cast members around the lagoon are native to the lands they represent. There is also some form of local entertainment at virtually every pavilion, and some are simply delightful.

At the end of each day here at the World Showcase, there is IllumiNations, a spectacular laser light fireworks show. Timed precisely to classical music, this dramatic display is the perfect end to an evening at Epcot. For more details, see Chapter 5, Live Entertainment and Nightlife.

The World Showcase Plaza is the gateway to the World Showcase. The two shops here, the Port of Entry and Disney Traders, offer the usual collection of Disney and Epcot logo merchandise and sundries.

Besides walking around the World Showcase, you can also take a boat or go by double-decker bus. Two Friendship launches make regular passages across the lagoon from the docks near the Showcase Plaza. The double-decker buses circle the lagoon continuously with stops at Norway, Italy, France, and Canada.

We'll take you clockwise around the lagoon, which is our favorite direction. We won't give you every detail about what you will see here; we'll give just enough information to help you make your own discoveries. Exploration is the operative word here. Spend time in each of the countries, sit awhile, and catch the entertainers. Check your entertainment guide for times. Look in every nook and alley. You never know what you'll find.

We'll briefly mention the table-service restaurants here. For details and our reviews, see Chapter 6.

Mexico

This pavilion resembles an Aztec pyramid and is surrounded by a lush, tropical jungle, complete with squawking parrots and colorful orchids. Inside, the world of old Mexico comes alive with the beat of mariachi music. Featured is a display of Meso-American artifacts of amazing beauty and workmanship. A plaza of colorful shops offer baskets, hats, piñatas, jewelry, and men's and women's fashions, all in great abundance.

Also inside is the stunning San Angel Inn, Mexico's restaurant. Set on the banks of El Rio del Tiempo (River of Time), it enjoys an atmosphere unique even at Disney World. Under a dark sky and surrounded by jungle, you can enjoy Mexican cuisine while a volcano smoulders in the distance.

Outside the pavilion is Cantina San Angel, a counter-service restaurant that has a small but south-of-the-border menu. The Cantina features Mexican beer and is a good place to sit and listen to one of the musical groups that perform here throughout the day. Check for show times.

El Rio del Tiempo (The River of Time)
✓ Boat ride
✓ Lasts 9 minutes
✓ Line moves very quickly

This ride reminds us of It's a Small World except that it travels through the history of Mexico.

GOOD, try not to miss it

Norway

This quaint pavilion features a cobbled town square, a lovely Norwegian stave church, and a formidable replica of Akershus Castle. From the sod roof to the tiled cottages, the detail work in this "village" is impressive. Don't miss the "Ends of the Earth" exhibit in the Stav Kirke. For browsers, Puffin's Roost offers an array of Norwegian products (toys, clothes, jewelry, and hats), making this one of our favorite World Showcase stops.

Inside the miniature castle is the Akershus restaurant, whose menu comes straight from Norway. Kringlas Bakeri og Cafe offers an interesting selection of Scandinavian open-faced sandwiches and pastries as well as Norwegian Ringnes beer.

The Maelstrom
✓ Boat ride and film
✓ Lasts 15 minutes
✓ Line moves quickly

An exciting voyage aboard a Viking ship, this ride is fun and offers one brief thrill. There is lots to see during the trip, and we even recommend a second look. The film is outstanding and has inspired us to put Norway on our list of places to visit.

EXCELLENT, don't be afraid of the thrill and don't miss this ride and film

China

The centerpiece of this beautiful pavilion is the ornate Temple of Heaven, re-created here in intricate and colorful detail. Music and landscaping come together to make the courtyard an exceptionally restful retreat. We recommend that you sit awhile and wait for the entertainment. Shopping is outstanding at the Yong Feng Shangdian Shopping Gallery. All things Chinese are found in this large bazaar. Set aside some time, as it is a unique browsing experience.

China features a sit-down restaurant, the Nine Dragons, and a counter-service eatery, the Lotus Blossom Cafe. The Lotus Blossom has a small and fairly uninspired menu that includes lo mein and sweet and sour pork. Food is acceptable and inexpensive.

The Wonders of China: Land of Beauty, Land of Time
✓ Film
✓ Lasts 20 minutes
✓ Line moves to fill theater

This beautiful and poetic 360-degree film delivers just what its title promises. Visitors stand against rails to watch. You'll be so entranced that you'll hardly notice you're standing.

EXCELLENT, not to be missed
Tips: Check at the door for the time of the next show and browse until a few minutes before it begins. The theater will almost always accommodate everyone waiting.

The Village Trader   Just beyond China and nearly to Germany is the Village Trader. This small shop features art, handcrafts, and clothing from both Africa and Australia. There's some interesting stuff.

Germany

Browse in the square here while the strolling accordion player is performing, and you'll feel as though you're in a travel documentary. The main attraction in this charming bit of Bavaria is the pavilion's restaurant, the Biergarten, which features a wild and zany rendition of German beer hall entertainment.

The quaint shops of this Bavarian village offer a large variety of handcrafted German merchandise: cuckoo clocks, glass and porcelain, authentic fashions, and even precision timepieces. There's even a European-style candy shop and a wine cellar with daily wine tastings.

Sommerfest is a counter-service German restaurant. Pick up a meal at the counter and find a nice place to sit in the square.

Italy

Some evening, we'd like to go for a ride in one of the gondolas parked out in front of Italy. It would be so romantic. Instead, we'll stroll in the shadow of the Doge's Palace and perhaps later will enjoy a dinner in the ristorante.

The shops in Italy offer the finest in Venetian glass and crystal, a colorful selection of Italian fashion wear, and a large choice of hand-crafted jewelry.

Culinary offerings here include a sidewalk vendor who sells pastries, desserts, and beverages from a small cart; there's also the large and bois-terous Italian banquet hall, L'Originale Alfredo di Roma Ristorante.

The American Adventure

The American Gardens Theater is, perhaps, what makes this pavilion the centerpiece of the World Showcase (it certainly isn't this area's culi-nary offerings). The theater features a variety of performances, some with well-known entertainers. Others include high school and college groups from across the country and around the world. There is always something going on here, so check your entertainment guide.

The colonial-style building is home for both the pavilion's attraction, the American Adventure, and its eatery, the Liberty Inn Restaurant. Heritage Manor Gifts features an attractive assortment of crafts that are uniquely American. For collectors and gift givers, this is a place to browse. Outdoors, on the side of the pavilion nearest Japan, is the American Adventure Rose Garden, a perfect place to rest and escape the throngs.

We don't know what went wrong here with food at the American Adventure. It is a mystery to us why Disney opted to serve mediocre fast food.

The American Adventure Show
✓ Audio-animatronic show
✓ Lasts 30 minutes
✓ Line moves to fill theater

This patriotic journey through American history is narrated by "Mark Twain." It is interesting and even stirring.

QUITE GOOD

Japan

This lovely pavilion is marked by the torii gate on the shore of the lagoon. We always marvel at the Disney imagineers' attention to detail. The bases of this gate are covered with "oysters," as though the tide had fallen. From the towering pagoda to the Bijutsu-Kan Gallery, the rest of Japan has been just as meticulously created.

The Japanese garden should not be missed during your Epcot visit. Try to get here before the crowds to enjoy its serene beauty. Visitors to Disney's Japan will enjoy a choice of three uniquely Japanese dining experiences as well as shopping in the fabulous Mitsukoshi department store. Kimonos, vases, lacquered bowls, and colorful masks are a few of the thousands of items offered in this large shop.

Tempura Kiku is Japan's tempura bar. The Teppanyaki Dining Room features grill-tables where performance chefs prepare your dinner with a sizzle and a flair. Japan is also home to the Yakitori House, a delightful and authentic Japanese fast-food restaurant that features a lovely garden dining area. The Matsu No Ma Lounge is a full-service bar, and its menu includes a variety of specialty drinks, sake, and a tempting selection of Japanese finger foods including sushi and Kabuki beef. The view of the lagoon from here has no equal in Epcot. Try watching IllumiNations from the Matsu No Ma ♥♥♥.

Morocco

This pavilion, of all the countries, seems to best capture the feeling of being in a foreign land. Back among its winding, narrow streets and shops, you could almost forget that you are at Disney World. This exotic land even reaches out onto the sidewalk with a lively festival of musicians and dancers.

Tons of handcrafted tiles were imported to create the Chellah Minaret, the towering landmark of Epcot's Morocco. There is even an ancient waterwheel that "irrigates" the beautiful gardens along the lagoon. The shops here at Morocco are especially interesting. All things Moroccan are offered in this bazaar: jewelry, native clothing, brassware, leather goods, and more. Prices are fairly reasonable.

Morocco features one of our favorite Epcot restaurants, Marrakesh ♥♥. This exotic eatery boasts a menu of Moroccan cuisine and live entertainment at both lunch and dinner.

France

This pavilion enjoys a perfect location. Set where the waterway from nearby Crescent Lake enters the lagoon, Disney's France captures a sense of the lovely River Seine and the City of Lights. Small boats and artists' kiosks dot the river's edge. The Eiffel Tower rises beyond the mansard roofs. It is not quite Paris, but it is no doubt Gallic.

As you would expect, the emphasis here is on cuisine. This pavilion features two restaurants, a cafe, a pastry shop, and a winery. The shops are distinctly French, with offerings such as men's and women's fashions, original artwork, and the finest of perfumes.

The sidewalk cafe in this small piece of Paris is Au Petit Cafe ♥♥. It is quaint and picturesque. The two restaurants are the Bistro de Paris ♥♥♥ and Les Chefs de France ♥. French foods and wines are featured, and the settings and menus vary. Boulangerie Patisserie was a big hit with one of our mothers, who can sniff out good pastries at great distances. Croissants, brioches, tarts, and heavenly eclairs are just a few of the tempting treats here. Beverages are also served.

Impressions de France
✓ Film
✓ Lasts 20 minutes
✓ Line moves to fill theater

This film is beautiful, romantic, and unforgettable ♥♥. The theater is cool and offers each guest a seat. Need we say more?

EXCELLENT, not to be missed
Tips: Ask at the door for the next show time. If there is no crowd, browse until just before it begins.

Sidewalk Artisans de Paris   Along the lagoon artists are at work. Some do sketches, some create chalk portraits, and yet others will snip your silhouette in black paper. The prices are all reasonable, and the work is good. One of these will make a much better souvenir than a photo taken in front of the geosphere.

The United Kingdom

Our favorite part of this pavilion is tucked away in a corner (which might be why we like it so much). The traditional English garden is the perfect spot for a rest after you've browsed the shops along the streets of London and visited Anne Hathaway's cottage. Pick a nice shady bench and enjoy this beautiful and relaxing hideaway.

We have always enjoyed shopping in Disney's Great Britain. There is something special about the Scottish woolens, fine English teas, and colorful assortment of wooden toys. A lot is here, and we suggest you give it a good looking over.

The U.K.'s restaurant is the Rose and Crown Pub and Dining Room. The pub has all the look and feel of the real thing as well as a selection of stouts and ales. The dining room features British cuisine and several different dining areas, one of which is outside overlooking the lagoon.

U.K. Food Carts   Two food carts are usually at each end of the pavilion. The cart nearest the International Gateway offers baked potatoes with a variety of toppings. After a potato, if you are still hungry, head over towards Canada and to the next cart. There you'll find a small assortment of desserts. (If you get there after one of our mothers, there may not be any eclairs left.)

Canada

We enjoy many things in Disney's Canada. The pavilion's 360-degree film is only part of the excitement. After the film, we like to take a walk through the mountain area, past its waterfall, and into the beautiful garden that re-creates the famous Bouchart Gardens of Vancouver Island, British Columbia. Colorful beds of flowers, willows, and maple trees make this a little slice of our neighbor to the north.

Back on the sidewalk along the lagoon, we listen for the Caledonia Bagpipes. In the shadow of the stone architecture of old Ottawa, this little musical group pipes away the folk tunes of Canada. Shopping here is good, too. The Northwest Mercantile has an intriguing selection of Canadian products. Maple syrup, Indian clothes and moccasins, and some real Innuit sculptures are only a few of the interesting items that you will find here. If you've ever wanted a Canadian Mounties hat, come and get it. La Boutique des Provinces, Canada's other shop, specializes in goods from the French province. Le Cellier is a moderately priced cafeteria-style restaurant.

O Canada!

✓ Film
✓ Lasts 20 minutes
✓ Line moves to fill theater

This is a CircleVision 360 (360-degree) film, like the one in China. All travel films should be this exciting.

VERY GOOD, no reason to miss this one
Tip: If it seems particularly crowded, ask one of the attendants if you'll make it into the next show.

ROMANCE AT THE WORLD SHOWCASE

- A meal or appetizers at San Angel Inn: ♥♥♥
- The garden of Japan: ♥
- A drink at Matsu No Ma Lounge during IllumiNations: ♥♥♥
- Lunch or dinner at Marrakesh: ♥♥♥
- Taking the *Breathless* Cruise from the marina at the Yacht Club (see Chapter 7 for details): ♥♥♥♥
- Having espresso and sharing a dessert in the evening at Au Petit Cafe: ♥♥
- Having a sketch done by a sidewalk artisan in France: ♥
- Dinner at the Bistro de Paris: ♥♥♥
- *Impressions de France:* ♥♥
- Spending a few quiet moments in the English garden: ♥♥

Disney–MGM Studios

This may be the smallest of the three theme parks, but it is a power-house of entertainment. With a modest amount of planning, you should be able to take in everything here in a few visits. Most of the attractions are geared to accommodate large numbers of visitors. The exception is Voyage of the Little Mermaid, and we will give you some tips for that show later.

DISNEY–MGM TIPS

- Disney–MGM Surprise Mornings are on Sunday and Thursday.
- Attractions to hit early are Star Tours, Twilight Zone Tower of Terror, Voyage of the Little Mermaid, and the Great Movie Ride.
- Some of the attractions ask for participants. Get involved. These are the moments that you will remember most fondly. Trust us on this. The attractions that feature guest participation are the Indiana Jones

BACKLOT THEATER

NEW YORK STREET

MUPPETVISION 3-D

STAR TOURS

SOUND STAGES

GREAT MOVIE RIDE

BACKSTAGE STUDIO TOUR

VOYAGE OF THE LITTLE MERMAID

MAGIC OF DISNEY ANIMATION

SUPERSTAR TV

MONSTER SOUND SHOW

INDIANA JONES STUNT SHOW

SUNSET BLVD.

HOLLYWOOD BLVD.

TWILIGHT ZONE TOWER OF TERROR

BEAUTY & THE BEAST STAGE SHOW

ENTRANCE

Disney–MGM Studios

Epic Stunt Spectacular, the Monster Sound Show, and SuperStar Television.

- Take advantage of the roving photographers who will take your picture and then enhance it with Disney characters. These FotoToons make great memories.

Hollywood Boulevard

Hollywood Boulevard, like Main Street, ushers visitors into the park along a themed street of shops. The architectural style is art deco, and it is carried off with the perfection typical of Disney attractions. Details include old mailboxes, bus benches, and, here and there, a curbside classic automobile. 1930s Hollywood comes alive along this amusing and fanciful avenue. There are some interesting shops here, but we suggest that you save them for later, when the attractions begin to get crowded.

Sunset Boulevard

Sunset Boulevard is one of the newest areas. Located at its far end is the "dilapidated" Hollywood Tower Hotel, home of the Twilight Zone Tower of Terror. Along this street is a variety of shops, attractions, and eateries.

The Shops on the Boulevards

If you enjoy movie memorabilia, then you've come to the right place. Sid Cahuenga's One-of-a-Kind is one of Disney's most unique shops. Don't miss it. The rest of the Boulevards are packed with shops that feature souvenirs of every sort, much of it Disney-related. There are several good clothing stores, one of which, Keystone Clothiers, offers a mouse-ears umbrella.

The Attractions of Disney–MGM Studios

We really like this park. There is a lot of thought behind each attraction, and nothing except for the *Honey I Shrunk the Kids* Movie Adventure Set is aimed solely at children. Things here are intelligent and thoughtful, not to mention fun. We suggest that you give everything a chance. In particular, we encourage you to see the Backlot Studio Tour and the

Magic of Disney Animation Tour. Both are excellent and seem, some-how, to be at the very core of the experience here. Disney–MGM Studios is more than a theme park—it is a working studio, and these attractions will bring you into these working areas to give you an intriguing look at the magic behind the movies.

Twilight Zone Tower of Terror
✓ Special-effects thrill ride
✓ Lasts 10 minutes
✓ Line moves slowly

If you don't mind being taken to the top of a 13-story building in an "elevator" and then dropped to street level, then you're ready for this. The special effects along the way are some of the best we've ever seen, and the story line is entertaining. The drop is over quickly and is not as bad as it sounds. (How many times have you heard that line?)

EXCELLENT, if the plunge doesn't frighten you off
Tips: This attraction is very popular and, since the line moves slowly, a long wait is likely. Usually open for Surprise Mornings.

Beauty and the Beast Stage Show
✓ Live show
✓ Lasts 30 minutes
✓ Line moves to fill theater

Real people perform this miniversion ♥♥ of the Disney classic film. The costumes, sets, and performances are all good, and the music is, we think, the best ever in a Disney animated feature.

EXCELLENT, do not miss
Tips: The 1500-seat Theater of the Stars will accommodate virtually everyone in line. The amphitheater is large, and all of the seats provide a reasonably good view of the stage. Seating begins 30 minutes prior to each show. Check for show times.

Star Tours
✓ Simulated thrill ride
✓ Lasts 7 minutes
✓ Line moves quickly

Based on the *Star Wars* films, this ride doesn't really go anywhere. It is a pod-like "ship" that merely simulates flight by coordinating film, sound, and a bit of rocking, tipping, and bucking. It is very convincing and very entertaining.

EXCELLENT, do not miss
Tip: Usually open for Surprise Mornings.

Voyage of the Little Mermaid
✓ Live Musical Show
✓ Lasts 20 minutes
✓ Line moves slowly to fill theater

This show combines live action and puppetry in a brief version of the Disney animated film. Everything about this show is excellent, especially the special effects.

EXCELLENT, do not miss
Tips: When you first get your entertainment guide, check for the time of the first show. Arrive 30 minutes before. Better a 30-minute wait early than a much lengthier one later. Only one theater-full of people is admitted at a time, and you may not be in line for the very next show; ask a cast member.

The Great Movie Ride
✓ Adventure "train" ride (slow)
✓ Lasts 20 minutes
✓ Line moves very quickly

This ride takes you through a series of movie scene re-creations. The sets, audio-animatronics, and special effects are all worth seeing again and again. There are even a couple of "live shows" staged along the way. (There are two different versions of the shows, shown to alternating cars.)

EXCELLENT, do not miss
Tips: This ride is usually open for Surprise Mornings. Parts of it may be too intense for very young children.

The Indiana Jones Epic Stunt Spectacular
✓ Live show
✓ Lasts 30 minutes
✓ Line moves quickly to fill large amphitheater

This is a live-action stunt show. The special effects and scenery are memorable. This is an attraction executed on a grand scale, and it is exciting and fun.

EXCELLENT, do not miss

The Backstage Studio Tour
✓ Tram and walking tour
✓ Lasts 1 hour, 15 minutes
✓ Line moves quickly

The tour is really divided into two parts, a motorized tram tour and a walking tour through the working studios. You do not have to go on the walking tour (which lasts one hour), but we strongly suggest that you do. This part of the tour is informative and entertaining. The walking tour concludes with previews of upcoming Disney films, some of which are genuine first looks at yet to be finished creations.

EXCELLENT, not to be missed

The Magic of Disney Animation Tour
✓ Film and walking tour
✓ Lasts about 30 minutes
✓ Line moves quickly

This tour begins with a film that you will not soon forget. Robin Williams and Walter Cronkite join forces in an introduction so hilarious that you will want to see it again. The tour then takes you through the Disney animator's actual working areas. It is interesting. The grand finale is another memorable film of animation clips from Disney classics.

EXCELLENT
Tips: The waiting area showcases cels, sketches, and artifacts from Disney's most recent animated features. Don't miss the Sorcerer's Apprentice topiary as you exit.

SuperStar Television
✓ Show with audience participation
✓ Lasts 30 minutes
✓ Line moves slowly to fill theater

This show puts costumed visitors on stage and right in popular television shows. It is especially memorable when one or both of you gets into the show. "Tryouts" are held 20 minutes prior to each show. Get involved in this fun.

EXCELLENT

The Monster Sound Show
✓ Film and show
✓ Lasts 15 minutes
✓ Line moves slowly

This is another wonderful audience-participation show. It demonstrates the art of creating sound effects. The show is wild and hilarious as well as interesting.

VERY GOOD

MuppetVision 3-D
✓ Film and more
✓ Lasts 20 minutes
✓ Line moves quickly to fill large preshow area, then theater

This 3-D film is a lot more than just a film. We'll leave the rest a surprise.

EXCELLENT, not to be missed
Tips: The line here seems to come and go with the flow of people from nearby attractions, such as Indiana Jones. Try it when there isn't much of a line at various times throughout the day. The preshow should not be missed.

"Honey, I Shrunk the Kids" Movie Set Adventure
✓ Playground for children
✓ No time limit
✓ Line moves very slowly

This is a playground where objects are much larger than usual. Much, much larger. Everything is "rubberized." for safety.

OK, for small children, otherwise avoid it

Tips: Lines here can be awful and awfully slow. If this is a must-see for your child, we suggest that you get here early.

"New York" Street Set
✓ Walk-through
✓ No time limit

Here on the backlot of the studio, Disney has created a huge facade of New York City. It presents some nifty photo opportunities. Parts of the set were used during the filming of Dick Tracy.

GOOD

The Pocahontas Stage Show
✓ Live show
✓ Lasts 25 minutes
✓ Line moves to fill theater

At the Backlot Theater, this rendition of the Disney animated film is entertaining, and the costumes are good.

VERY GOOD
Tip: Seating begins 25 minutes before the show.

The Restaurants at Disney–MGM

Dining at Disney–MGM is better than at the Magic Kingdom. Here you will find the fine as well as the fun. There are four interesting table-service restaurants. The Hollywood Brown Derby ♥ is fine dining in a charming re-creation of the famous Hollywood eatery. The 50's Prime Time Cafe offers American food and fun, and Mama Melrose's is Disney's neighborhood Italian eatery. The Sci-Fi Dine-In Theater will put you in the back (or front) seat of a car at the drive-in. For our reviews and more information, see Chapter 6. Reservations for these restaurants are strongly recommended.

The Studios has a large selection of counter-service restaurants. Hollywood & Vine Cafeteria of the Stars serves breakfast, lunch, and dinner. Meals are acceptable and inexpensive. The Soundstage features a themed character buffet breakfast (Pocahontas and Friends are currently appearing) and a large variety of counter-service foods for lunch and dinner. The Commissary offers a modest variety of interesting sandwiches in a fairly standard fast-food setting.

The Backlot Express, located near the Indiana Jones show, features grilled chicken, burgers, and hot dogs in a pleasant outside sitting area, while Min and Bill's specializes in subs, pasta salads, and cold sandwiches. The Sunset Ranch Market is really a group of food outlets that are set in an outdoor farmer's market. From fresh fruits and salads to hot dogs and chili, there's a lot to choose from here. For snacks and desserts, you can go to Dinosaur Gertie's or Starring Rolls. Starring Rolls is a little bakery around the corner from the Brown Derby, and it offers hot cocoa and tea; it's a nice spot for a light breakfast.

Lounges at Disney–MGM

Because this theme park is geared more towards adults, there are lounges here at Disney–MGM Studios. So drop in for an afternoon cocktail or an evening sip of wine.

- The Catwalk Bar is located upstairs from the Soundstage restaurant. It is very colorful and full of movie props. Seating is equally interesting. Beers, wines, specialty drinks, and espresso are offered along with a pretty interesting assortment of appetizer-like foods. It's a nice escape.
- The Tune-In Lounge is part of the 50's Prime Time Cafe and has a good selection of beers and wines.
- Mama Melrose's Bar, located right alongside the kitchen, will give you a great view of the chefs at work as you quaff your beer or enjoy your wine. The selection here is small but interesting.

DISNEY–MGM ATTRACTIONS NOT TO MISS

- The Backstage Studio Tour
- Beauty and the Beast Stage Show
- The Great Movie Ride
- The Indiana Jones Epic Stunt Spectacular
- The Magic of Disney Animation Tour
- MuppetVision 3-D
- Star Tours
- Twilight Zone Tower of Terror
- Voyage of the Little Mermaid

ℛomance at Disney–MGM Studios

- Beauty and the Beast Stage Show: ♥♥
- Sorcery in the Sky fireworks: ♥♥ (see Chapter 5)
- The Hollywood Brown Derby Restaurant: ♥

Other Walt Disney World Attractions

Discovery Island

This small island, located in Bay Lake, is unlike any of Disney's other attractions. The focus here is on wildlife. Real, live wildlife. There are no audio-animatronic birds and no robotic reptiles. This beautiful and densely tropical isle is Disney's own zoological park, certified and accredited by the American Association of Zoological Parks and Aquariums.

A short boat ride from the Magic Kingdom, Discovery Island seems a world away. This overlooked Disney gem offers a unique getaway from the hustle and bustle of the other attractions. Take a lazy stroll down a shady path. Watch hundreds of rare birds in one of America's largest walk-through aviaries. Come prepared to explore, and don't forget a picnic lunch from your favorite restaurant.

Discovery Island is an 11-acre sanctuary for more than 250 species of reptiles, mammals, and birds. While this may not be a place that you would wish to spend an entire day, you will find that there are plenty of things to fill a morning or afternoon. This is a small and quiet place, which is precisely what makes it so attractive. Not only is there no need to hurry here, but there is no temptation to.

What you will find are shady paths that wind lazily through bamboo thickets and under a dense canopy of trees. There are toucans, kookaburras, macaws, and dozens of other birds. In fact, there are whole flocks in natural aviaries. You may even be lucky enough to spy Discovery Island's resident bald eagle. The island also enjoys a small population of exotic mammals and reptiles. From the lumbering Galapagos tortoises to the miniature Asian muntjac deer, Discovery Island provides one delight after another. The three shows here are small and intimate, like the rest of the island. The Thirsty Perch, the island's store, offers a selection of beverages, snacks, and souvenirs. Several nice picnic areas are available.

OUR RECOMMENDATIONS FOR DISCOVERY ISLAND

- This place is especially nice and especially deserted during the fall months.
- Make arrangements with one of your favorite restaurants to prepare a picnic lunch ♥♥.
- Nesting season for the island's feathered inhabitants runs from February to early fall.
- Feeding time at Pelican Bay is 3:30 P.M.
- This attraction is closed annually from mid-February to mid-March.

The Disney Water Parks

So far, Disney has built three water parks, and each one seems to get better. River Country was the first, followed by Typhoon Lagoon. Just when you thought they couldn't get much grander, along comes Blizzard Beach. Whether you're young or old, visiting with your family or as a couple, these parks will very likely provide a day's worth of excitement and entertainment. Each has kiddie pools, slides both tame and wild, raft rides, and wave pools.

Admission to all of the water parks is included in the Length of Stay Pass and the Five-Day World Hopper Pass. A separate admission ticket is sold for River Country for $16, while the way to get into either Typhoon Lagoon or Blizzard Beach is to buy a $24 Water Park Hopper Pass that provides admission to all three for one day; you can visit any or all of these parks during the one-day admission.

All three parks suffer from the same problem: too many people. At peak times, you will find yourselves spending more time in line than having fun. Here are a few ways to avoid the crowds:

- Arrive early. Get there 30 minutes before the park opens, and use the first few hours for the slides and raft runs.
- Arrive late. During the summer months, the water parks stay open until 8 P.M. Arrive around 4 P.M., when the crowds are starting to thin out. Most offer a discounted afternoon rate. In the summer, the late afternoon is cooler and the sun is kinder.
- Try a water park when the weather is "less than ideal." The water is heated to 80 at each and, in inclement weather, it may be brisk, but the park will be all but empty.
- Arrive right after an afternoon thundershower. The rain will have driven the crowds away.

$\mathcal{M}$ORE WATER PARK TIPS

- The hours to the water parks vary with the seasons. Check with Guest Services or the "World Update" for the operating hours.
- Towels are available as rentals. Wear shoes or flip-flops. For women, one-piece bathing suits are best for the slides. There are changing rooms, but, if you like, you can wear your suit under your clothing to avoid having to change.
- Do not forget sunblock or sunscreen. The Florida sun is brutal, even on an overcast day. Besides being dangerous, a sunburn is uncomfortable. You don't want to spend your romantic Disney vacation being too sore to be touched. We usually wear light T-shirts to protect ourselves from the sun.
- The food at Disney aquatic theme parks is typical fast food. Have one of the restaurants in your resort pack a nice lunch.
- Leave jewelry and watches back in your room. This stuff tends to fall off while you're zooming down slides. No personal swim gear is allowed in any of the parks, including mask, fins, rafts, and floats.
- As soon as the park opens, go stake out a place with lounge chairs. Some spots are in the shade, and some are not. Take your pick and deposit a few of your things on enough lounges to provide each of you with one. If you don't, someone else will.
- Rental lockers are available at all of the water parks. If you have valuables with you, such as a camera or a bag, you can't leave them lying around. This may be Disney World, but it is still planet Earth.
- Use the first few hours after opening to hit all of the fast-moving slides and raft rides. Save the lazy tubing, swimming, and surf-riding for later.

River Country

The first of Disney's water recreation parks, River Country is also its smallest. This is the "ol' swimmin' hole" a la Huck Finn, and while it's not executed on the grand scale of Typhoon Lagoon or Blizzard Beach, it has its charm.

Not far from Discovery Island, River Country is set perfectly on the shore of Bay Lake. The cool breezes from the lake make it particularly nice. There is more emphasis here on landscaping and beauty than on exciting slides. Huge man-made boulders, waterfalls, and lots of trees make this place seem less of an attraction and more like a natural occurrence. River Country consists of several areas. Bay Cove is the large swimming area and the heart of the attraction. It is actually an area of the lake that has been walled off. The water here is kept clean and circulating, making it a large, sand-bottomed swimming pool. There is a lot of fun to be had here, though mostly for the younger set. Rope swings and a large boom are several ways to enter the cove. There are also two pretty decent water slides, Hoop 'n Holler Hollow, and a gentle raft ride, oddly misnamed White Water Rapids. If you are looking for excitement, this may not be the place for you.

River Country also has a large swimming pool. Upstream Plunge is not far from Bay Cove. It features two steep slides. And Cypress Point Nature Trail is a short and scenic stroll through the wetland area along the lake.

There are two counter-service restaurants. Pop's Place is the larger of the two, offering burgers, hot dogs, salads, and a variety of snacks. The Waterin' Hole, a snack bar, opens only during the busier seasons. Picnicking is permitted at River Country, which may be the best way to get some good food.

River Country is located at Fort Wilderness. Buses make the trip from the Ticket and Transportation Center (TTC) throughout the day. The water park can also be reached by taking the Fort Wilderness boat from the Magic Kingdom dock.

Typhoon Lagoon

Typhoon Lagoon tells the story of a small fishing village hit by a typhoon. The storm has left the village in ruins—creating the perfect aquatic theme park. Mount Mayday is the most prominent feature of the crazy world of Typhoon Lagoon. Speared atop its peak is an old shrimp boat. Every half hour, a fifty-foot geyser of water spews from its smoke stack. Look around, and you can't help but notice that things are are way out-of-whack. The storm has left this place utterly askew. Buildings lean this way and that, seemingly about to topple.

These delightful effects are everywhere. Nothing has escaped the wrath of the typhoon or the notice of the Disney imagineers. There is more here than just a cute story and some nifty props, though. Typhoon Lagoon's 56-acres is jammed with slides, creeks, raft rides, and a rumbling surf pool.

Of all the attractions here, Humunga Cowabunga is the only one that we would hesitate to recommend for everyone. This steep, 50-foot, high-speed water slide is a bit too vertical. If this kind of speed is your thing, you'll love it. Six other slides here range from mild to exciting. None approaches the speed or height of Humunga Cowabunga, and we think that you'll like them all. Three of them are raft runs of varying lengths. The remaining slides are body slides: Rudder Buster, Stern Burner, and Jib Jammer are each exciting and fairly fast.

Castaway Creek winds lazily around the park, and you can hop aboard a tube almost anywhere and float to your heart's content. This little river takes you through some amusing effects: a tunnel, a waterfall, and under a leaky bamboo pipe.

Ketchakiddie Creek is a miniversion of this park, and it is just for kids (adults admitted only when accompanied by a child). Shark Reef offers a snorkeling experience through a lagoon of live fish. The water in this pool is much cooler than the rest of Typhoon Lagoon.

Typhoon Lagoon offers two counter-service restaurants, the Leaning Palms and Typhoon Tilly's. There are also two "beach shacks" that serve snacks, soft drinks, beer, and wine coolers. And of course, no theme park would be complete without shopping. Here at Typhoon Lagoon, you have Singapore Sal's, which carries souvenirs, Typhoon Lagoon merchandise, and a variety of sundries.

Blizzard Beach

Disney imagineers like to give every place a "spin," and this could be the tallest tale of all. Blizzard Beach, so the story goes, is the result of a freak winter storm that blasted this piece of Walt Disney World with snow and ice. It was too great an opportunity to pass up, so work was begun immediately on a ski resort. Before the resort was completed, however, the temperature returned to normal. Hopes for a Disney ski complex were dashed.

Ready to shut the whole thing down, the resort operators noticed an alligator frolicking in the water from the melting snow. The place would, they quickly realized, make for the perfect water adventure park. So, what had once been ski slopes, slalom courses, and bobsled runs were hastily converted into some of the wildest and tallest water slides anywhere. And so began Blizzard Beach.

We have told you more than once that Disney's creations continue to get better and better. Blizzard Beach is certainly proof of this. Words like wild, crazy, and zany only begin to describe it. The Disney imagineers must have had a lot of fun thinking up this one.

The cluster of buildings at the entrance to Blizzard Beach resembles alpine lodges. Here and there are banks of melting "snow." Icicles hang from the eaves, and racks of skis sit useless in the sun. The centerpiece of the park is Mount Gushmore. A real chairlift runs to the small chalet on its snow-covered summit. From there, a steep staircase leads up to the nearly vertical ski jump/water slide. Other slides and chutes run down the mountain, twisting and turning in all directions. Ice and snow glitter realistically in the bright sun. Comic details are everywhere: the Avalunch snack bar, a lone ski sticking out of a snow bank, and a potbellied stove.

Summit Plummet is the high-speed water slide that claims to be the tallest and fastest in the world. Or jump aboard a large raft at Teamboat Springs and zoom down the mountain. The six-passenger raft twists and turns along 1,200 feet of splashing waterfalls.

Runoff Rapids is a tube ride down a choice of three flumes. Slush Gusher is a slide nearly as high as Summit Plummet but nowhere near as steep. Snow Stormers runs through a zigzag slalom course, complete with banks of snow and flag gates. Toboggan Racer is a rather tame eight-lane slide down one of the gentler slopes on Mount Gushmore.

If the slides of Blizzard Beach get too crowded, head off to explore Tike's Peak, a scaled-down and pint-sized version of the park. It won't be hard to find Melt-Away Bay, a one-acre swimming area with a sand beach. Here in the shadow of Mount Gushmore, waders and swimmers splash away the day. The Blizzard Beach Ski Patrol Training Camp, about halfway up the slope, is an area designed for preteens. Here, a series of events such as Mogul Mania and the Ice Flow Walk present comical challenges at this goofy training camp. Or, as an alternative, hours can be spent drifting lazily around the park in tubes along the wonderful Cross-Country Creek.

Blizzard Beach has two snack bars, Avalunch and the Warming Hut, and one rather large counter-service restaurant called the Lottawatta Lodge. With seating either inside or in a pleasant courtyard, this Caribbean-style ski lodge is the place to take your appetite. Pizza, hot dogs, hamburgers, and other fast Disney foods are available at the many counter windows. (Even with a large opening week crowd, the wait was minimal.) The Beach Haus offers a large selection of Blizzard Beach memorabilia, Disney character merchandise, and even some interesting apparel.

$\mathcal{L}$ ive Entertainment and Nightlife

Don't ask us why Walt Disney World is not known for its live entertainment. By our reckoning, Disney could be the single largest employer of talent anywhere. While we enjoy the make-believe part of Disney, we also spend time seeking out the numerous and unusual forms of live entertainment. No matter how many times we visit, the World has something to offer that is new and exciting. Whether it is a puppet show from Great Britain, a country and western band, or the orchestra in the lobby of the Grand Floridian, we are certain that you too will find much to enjoy.

In this chapter, we'll give you the scope of the performances available along with details about them. And of course, we'll tell you where and when to find them. And since the Disney imagineers are continually inventing new and exciting things, we'll give you some tips on how to keep abreast of anything special that may be happening during your trip.

Live Entertainment in the Theme Parks

Each of the theme parks offers a lot of live entertainment. Since these performances are all over the place, you'll need a guide to help you locate them. We've already told you about the theme park entertainment guides. Updated weekly, these will be your tickets to locating Disney's live entertainment. The guides include parades, fireworks, live performances, and unique events, as well as Disney character appearances. Since many of the events and performances occur only on certain days of the week, we suggest that you get all three entertainment guides early in your Disney visit so that you can plan your time in the theme parks.

Live Entertainment in the Magic Kingdom

Main Street USA   The Walt Disney World Band performs every morning in Town Square on Main Street. During the busy summer months, they usually give several concerts.

One of our favorite Main Street groups is the Dapper Dans, Disney's tap-dancing barber shop quartet. They usually begin around 10 A.M. and wander Main Street, performing at unannounced times. It's just hit or miss; we recommend "hit."

Another group of musicians found here are the Rhythm Rascals, a zany washboard and banjo troupe that will have you laughing while you tap your feet. This gang reminds us of Spike Jones and his band (if you are old enough to remember them). At Casey's Corner, a ragtime pianist will bring the old days alive, and the Kids of the Kingdom offer musical shows at the stage in front of Cinderella's Castle. They are particularly popular with children but are not among our favorite performers in the Magic Kingdom.

Adventureland   J. P. and the Silver Stars ♥ is a steel band that performs authentic Caribbean music at the Caribbean Plaza, near Pirates of the Caribbean. Check out the unique instruments used by this rhythmic group as they offer up a touch of the islands. If you've never heard this kind of music, don't miss it. And while you're in Adventureland, check out the "drum machine" in the plaza near the entrance to the Jungle Cruise.

Frontierland   The Frontierland Stuntmen stage a Wild West shoot-out daily in the streets and on the rooftops of Frontierland, usually near Country Bear Jamboree. The Stuntmen appear seasonally.

Fantasyland   The Sword in the Stone Ceremony is scheduled throughout the day in the plaza near the castle. This reenactment of the King Arthur legend is performed with the participation of a young guest selected from the audience. It is cute and heartwarming, especially if the youngster is yours.

A variety of bands from all over the U.S. perform each week at the Fantasy Faire Stage. On special occasions, you are likely to catch the Walt Disney World Band here as well.

Tomorrowland   For out-of-this-world entertainment, try the Galaxy Palace in Tomorrowland. Imagineers have been beating the bushes for something a little, well, alien. Silly and largely for children.

Live Entertainment in Epcot

Epcot offers a large assortment of unique and talented performers from all over the world. Each country in the World Showcase has its own offering. Some performers seem to be permanent fixtures, others are guests. The guest artists come to Disney World for a year or two, usually in the "country" of their origin in the World Showcase. These are some of the most interesting performances at Walt Disney World, and we urge you to seek them out, not only to enjoy their performances but also to chat with the artists. It is a rare opportunity for cultural exchange.

Epcot also offers a variety of guest artisans that might include a Persian rugmaker or a French glassblower. Such craftsman can be found in the countries around the World Showcase and are usually mentioned in the entertainment guide. Here and there around Epcot, you'll also find high school and college bands and choruses from all over the U.S. and the world.

First we'll discuss entertainment at Future World, then we'll cover the World Showcase.

Future Corps   This drum and bugle group plays a variety of popular tunes. They are entertaining and, being professionals, are outstanding. Performances are usually at Innoventions Plaza.

The Anacomical Players   This impromptu theater group performs in the Wonders of Life Pavilion. Their sketches about health often involve the audience. Look for the Anacomical Players stage area on the main floor of the pavilion.

Dreamfinder   Dreamfinder and his companion Figment appear outside the Journey Into Imagination Pavilion. These characters are part of the show inside and appear throughout the day, largely for the enjoyment of young children.

Following are the live entertainment shows available at the World Showcase.

Mexico   Marimba Mayalandia and Mariachi Cobre are two musical groups. They are entertaining and colorful. Try timing a performance with a snack or a drink in the sidewalk cafe ♥.

Norway   The entertainment in Norway is usually traditional Scandinavian folk song and dance. We have had some of our most memorable entertainment moments in this lovely village. We have usually been able to chat with the performers, and it has been entertaining, personal, and informative. What more could we ask for? The performances can be found near the Kringla Bakery. Pick a bench and sit awhile before the musicians arrive.

China   The performances are typically a solo musical performer and a small group of Chinese acrobats. We suggest that you stroll by to see where they will be and then return for a later show, finding a bench nearby. Arrive early enough to sit and enjoy the courtyard. The piped-in music in China is particularly pleasant. If you take the time, you will see a lot that a walk-through would miss. By the time the performers arrive, you'll feel as though you're in China.

Germany   Entertainment in Germany includes a courtyard accordionist and a wild and musical dinner show at the Biergarten restaurant. Strolling around the German pavilion while the accordion player is performing will provide the proper mood for your "visit to Germany." Check the entertainment guide for times and make your arrival on cue.

Italy   There are two groups of live entertainers here in Italy. The Commedia di Bologna are actor-comedians that put on a show in the square. They are crazy, fun, and typically corny. The other group plays and sings at Alfredo di Roma Ristorante. This restaurant is a little slice of Italy: gay, colorful, and noisy. A good choice for a fun and festive meal.

The United States   Inside the rotunda are the Voices of Liberty, an a cappella choral group performing medleys of traditional American ballads. Arrive a few minutes early. It is a good show, especially if you have a place to sit down. In front of the pavilion, check out the Sons of Liberty, Disney's fife and drum corps, complete with traditional costumes.

The American Gardens Theater, a large stage near the pavilion, offers a selection of performing artists and groups. Often, you will find a high school band or chorus or a big-name performer. During the course of a Disney week, the variety of entertainment here is pretty impressive. Check your entertainment guide. If someone well known is performing, give yourselves plenty of time to get a seat.

Japan   There are usually several different performances here, one of them being our favorite Epcot entertainer, the Fantasy DreamMaker. The good news about this man is that he appears to be permanent. He is a Japanese street entertainer that performs tricks, jokes, and carves tiny sculptures out of little globs of brown rice gum. The Fantasy

DreamMaker is precisely the kind of thing that you might not even be lucky enough to see if you visited Japan. The bad news is that he appears only a few days a week and at times not specified in the entertainment guide. He usually doesn't appear before 11 A.M. Watch for a small, wizened fellow pushing a cart with a large banner and lantern. This is one performer who is definitely worth the wait. The other performance here in Japan is usually a formal type of entertainment such as a dance or drum group.

Morocco   There's almost always something exciting going on in the bazaar of Disney's Marrakesh. Check your entertainment schedule and get there in time to wander around the marketplace while the dancers and musicians do their thing. This instant street festival features a group of Moroccan artists who will dazzle you with their exotic music and dance.

Inside Restaurant Marrakesh ♥♥ is a belly dance show during both lunch and dinner. In both cuisine and atmosphere, the Marrakesh delivers a truly exotic restaurant experience.

France   Entertainment at this pavilion is usually a trio of musician-singers who offer a selection of standard French ballads. At other times, a small band of street comedians perform. The entertainment is quite pleasant, especially in this beautiful pavilion.

The United Kingdom   Street entertainment is the main attraction here. The Old Globe Players put on short comedies that are entertaining and corny. Recently, though, we have been enjoying Sue and Peter Barbour, two British puppeteers who perform on stilts. They are clever and talented. Their show is very entertaining, and we hope that they will be there for you to enjoy.

Canada   The Caledonia Bagpipes also appear to be a permanent feature here in the Canadian Pavilion, and the Canadian Comedy Corps, often in the company of a kilted Goofy, performs its slapstick act at various times throughout the day.

Live Entertainment at Disney–MGM Studios

Hollywood Boulevard Street Performers   Along Hollywood Boulevard, a band of wacky street entertainers perform unannounced throughout the day. These zany characters are dressed in the weirdest of costumes, and their comic routines often involve unwary onlookers. These are the denizens of Disney's 1930s Hollywood. It is easy just to rush down Hollywood Boulevard to the rides and shows, never realizing that something's happening here. Don't forget to come back later and catch the shows.

Star Today   Each week, Disney brings a television or movie personality to Disney–MGM for a motorcade and handprint ceremony. The celebrity is usually available for autographs and a brief "star conversation." Check to see who is appearing during your Disney visit.

The Studio's Soundstage   This theme park is also a working studio. During the year, television programs are produced in its three large sound stages. Often, they involve audiences. Check at the Production Information Window just inside the front gate for ticket availability and show times.

Street Musicians   A variety of bands play at various places throughout the park. The Tubafours Quartet, Toon Town Trio, and Hollywood Hitmen offer their own brand of musical entertainment and street comedy.

Muppet Characters   The Muppets can be found around the back of the Muppet Theater. Always fun, these characters are especially entertaining for young children.

Beauty and the Beast Stage Show ♥♥   This lavish stage production takes place in a large theater on Sunset Boulevard. Beautifully costumed performers dance and lip-synch to the memorable music of the animated Disney classic.

Backlot Theater   Long the home of the Ninja Turtles, good taste has at last prevailed here, and the pizza-loving reptiles have been sent packing. Featured this year is the Spirit of Pocahontas Stage Show, a live version of the animated film. Make plans to see it.

Live Entertainment at Pleasure Island

Pleasure Island is Disney's adult nightspot. It is a six-acre island with seven nightclubs, some of which feature outstanding live bands. You'll find the groups at the Pleasure Island Jazz Company, the Neon Armadillo, and the Rock 'n Roll Beach Club. If you're looking for live comedy, don't miss the Comedy Warehouse. And if you're looking for something, well, completely different, plan on spending some time at the Adventurer's Club. For more information about these clubs, see "Nightlife at Walt Disney World" later in this chapter.

Live Entertainment in the Disney Resorts

The Grand Floridian

Each day from 3 to 6 P.M., a pianist plays in the grand lobby. In the evenings, from 9 to 11 P.M., a small orchestra performs on the landing outside of Mizner's Lounge on the second floor. The music is pleasant and can be heard from anywhere below. Either entertainment is reason enough to drop by to see this elegant place ♥.

The Polynesian

Another form of live entertainment to consider is one of the three dinner shows at the Poly. The Luau ♥, Mickey's Tropical Revue, and 'Ohana each have something interesting to offer. For details, see Chapter 6.

Fort Wilderness

Yes, even Fort Wilderness offers live entertainment. The Hoop-Dee-Doo Musical Revue could very well be Disney World's most popular dinner show. While not exactly a performance, the Campfire Singalong is definitely entertainment. This nightly event is held near the Meadow Trading Post and is free to all Disney resort guests. It features Disney movies on an outdoor screen, a marshmallow roast, a campfire sing-along, and a visit by Chip and Dale.

Port Orleans and Dixie Landings

Both resorts feature entertainment in the lounges of their central areas. The Cotton Co-Op and Scat Cat's Club each usually have a singer/ entertainer in the evenings. Performances usually beginning after 9 P.M. Drop in for a drink and enjoy.

The Swan and The Dolphin

Juan and Only's Cantina and Bar, at the Dolphin, frequently features a Flamenco guitarist in the evenings, and the Lobby Court Lounge at the Swan has its own pianist in the evenings, Thursdays through Saturdays.

Disney Parades

The Magic Kingdom is famous for its parades, and there's one every day along Main Street. A celebration of Disney characters and Mickey Mouse in particular, this incredible parade always features floats, spectacular costumes, and lots of music and special effects. It usually begins at 3 P.M. Check your entertainment guide to be sure. It is definitely worth seeing once.

Disney–MGM Studios also features a daily parade. The currently running Aladdin's Royal Caravan is slated to end with no replacement as yet announced. Rumor has it that the animated film, the Toy Story, will furnish the theme for the new parade.

Walt Disney World's Twenty-Fifth Anniversary Celebration

In October of 1996, Disney promises to kick off a year-long, "once-in-a-lifetime" celebration of its twenty-fifth anniversary. Shows, parades, and special attractions are being planned. The party begins on October first, and it sounds to us like a reason to go.

Some Romantic Live Entertainment

- Have a drink at Mexico's sidewalk cafe during a Mariachi performance: ♥
- The belly dance show during a meal at Morocco's Restaurant Marrakesh: ♥♥
- The Beauty and the Beast Stage Show at Disney–MGM Studios: ♥♥
- Musical entertainment at the Grand Floridian: ♥
- The Polynesian Luau at the Polynesian Resort: ♥

Nightlife at Walt Disney World

During your romantic getaway at Walt Disney World, you'll most certainly want to get out in the evening and have some fun. This is the Vacation Capital of the World, and that means there'll be lots to do. During the busy times of years, the parks are all open late and Disney World is running at full-throttle. Finding something to do in the evening will be a matter of choice. Whether you want to follow dinner with SpectroMagic or the Twilight Zone Tower of Terror, or whether you wish to take a dip in the pool or go out dancing, you'll find plenty to do after dark.

During the off season, there is not quite so much going on. The theme parks and attractions all close relatively early. The Magic Kingdom and Disney–MGM Studios usually close at 6 P.M. and the World Showcase at Epcot closes at 9 P.M. While Epcot features IllumiNations every night, the other parks stay open late with nighttime parades and fireworks only on weekends.

We like the off season because it fits our pace. With fewer people in the parks during the days, we have plenty of time for theme park excitement. We then use the evening to ease back, spend some time together, and to get out in search of that something special. Whether it's the busy season or not, you'll both find lots of nightlife at Walt Disney World. Besides dining out, you will be able to enjoy Pleasure Island, dinner shows, the movies, great shopping, hot tubbing, special and seasonal events, and "resort hopping." After the parks close, you still have a whole other world of Disney magic, and after July of 1996 Disney's BoardWalk will be available as well.

Fireworks over Disney

Most Disneymaniacs think that Disney–MGM's Sorcery in the Sky ♥ is the finest fireworks show at Disney World. Set to the most memorable of Hollywood film scores, this is indeed an extraordinary pyrotechnic display. It's not simply the magnitude of the show that makes it so special; the rockets themselves seem especially beautiful. It is staged only when the park is open late, during the busier months or on holidays. If it is scheduled during your visit, don't miss it.

IllumiNations   ♥♥ is a spectacular laser and fireworks show that takes place each night on the World Showcase Lagoon at Epcot. Featuring a perfect orchestration of blazing rockets, colored fountains, and classical music, this is a one-of-a-kind event. The sound system is unbelievable. Come early to get a good viewing. Our favorite spot is on the bridge between France and the United Kingdom or in the garden area right below it. Other good places to see this show are near Mexico, the United Kingdom, and near the World Showcase Plaza, which is the entrance to the World Showcase Lagoon. Be sure that you are able to see the huge ball in the center of the lagoon and that you have as good a view as possible of the various pavilions. Do your best to avoid being downwind of the show, unless you like smoke. No view is perfect. Stake out your place at least 30 minutes before the show.

On evenings when the Magic Kingdom stays open late, there is Fantasy in the Sky ♥, a fireworks spectacular set to music. Most people flock to Main Street to see this, but we suggest that you try Mickey's Starland, where the crowds are fewer and the viewing is nearly as good. With the park closing right after the show, simply hop aboard the train that will be waiting at the station there and ride around to the Main Street Depot for an easy exit.

The SpectroMagic Light Parade

SpectroMagic ♥♥♥ is the Magic Kingdom's fantastic light parade. It takes place after dark during the busier times of year and on weekends year-round. It's like nothing you've ever seen before. When the park is open until midnight, it's done twice, at 9 P.M. and again at 11 P.M. Parades will never be the same for you after this one, we promise. For a good viewing place for either of the Magic Kingdom parades, try Liberty Square or Frontierland.

Pleasure Island

We admit it. We exaggerated about the theme parks all being closed early. Once you see this place, you'll see that it is really a Disney theme park. The theme here is adult, nighttime entertainment. Pleasure Island is an island of nightclubs, shops, theaters, and restaurants. The Island features seven completely unique clubs, and a nonstop street party. Each evening is capped off with an explosive New Year's Celebration. There's likely more than just a little something here for the two of you. Be forewarned that the music in the dance clubs is quite loud.

This is a Disney attraction, which means a single admission charge gets you into any or all of the clubs.

𝒫LEASURE ISLAND ADMISSION

- $16 per person
- Included with Length of Stay Pass or Five-Day World Hopper Pass
- Magic Kingdom Club admission is $14
- Annual Pleasure Island passports available

Getting to Pleasure Island   In the evenings, buses run directly to Pleasure Island and the Village Marketplace from every resort area except Fort Wilderness. From there, you'll have to take a bus to the TTC (Ticket and Transportation Center) and then transfer. Driving to Pleasure Island is simple. Parking, however, becomes more of a challenge as the evening progresses. There is valet parking for $5, and this may be your only choice late in the evening.

Busing always seems best to us, especially if we are planning on having a few drinks. After an evening of partying on the Island, it's nice to have a designated driver.

Next, we'll describe the different clubs of Pleasure Island.

The Neon Armadillo Music Saloon   The 'Dillo is a country and western club and the place to go for line dancing. Plank and barrel tables and Southwestern decor are not what really makes this place, it is the music. Not even lovers of this musical style, we are always drawn to the Armadillo. The songs are singable and danceable and, before long, the small dance floor comes alive.

The club features a good selection of beer, a full-service bar, and some light foods, including nachos, Buffalo wings, chili, and burgers.

The Pleasure Island Jazz Company   This is the latest addition to Pleasure Island, and one that we welcome. The Jazz Company makes an effort to be more of a nightclub. It is cozy, the lighting is low, and patrons sit at small cocktail tables in front of the stage. Besides wines, specialty drinks, and champagne, the Jazz Club has an interesting menu of appetizers. Here are some of the offerings: shrimp quesadillas, crab cakes with roasted red pepper remoulade, Caesar salad, grilled red snapper with green peppercorn sauce, and lemon-caper chicken. Prices range from $5 to $10. There is also a variety of rich desserts. Couple this with a few hours of outstanding entertainment, and you have a real 1930s-style nightclub. The club features various groups and occasionally has well-known artists. The music is not too loud and conversation is still a possibility. There really isn't any other place like it here.

The Rock 'n Roll Beach Club   With hundreds of flashing and blazing lights and special effects, this club is a dazzling place. There is even a smoky mist that occasionally covers the dance floor. The effect, as we used to say in the sixties, is pretty far-out. We guess, too, that it may be a generational thing that we enjoy this club. The music more reflects our time: Beatles, Rolling Stones, and other familiar sounds make this our kind of dance place. The bands are always good, both instrumentally and vocally. If you want to dance to some good old rock 'n roll, you can hardly go wrong with this club. The Rock 'n Roll Beach Club has a full-service bar and also offers pizza, subs, and a small selection of sandwiches.

The Comedy Warehouse   This is one of the most popular clubs on the island and features a handful of improvisational and stand-up comics. The humor is clean and harmless; vulgarities are not part of this or any other Disney show. The riskiest these folks get is to poke some fun at the Disney experience, some of which is actually quite funny. Occasionally, a well-known comic appears and, for this, a $5 charge may be added. There are five shows nightly. Specialty drinks, beer, and wine are featured as well as a small selection of finger foods.

8TRAX   This dance club specializes in the sound of the seventies. We're not sure what we were listening to back then, but it sure wasn't this stuff. Still, this place may be just your thing. There are no live bands here, but the sound system is just as spectacular as you'd expect. Ambience is futuristic, and 8TRAX features a multilevel dance floor and a full-service bar. Burgers, fries, and a selection of sandwiches make up the menu.

Mannequins Dance Palace   This place was voted the number one contemporary dance club in the southeast U.S. We wonder who voted. Decorated with mannequins dressed in a variety of weird leather garments, Mannequins is the only Pleasure Island nightclub that requires its patrons to be at least 21 years of age. The main dance floor is a huge turntable, and the special effects and light show are state of the art. All this, plus the sounds of the mostly contemporary music, makes this club *the* place for the younger crowd.

The Adventurer's Club   Take a good look at the outside of this place before you enter. The Adventurer's Club pretends to be one of those stuffy British gentlemen's clubs of the 1920s. You know the type: members sit around in the wood-paneled library or enjoy an exotic drink in the comfort of a stuffed chair. These are the places that have been featured in countless old films, in which world-weary explorers come home to the British aristocracy. This club only *looks* like one of these places. And there is more here than meets the eye.

The Adventurer's Club is absolutely crammed full of the strangest assortment of interesting artifacts that we have ever seen in one place, and the club's inhabitants are every bit as eccentric. The Adventurer's Club offers a totally different kind of entertainment than the other Pleasure Island clubs.

It is staffed by a group of actors and comedians, all in costume, who stage radio broadcasts, award ceremonies, and interact with guests. You'll meet mysterious maids, an eccentric butler, and the famous explorer Hathaway Brown. A lot of crazy stuff is going on in all of the rooms, and you'll need a program card (you can get one at the door) to keep up with all the events.

The Shops of Pleasure Island   Pleasure Island has eight interesting shops along the street. Most of this stuff is not available elsewhere at Walt Disney World. Avigator's Supply features a collection of men's and women's clothing and accessories, the type of which might be worn by habitués of the Adventurer's Club. Other shops offer movie and music memorabilia, jewelry and trendy fashions, and Disney character merchandise. One of our favorite shops is Suspended Animation; original and limited-edition animated cels are this shop's stock-in-trade, and they are definitely worth a look.

The Pleasure Island Midway   A midway adds to the carnival atmosphere of the island, with several booths, games of strength, a Velcro jumping wall, and two rather interesting "rides." The Orbitron is a huge gyroscope mounted on a fixed base. Participants are strapped into the center of it and, by shifting their weight, rotate rapidly in several planes. It looks like fun, although we've never given it a spin. The other ride is also an Orbitron, but this one adds a virtual reality helmet and computerized battle to an already fascinating ride.

Everywhere throughout the island are street vendors of every sort, hawking espresso, stick-on tattoos, beer, wine, and jewelry. There is a lot going on everywhere.

Dining at Pleasure Island   As we have already mentioned, the clubs feature a variety of edibles—some more edible than others. A few other sidewalk vendors and shops offer food. There is the Hill Street Diner for deli, pizza, burgers, or hotdogs and D-Zerts, which features a decent array of desserts, soft-serve and frozen yogurt, as well as espresso or cappuccino.

For a real meal, you have several good choices. Portobello Yacht Club and the Fireworks Factory are two of our favorites. Both are run by Levy's Restaurants of Chicago. Early in 1996, the nearby *Empress Lilly* riverboat will reopen as a crabhouse-style eatery. Right next to Pleasure Island is the famous Planet Hollywood. It is likely the most incredible of the stylish chain. The building itself looks more like a Tomorrowland ride. Inside is an eclectic collection of real movie artifacts. The food is actually quite good. This restaurant is very popular.

For more information about these restaurants, see Chapter 6.

The West End Stage   Each night, a band is featured here. Located at the end of the street that runs along the Island, the West End Stage keeps the street party going. The music is good, and people dance and enjoy themselves. As the time for the nightly New Year's celebration approaches, this is right where you'll both want to be. Don't miss it.

New Year's Eve   Yes, it's New Year's Eve every night on Pleasure Island. The celebration includes a live band, dancers, special effects, fireworks, and confetti cannons. It alone is just about worth the price of admission. Find out what time this happens (midnight isn't always midnight at Walt Disney World), and don't miss it. It is the highlight of the evening.

The AMC Pleasure Island Theaters   Located next door to the clubs of Pleasure Island, this complex features 10 of the very latest feature films running in state-of-the-art theaters. A great romantic comedy may just fill the bill for one of your evenings out.

Seasonal Nightlife

During the course of each year, Walt Disney World offers a variety of special events. Many of these happen during the evening hours, further spicing Disney nightlife. From the Jolly Holidays Dinner Show to the Walt Disney World Wine Festival, there's almost always something interesting going on. Other seasonal events include the Pleasure Island Mardi Gras Celebration, Mickey's Very Merry Christmas Party, the Haunted Village Halloween, the Annual Jazz Festival, Chinese New Year, and Epcot Swingin' Summer Nights. New events are added each season, so check to see what's going on during your visit.

Resort Hopping

Any visit to Disney World is not complete unless you get the chance to check out the Disney resorts. If you have never seen the Grand Floridian, the Polynesian, or the Contemporary, take a monorail ride and do some exploring. There is plenty to see, and you can look these places over for your next visit. Don't leave out the Wilderness Lodge and its award-winning lobby.

While you're out in the evening at any of the Magic Kingdom resorts, don't forget to look for the Electric Water Pageant on the Seven Seas Lagoon. This display of electrical and musical magic passes by each resort on the lagoon around 9 P.M. Check at any resort for the exact time. There are good viewing places all along the beach areas of the Polynesian, the Grand Floridian, the Contemporary, the Wilderness Lodge, and Fort Wilderness. Try the fourth-floor lake overlook at the Lodge for something especially nice.

Resort hopping is especially fun during the weeks between Thanksgiving and Christmas, when the World is decked out in its Christmas finery. Nearly every resort has a beautifully decorated tree in its lobby, and there are tree lighting ceremonies each night. Disney characters and free refreshments are almost always part of the entertainment. Last year, we caught a chorus of bell ringers playing Christmas carols at the Wilderness Lodge.

Even if it's not the holiday season, many of Walt Disney World's lounges are quiet and romantic places and offer interesting selections of appetizers and hors d'oeuvres. Try skipping dinner and traveling around the World in search of tasty treats. Some of our favorite spots are Martha's Vineyard at the Beach Club, the Territory Lounge at the Wilderness Lodge, Scat Cat's at Port Orleans, and the Copa Banana at the Dolphin. There are lots of others, and we'll leave them for you to discover.

Disney's BoardWalk

When it opens in the summer of 1996, the BoardWalk promises to become yet another landmark for Disney nightlife. Besides several good restaurants and a promenade of shops, a number of interesting attractions will be added to Disney's evening entertainment. We are eagerly awaiting the Atlantic Dance Hall. Dancing will be to popular music from the thirties to today, played by a 10-piece orchestra. We hope this is as interesting an alternative to Pleasure Island as it sounds.

Another great nightspot will be Crazy Fingers Dueling Piano Bar. This neighborhood-style bar will feature lively entertainment with sparring pianists. The Big River Grill and Brewing Works will be Disney World's first microbrewery, offering a variety of fine beers and ales and a menu of grilled seafood and steaks.

As if this were all not enough, there will also be a state-of-the-art sports bar. Partnered with ESPN sports network, Disney is creating the largest and most elaborately equipped sports bar anywhere. Sixteen satellite feeds and the largest collection of virtual reality games are just a few of the attractions to be offered here, come summer of '96.

The BoardWalk promises to be like no other area of Walt Disney World: a combination of entertainment, shopping, restaurants, and resort rooms.

The Romance of Disney Nightlife

- Relax in the afternoon before your Disney evening out: ♥♥
- Have a nice hot tub before you go out for the evening: ♥♥
- SpectroMagic Light Parade at the Magic Kingdom: ♥♥♥
- Watch the Magic Kingdom fireworks or the Electric Water Pageant from one of the swings on the beach at the Grand Floridian or the Polynesian: ♥♥♥♥
- Dine at Portobello and have an evening out at Pleasure Island: ♥♥
- A light dinner at Pleasure Island's Jazz Company: ♥♥
- "Resort Hopping" at Christmas time to see the decorations and tree lighting ceremonies: ♥♥
- Have a wine flight at the Beach Club's Martha's Vineyard lounge: ♥♥♥

$\mathcal{D}$ining at
Walt Disney World

The first time we went to Disney World, we brought sandwiches. We don't do *that* anymore. In fact, Walt Disney World doesn't even provide areas in the three theme parks where visitors can picnic on their own food. What Walt Disney World does provide, however, is an astounding array of nearly 200 places to eat. It is an amazing assortment that is guaranteed to make happy any palate or purse. From a hot dog at Casey's Corner on Main Street to the gourmet elegance of Victoria and Albert's, the imagineers and the chefs of Disney have conjured up an impressive diversity of culinary experiences. If you think that eating at Disney means overpriced fast food, then let this be your wake-up call.

Interested in a dinner show or a western barbecue? Our specialty. We've been everywhere and can tell you all you need to know if you want to fix your own breakfast or get dressed up for Victoria and Albert's. Looking for exotic cuisine or an intimate cafe? Singing waiters or strolling musicians? From breakfasts to midnight snacks, we have gone after the Disney dining experience with an appetite and a vengeance. If we sound a bit excited about this, it is because we are. The restaurants of the World have provided us with some truly memorable meals as well as many unforgettable moments. So, put on your turn signals and pull out of the fast-food lane to join us on a delicious tour of Disney dining.

Making Reservations

We don't really like to make reservations. They always make us feel as though we're tied to a schedule. At Disney, however, you will find that you'll have to make at least some. It's inevitable. You won't ever get into some places if you fail to make an appointment. Also, you will probably want to eat during a busy time of day, and you will be glad to have a reservation then.

- Dining reservations may be made anytime within 60 days of the date of your meal. For Disney dining reservations, call (407) WDW-DINE (939-3463). Hours are 7 A.M. to 10 P.M., seven days a week.
- Same-day, theme park dining reservations by telephone are available only to Disney resort guests. Touch 55 on your room phone.
- Guest Services is a good way to make reservations. They have a variety of menus. Look them over, then let Guest Services make your reservation.
- Reservations are most necessary during the regular mealtimes. If you are without reservations, try eating early. For dinner shows, reserve when you make your room reservation.
- For character breakfasts, it is wise to make reservations. King Stefan's will accept reservations no more than seven days in advance, and both Olivia's and the Soundstage will only take reservations 30 days ahead. All other character breakfasts can be reserved up to 60 days in advance.
- It is wise to reserve ahead when dining in one of the theme parks. If you haven't, most theme park restaurants will take same-day reservations at the front door during the morning hours.

Dining Tricks and Budget Tips

Over the years, we have learned to be imaginative with our approach to the pleasures of dining at Walt Disney World. Here are some of our ideas.

OUR TIPS FOR BREAKFAST

- Virtually all table-service restaurants and room services will fix anything that you desire. To get what you usually eat for breakfast, all you have to do is ask.
- For luxury and convenience, try room service and breakfast in bed ♥♥♥♥. It's only a little more expensive and will leave you feeling as pampered as you should feel.
- Try sharing a breakfast. The portions at most table-service restaurants and room service are large enough for all but the hardiest of eaters.
- Enjoy a poolside breakfast ♥. Pick up your breakfast at the food court and find a nice table on a patio or out by the pool.

- Fix your own breakfasts. Get a refrigerator from housekeeping ($5 a day or free, depending on your resort), and make a simple breakfast right in your room. Ingredients and supplies can be found either at the Gourmet Pantry at the Village Marketplace or nearby at Gooding's at the Crossroads Plaza.
- Watch out for food courts if you are in a hurry for breakfast. The usual hours for breakfast are very crowded, and you can find yourself standing in line for pancakes instead of Splash Mountain. Try having breakfast earlier or later. Food courts usually open at 6 A.M.

OUR TIPS FOR LUNCH

- Eat dinner for lunch. One bonus is that the same food served at dinner is cheaper at lunchtime.
- Have some appetizers for lunch. Pick a fancy, expensive restaurant and share a salad and an appetizer ♥. One of our favorites is to split the seafood nachos at Narcoossee's.
- Room Service ♥♥♥. Need we say more?
- Avoid the crowds and have an early lunch, as soon as places begin to serve, usually 11 or 11:30 A.M.
- Have a breakfast buffet for an early brunch. These are usually character meals and offer many foods appropriate for midday dining. Most usually serve until 11:30 A.M.
- Plan a picnic ♥♥. Have your favorite restaurant pack a lunch and head off to Discovery Island, Typhoon Lagoon, or some other outdoor Disney attraction.

OUR TIPS FOR DINNER

- Share a meal at one of the fancier dining spots. Try sharing a salad, a couple of appetizers, one entree, and a dessert.
- Pull out all the stops at least once during your vacation. Dress up and go someplace extravagant and intimate.
- Disney offers "early bird" specials at most of the restaurants at Epcot's World Showcase. Disney calls them Early Evening Value Meals. Seatings begin at 4:30 P.M. and last until 6 P.M. These meals usually feature a soup or salad, choice of selected entrees, and a dessert. Prices for each meal are usually less than $17, and many are much lower. There is also an attractive early bird special at the Hollywood Brown Derby.

Dining in a Lounge

Many of the lounges around Disney feature appetizers and finger foods from the restaurants adjacent to them. Lounges at Walt Disney World are not what you find in the outside world. Usually, they are quiet, comfortable, and often quite intimate. For a light meal or simply a large variety, dining in a lounge will likely be quite pleasing. Some even feature live entertainment. Martha's Vineyard at the Beach Club, the Matsu No Ma Lounge in Epcot, the Crew's Cup at the Yacht Club, and the Territory Lounge at the Wilderness Lodge are just a few of the many interesting choices.

Special Dietary Needs

In recent years, we have witnessed a "World"-wide change in menus all across the spectrum of Disney eating establishments. Menus have been revamped to include foods that more reflect what people are eating today. It is a simple matter to find low-fat meals, vegetarian entrees, and a host of healthier and lighter meals. Such foods can be found virtually everywhere, from counter-service eateries to the most elegant of gourmet dining spots. Fast-food outlets are even offering fruit as an option to French fries. Walt Disney World has become committed to satisfying the dietary needs of virtually every guest.

To test this commitment, we brought Aunt June and Uncle Jake to Walt Disney World. These folks are on a no fat, vegetarian diet. No fat, no nuts, no olives, no cheese, no fish. If you are wondering what that leaves, we can tell you how surprised even we were at what the chefs of Disney created. By notifying the kitchens when we made our reservations, Jake and June enjoyed dinners created especially for them. From cold melon soup to grilled vegetables and couscous, each entree was handcrafted. After a few meals, we were saying, "We'll have whatever they're having."

For kosher requirements, 24-hour notice is needed. Note that kosher foods arrive at Walt Disney World prepared and frozen.

Disney Character Meals

These delightful experiences are usually buffets. Disney characters make the rounds during mealtime, visiting each table. Not just for kids, character meals can be fun and provide some great photo opportunities, too.

WHERE TO HAVE CHARACTER BREAKFASTS

- Artist Point, Wilderness Lodge, with Chip and Dale, Goofy, and Pluto
- Baskerville's, the Grosvenor (Tuesday, Thursday, Saturday)
- Cape May Cafe, the Beach Club, with Admiral Goofy and crew
- Contemporary Cafe, the Contemporary, with Goofy and his gang
- Concourse Steakhouse, the Contemporary, with Winnie the Pooh and friends
- Country Fair, the Hilton (Sunday)
- Garden Grove Cafe, the Swan (Wednesday and Saturday only)
- Harry's Safari Grill, the Dolphin (Sunday brunch)
- King Stefan's, Fantasyland, with Cinderella and friends
- Olivia's, the Vacation Club (Sunday and Wednesday), with Winnie the Pooh and Tigger
- 1900 Park Fare, the Grand Floridian, with Mary Poppins and friends
- 'Ohana, the Polynesian, with Minnie Mouse and friends
- The Soundstage, Disney-MGM, with Pocahontas and friends
- Garden Grill, the Land, Epcot, with Farmer Mickey and Minnie
- The new and as-yet unnamed restaurant aboard the *Empress Lilly* riverboat with Mickey, Minnie, Donald, and Pluto
- Contemporary Cafe, the Contemporary, featuring Safari Goofy and friends

WHERE TO HAVE CHARACTER DINNERS

- Baskerville's, the Grosvenor (Wednesday)
- Garden Grove Cafe, the Swan, (Monday, Thursday, Friday)
- Garden Grill, the Land, Epcot
- Liberty Tree Tavern, Liberty Square, Magic Kingdom
- Mickey's Polynesian Revue, the Polynesian (dinner show)
- 1900 Park Fare, the Grand Floridian, featuring Mickey and Minnie
- Contemporary Cafe, the Contemporary, featuring Safari Goofy and friends

Dinner Shows

For an evening of fun and food, try one of Disney's dinner shows. We suggest that you set aside some time for one and make a reservation when you book your room.

The Polynesian Luau

Unlike many of the cute and typical Disney productions, this one features authentic South Pacific entertainment. The colorful show features performers from a variety of South Sea islands. There is hula dancing, fire dancing, and the authentic music of the South Seas. This is just the kind of thing that we like best: authentic and exotic entertainment.

You'll be seated at long tables and fed endless amounts of chicken, ribs, and seafood. Tropical drinks (alcoholic or nonalcoholic) are included in the price. The food is acceptable, though not memorable.

Adults, $33; juniors (ages 12 to 20), $25; children (ages 3 to 11), $17; children under 3, no charge. Gratuity is not included. There are two shows, at 6:45 and 9:30 P.M. A 10% discount is available with a Magic Kingdom Club or American Express card.

This show is a lot of fun. It's even romantic ♥♥.

Mickey's Tropical Revue

This is a late-afternoon children's version of the Polynesian Luau, featuring a mix of South Sea performers and Disney characters. It is fun if you have small children. At the end of the show, the performers bring the kids onto the stage to teach them Polynesian dancing. The food is the same as the Luau. Don't forget your camera.

Adults, $29; juniors (12–20), $22; children (3–11), $13. Gratuity is not included. One show at 4:30 P.M. 10% discount is available with Magic Kingdom Club or American Express card.

The Hoop-Dee-Doo Musical Revue

This saloon-style show has been a regular feature at Fort Wilderness for many years. It is very popular, and tickets to it do not come easily. Pioneer Hall, the setting for the Hoop-Dee-Doo, is an amusing recreation of an Old West dance hall, complete with velvet curtains, rough-hewn beams, and saloon-like tables and chairs.

The cuisine is country cooking: barbecued ribs, fried chicken, salad, bread, corn on the cob, baked beans, and strawberry shortcake. Beverages include beer and wine. The show is memorable—a delight of song, dance, and corny laughs—and the food is much better than that of the Luau. The performers are obviously talented, and their timing is flawless. This is not sophisticated entertainment, mind you, but it is good, wholesome Disney fun.

Adults, $35; juniors (12–20), $25; children (3–11), $17. 10% discount for American Express and Magic Kingdom Club.

Tip: Transportation to this show is tricky. Check with your Guest Services.

The Jolly Holidays Dinner Show

This seasonal show is one of our favorite Disney events. We rarely miss it. It is always offered during the weeks between Thanksgiving and Christmas. Part of a package including accommodations, tickets to this dinner show are usually available to the public only for the shows on December 22, 23, and 24. The feast is a traditional Christmas dinner of turkey, ham, and all of the accompaniments. The food is amazingly good.

The show features nearly 200 costumed performers in a Christmas tale. The music, song, and dance are all memorable, and the costumes are magnificent. Given that the Jolly Holidays package also features some of the year's most outstanding resort discounts, this is one event not to miss.

The price is included in the package. If tickets are sold separately, the prices should be about $58 for adults and $32 for children.

A Bit of Dinner Entertainment

If you are looking for a bit of entertainment during dinner instead of a production, you can choose from among a number of restaurants that feature live dinner music.

- Flagler's at the Grand Floridian ♥♥: strolling musicians and singer waiters and waitresses
- The Grill at the Garden Grove at the Swan: strolling guitarist on Tuesday, Wednesday, and Saturday nights.
- Hollywood Brown Derby at Disney–MGM ♥: a pianist
- L'Originale Alfredo di Roma Ristorante at Epcot: a group of musicians and singers
- Palio at the Swan ♥♥♥: strolling violinist or guitarist (or both), Tuesday through Saturday only
- Marrakesh restaurant at Epcot ♥♥: Moroccan musicians and belly dancer, for lunch and dinner
- Victoria and Albert's at the Grand Floridian ♥♥♥♥: a harpist
- The Biergarten at Epcot: shows during lunch and dinner

Not Your Unusual Dinner Shows

The following restaurants do not feature song or dance during dinner. What they do offer, however, are talented performing artists. What we are talking about here is restaurants with seating that is in or adjacent to the kitchen. This is not everyone's cup of tea, but we find these nearly as exciting as the usual shows. For us, it is a real thrill to watch master chefs at work and to see how the restaurant works from the inside out. Samples and nibbles of various foods are inevitable. Conversation with the chefs is fascinating and friendly. There are three restaurants at Walt Disney World that currently feature "performance kitchens":

- The California Grill features a counter that overlooks all of the action. Try our regular seats at Yoshi's sushi bar.
- Sum Chows features a chef's table in the kitchen of renowned chef Christopher Salansky.
- Victoria and Albert's has a table right in the kitchen with chef Scott Hunnel and his culinary team. A prix fixe dinner is $100 per person; with wine paring, $125. For reservations, call (407) 824-1089.

Restaurants of Walt Disney World

We didn't take any surveys to come up with the following reviews. We didn't poll other diners, and we didn't consult other restaurant reviews. Simply, we just ate everywhere—many places more than once, and some places many times. These are not all of Disney's eateries, simply those we felt were worthy of mention.

We expect that menus will change from time to time. Such is the way of good restaurants. Some of our favorite dishes may no longer be available. Quality and service may vary too, one of the unfortunate realities when it comes to restaurants. However, the following should give you a pretty good idea of what each restaurant is like and just how good the food is.

THE RATINGS

$ Inexpensive, less than $15 per meal
$$ Moderately priced, $15 to $25 per meal
$$$ Expensive, more than $25 per meal

We have also included the price range for dinner entrees. Remember, many of these restaurants serve pretty much the same food at lunchtime for about 25% less. For the quality of the food, we have used the following guidelines:

★ Acceptable means simply OK. This is our lowest rating.

★★ Good food means tasty but not memorable. This is the kind of meal that leaves you satisfied but that you won't go home talking about.

★★★ Very good food is memorable, well prepared, even creatively conceived. A find, indeed, if it is moderately priced.

★★★★ Outstanding food is the stuff of memories: imaginative, perfectly prepared, and artfully presented, the creation of a world-class chef and a first-rate kitchen. A culinary experience.

AKERSHUS

$$ ★★★

✓ Norway Pavilion, Epcot
✓ Table-service buffet, lunch and dinner
✓ Norwegian beer, wine, full-service bar
✓ Reservations suggested
✓ Atmosphere is quaint and medieval. One of the best lunching places around the World Showcase Lagoon.

The Akershus restaurant is in Norway's charming re-creation of a medieval fortress. The buffet is a Norwegian "koldtbord." Featured foods include the outstanding breads and cheeses of Norway and a variety of cold herring and smoked salmon. There are also a few hot dishes (including meatballs, smoked pork, and lamb), but except for the rutabagas, we really did not care for them—all had been a bit too long in the steam table. We would suggest sticking to the "koldt" dishes. Other wonderful cold foods include vegetable salads, sliced roast beef, and smoked salmon and egg mousse. Neither of us ever loved herring until we tried Akershus. Both the herring and salmon are outstanding. Akershus also serves Norwegian Ringnes beer, on draught. It's very good.

The interior of Akershus is what you would expect if you dined in a castle: high, beamed ceilings; arched, cut-glass windows; and heavy wooden furnishings. Cast members here are young Norwegians dressed in traditional Norwegian garb.

ARIEL'S

$$$ ★★

✓ The Beach Club
✓ Table service, dinner only
✓ Full-service bar, an award-winning wine list

✓ Reservations suggested

✓ Atmosphere is pleasant, though a bit noisy

✓ Tips: Stick with grilled fish, lightly sauced, and you'll be pleased. Dining here will give you free child care, while you dine, at the Beach Club's Sandcastle Club children's center. Call the Sandcastle Club for a reservation at (407) 934-6290.

This lovely restaurant enjoys an "Under the Sea" theme from Disney's animated film *The Little Mermaid*. The motif begins with a 2,000-gallon aquarium of tropical fish at the eatery's entrance. Stylized fish mobiles hang from the ceilings, and there are lots of other nautical touches, from artwork on the walls to table settings.

Ariel's is a popular place for families and can be noisy. As you would expect, this is a seafood restaurant. The menu varies to accommodate what is freshest and in season. The house salad was good and the crab cakes were even better. The shellfish gumbo was outstanding. Entrees include the usual surf and turf, two-pound Maine lobster, and several competent cuts of beef. The food was uneven, with the paella a bit dry and the grilled fish very good.

ARTHUR'S 27

$$$ ★★★★ ♥♥♥♥

✓ The Buena Vista Palace

✓ Table service, dinner only

✓ Full-service bar, award-winning wine list

✓ Reservations required

✓ Atmosphere is sublime and unforgettable.

✓ Tips: Valet parking is complimentary for patrons of Arthur's. This restaurant is worth the trip. Evening attire is appropriate.

Arthur's is an elegant and award-winning gourmet restaurant. Located high atop the 27-story Buena Vista Palace at Hotel Plaza, this modern restaurant manages to feature large expanses of glass and crystal chandeliers without sacrificing warmth and comfort. Diners are seated at private tables that each enjoy amazing vistas of Walt Disney World. A dining experience here during fireworks will be unforgettable.

The food is well prepared and imaginative. Service is flawless. Arthur's 27 is a first-class dining experience with all of the accoutrements. The menu is large and intriguing, and the wine list is exceptional. Truffle ravioli with veal and mushrooms, baked salmon in strudel leaves, and herb-crusted tuna are typical of the many fine offerings.

One of the nicest things about this restaurant is that it offers three prix fixe dinners. For a set price, you can create your own gourmet meal. Prices range from $50 per person for the four-course Excitement Dinner to $60 for the six-course Gourmet Dinner. Expensive, yes, but really a value if you compare it to the a la carte prices.

ARTIST POINT
$$ ★★★ ♥♥
- ✓ The Wilderness Lodge
- ✓ Table service, breakfast and dinner
- ✓ Full-service bar, good wine list from the Pacific Northwest
- ✓ Reservations suggested
- ✓ Atmosphere is woodsy and very pleasant.
- ✓ Tip: This eatery excels at grilled fish.

This handsome restaurant is set amidst the splendor of one of Disney's grandest creations, the Wilderness Lodge. Inlaid wooden tables and huge canvases of western vistas make this a very pleasant place. Large windows overlook the courtyard and geyser, giving it a high-timber ambience.

The Artist Point features the fare of the Pacific Northwest. The emphasis here is on fresh and natural, and the Artist Point has managed it well. A simply superb Caesar salad and a Northwest Salmon Sampler would be the perfect beginnings to any meal. The menu varies to accommodate the season. During our visits, dishes such as smoked prime rib, maple-glazed king salmon, and an unforgettable Dungeness crab filet were just a few of the interesting choices. Servers seem willing, but the food comes slowly, which is acceptable if you're not in a hurry. The Artist Point offers an all-you-can-eat character breakfast.

AU PETIT CAFE
$$ ★★★ ♥♥
- ✓ France Pavilion, Epcot
- ✓ Table-service sidewalk cafe, lunch and dinner
- ✓ Full-service bar, French wines
- ✓ Reservations not accepted
- ✓ Pleasant, even romantic atmosphere if not too crowded.
- ✓ Tip: A nice place for a shared dessert and espresso in the evening before the park closes.

The menu here is basically the same as that of Les Chefs de France, with a few additions such as quiche. The setting for this delightful cafe is along the lagoon promenade, and in the evening it is memorable indeed. It is shaded and quite comfortable in all but the hottest of weather. Service can be brusque, and this place can be too crowded.

BEACHES AND CREAM

$ ★★
✓ The Beach Club
✓ Table service with take-out, breakfast, lunch, snacks
✓ Reservations not accepted

This fifties-style soda shop is one of our regular haunts when we are at the Beach or the Yacht. For us, a stay at either of these resorts is simply not complete without a swim and a great double-chocolate ice cream soda. Hamburgers and turkey burgers are very good, and the hot dogs are easily Disney's finest. Also a terrific assortment of soda-fountain concoctions. Beaches even has an egg cream. Nothing elaborate here, just good old American fare and someplace fun to enjoy it. Breakfasts here are fairly ordinary fast food or continental-style.

BIERGARTEN

$$ ★★★
✓ Germany Pavilion, Epcot
✓ Table-service buffet, lunch and dinner
✓ Beck's beer and good German wines
✓ Reservations recommended
✓ Atmosphere is quaint and well themed.

We resisted eating here for a long time. It just didn't sound like our kind of food or our kind of entertainment. Both were then highly recommended by family members who had lived for several years in Germany. We gave in, gave it a try, and found it quite pleasant. Seating was at long tables with other Disney guests, beer hall–style. Huge steins of Beck's beer were served and the meal was a German buffet. Sauerbraten, rotisserie chicken, and smoked pork loin were just a few of the offerings. There was also a marvelous red cabbage dish, salad, and breads. We thought that everything was well prepared and tasty, one of our better eating experiences at Epcot. By the time the show ended, we realized how wrong we had been about this place.

Biergarten is zany and fun. The costumed performers sing and dance and even play musical instruments. The stage is a small Bavarian village, complete with building facades and even trees. We had a memorable time, finding it difficult to believe that we had refused to try it for so long.

BISTRO DE PARIS

$$$ ★★★★ ♥♥♥
- ✓ France Pavilion, Epcot
- ✓ Table service, dinner only
- ✓ Full-service bar with a good selection of French wines
- ✓ Reservations required
- ✓ Atmosphere is intimate, romantic, and very Gallic.
- ✓ Tip: Ask for a table for two by a window.

This is definitely classic French fare, and it is served in an intimate and romantic bistro setting. The menu here, as well as in the other two restaurants of Disney's France, has been designed by three well-known Gallic chefs: Roger Verdé, Paul Bocuse, and Gaston LeNôtre. Appetizers run the course from foie gras to salmon tartare. Seafood casserole, grilled tenderloin of beef with mushrooms and green peppercorn sauce, breast of duck with cherries and red wine sauce, and rack of lamb for two make up this small but interesting menu. The Bistro is the "upstairs place," located above Les Chefs de France.

BOATWRIGHT'S DINING HALL

$$ ★★★
- ✓ Dixie Landings
- ✓ Table service, breakfast and dinner
- ✓ Bar features a variety of regional beers
- ✓ Reservations recommended only during peak mealtimes
- ✓ Atmosphere is themed but not unforgettable.

This is Dixie Landings' only table-service eatery, and it is surprisingly good. This is not fine dining, but it is good, hearty fare for a reasonable price. The setting is a large, warehouse-like boat factory. The walls are covered with real antique boatwright gear, from giant augers to chisels and mallets. Overhead, you see a partially completed keel and framed-out vessel. Boatwright's is decorative and comfortable.

The cuisine has a definite bayou flair. Servings for both breakfast and dinner are large. If you are inclined to share an entree, this is a place to do it. Tin Pan Breakfasts are complete and hearty breakfasts served in a large pan. Dinners range from burgers and fried catfish to ribs and grilled pork loin. There are even more elaborately prepared Cajun specialties, such as Bayou Bouillabaisse and pirogue of pasta and seafood.

BONFAMILLE'S CAFE
$$ ★★★ ♥♥
✓ Port Orleans
✓ Table service, breakfast and dinner
✓ Full-service bar, regional specialty beers
✓ Reservations suggested during peak mealtimes
✓ Atmosphere near the garden is quite nice.
✓ Tip: Order the Shrimp Orleans appetizer as an entree. It is outstanding.

The first time we visited Bonfamille's, it took us by surprise. The restaurant features a glassed-in garden area, and sitting by it was quite romantic. We were really expecting bland, manufactured food—wrong again. We were delighted to find a menu that features a mix of American and Creole entrees, even an intriguing variety of inexpensive sandwiches. Breakfasts feature a wide array of standards plus Skillet Combos, which are gigantic meals featuring eggs, potatoes, and ham, chicken, or Andouille sausage. Dinners run the gamut from T-bone steak and tortellini with vegetables to jambalaya. We loved the Dixie Blackened Voodoo lager and the Bourbon Street bread pudding. Not the finest dining at Disney, but good dining at a reasonable price.

CALIFORNIA GRILL
$$$ ★★★★ ♥♥
✓ The Contemporary
✓ Table service, lunch and dinner
✓ Full-service bar, good wine list
✓ Reservations suggested
✓ Tips: If the park is open late, try having a late meal during the fireworks show. Don't miss the citrus soufflé. Ask for a table by the window.

Set atop the Contemporary, this wonderful restaurant occupies the top spot of our favorites list as well. From our regular seats at Yoshi's sushi bar, we come to the Grill to watch a great show, chat with chef Cliff and his kitchen staff, and to sample the imaginative and well-prepared fare. The cuisine is Californian, and that means light, fresh, and creative.

From the opening basket of focaccia, baked in the Grill's own special oven, to the heavenly citrus soufflé, the voyage here is most memorable. First courses of alderwood-smoked salmon, sushi, and goat cheese ravioli are sublime beginnings. We move on to wood-baked pizzas of asiago cheese, chicken and wild mushrooms, and fresh mozzarella. Next comes the main course: should we get the grilled pork tenderloin with polenta and balsamic-smothered mushrooms or pan-seared yellowfin tuna with Asian slaw and blackbean cake? How about oak-fired filet of beef with Sonoma foie gras and Zinfandel glaze or roasted chicken with lemon-mustard dressing?

Foods, wines, desserts, and a personable staff of professionals makes the California Grill a memorable dining experience. Whether you catch the action kitchenside or take a seat by the window on top of the World, we think that this is one place worth making a reservation for.

CAPE MAY CAFE

$$ ★★

✓ The Beach Club
✓ Table-service buffet, breakfast and dinner
✓ Full-service bar
✓ Reservations suggested
✓ Atmosphere is pleasant, though hardly memorable.

A character breakfast with Admiral Goofy and friends is featured here each morning. The spread is large, and the quality is quite good. If you can't find something here, they'll be glad to fix it for you.

We wish that the Clambake Dinner were as good as it sounds. Promising a buffet of New England-style seafood, Cape May delivers instead a large selection of food that is simply adequate. As good an idea as a seafood buffet may sound, this kind of delicate food just doesn't stand up well to large batches and steam tables. Still, while this is not seafood dining at its best, Cape May offers a moderately priced, all-you-can-eat buffet that includes chicken, shrimp, fish, clams, and much more.

CAP'N JACK'S OYSTER BAR

$ ★★★ ♥

✓ The Village Marketplace
✓ Table service, lunch and dinner
✓ Full-service bar
✓ Reservations not accepted
✓ Atmosphere is charming, especially if you sit by a window overlooking the water.

Cap'n Jack's is almost more of a bar than a restaurant. Almost. Overlooking the lake and Pleasure Island, this cozy little eatery is immersed in nautical decor. Fish nets, polished brass, leather, and the usual seaside amenities make this place rather inviting.

The menu isn't large, and most entrees tend to be on the small side, so this is not a good place to share. Jack's Shrimp Ziti, Zesty Crab Cakes, and shrimp or clams from the steamer are some of the offerings. There are also chowders and salads. The food is well prepared and tasty. This is a nice place for a light meal.

Captain's Tavern

$$ ★★

✓ Old Port Royale, the Caribbean Beach
✓ Table service, dinner only
✓ Beer and wine
✓ Reservations suggested during peak meal times
✓ Atmosphere is comfortable, not unusual.

This is the only table-service restaurant at the Caribbean Beach. It offers a limited selection of seafood, poultry, and even a prime rib of beef. Nothing memorable here, but at these prices, you would not expect it.

Concourse Steakhouse

$$ ★★

✓ The Contemporary
✓ Table service, breakfast, lunch, and dinner
✓ Full-service bar
✓ Reservations suggested for dinner only
✓ Atmosphere is nothing special.
✓ Tips: A very good hamburger. For any of the meals, get here early and beat the crowds. This restaurant can get busy.

The Concourse Steakhouse offers a large selection of well-prepared foods for each of the day's meals. While this is not fine dining, it is definitely good eating.

Breakfasts include either a large selection of a la carte offerings or a character breakfast buffet. The lunch menu offers steaks, several good lunch salads, and a selection of well-prepared sandwiches. The

Concourse Steakhouse's burger wins our Best of Disney award. Dinners become a bit more involved with prime rib, a selection of beef cuts, roasted chicken, grilled pork, and a tasty grilled salmon. The food is all competently prepared and service is good. If you are looking for a simple, good meal, the Concourse Steakhouse is a good choice.

CONTEMPORARY CAFE

$$ ★
✓ The Contemporary (fourth floor)
✓ Table-service buffet, breakfast, lunch, and dinner
✓ Wine and beer
✓ Reservations recommended for character breakfast and peak mealtimes
✓ Atmosphere is comfortable but not interesting.

The character breakfast is pretty typical for Disney World. If you have been to one elsewhere, you probably won't notice much difference. Character-wise, there are lots of Disney characters, and they spend a lot of time with guests.

Dinner is another buffet. The American Harvest Buffet dinner is reputedly one of the best bargains of its type, but don't come expecting to find a large assortment of foods memorably prepared. The selection, which includes roast beef and shrimp, is not large. The quality is merely acceptable.

CORAL CAFE

$ ★
✓ The Dolphin
✓ Table service, open 6 A.M. to midnight
✓ Beer and wine
✓ Reservations not required
✓ Atmosphere is not memorable.

"All-day dining" is this restaurant's claim. Both buffet and a la carte breakfasts have the usual assortment. Specialty pizzas, salads, and sandwiches make up the lunch menu, and dinners add entrees such as pastas, steak, and Key West chicken. Sandwiches and entrees show a bit more imagination than most restaurants.

CORAL ISLE CAFE
$$ ★★
- ✓ Great Ceremonial Building, the Polynesian
- ✓ Table service, breakfast, lunch, and dinner
- ✓ A few wines
- ✓ Reservations suggested during the peak mealtimes
- ✓ Atmosphere is pleasant.

As we have said, the premium resorts each have an all-purpose restaurant that serves all three meals without a lot of fuss. This is the Polynesian's, and it is a pleasant place to enjoy a meal. This is not fine dining, and it makes no pretense to be.

The house specialty for breakfast is Auntie Kaui's Tonga Toast, a banana-stuffed French toast. From cereal and pancakes to omelettes, you will likely find something here. Lunches include some specialty sandwiches and salads, each with a Polynesian flair. Dinners include everything from sandwiches to fairly expensive entrees such as New York strip steak. Most entrees are priced moderately, and sandwiches are inexpensive. The Coral Isle features a selection of ice cream desserts. All in all, this is a pretty good value when eating at Walt Disney World.

CORAL REEF
$$$ ★★★ ♥♥
- ✓ The Living Seas Pavilion, Future World, Epcot
- ✓ Table service, lunch and dinner
- ✓ Reservations required
- ✓ Atmosphere is especially nice by the aquarium.

The Coral Reef is a beautiful and romantic place to dine. This is not the finest seafood at Disney, but the atmosphere more than makes up for it. The restaurant is adjacent to the Living Seas aquarium, and diners can enjoy a thrilling view. Entrees include Dover sole, grilled tuna, Maine lobster, beef tenderloin, and grilled chicken.

CROCKETT'S TAVERN
$$ ★★ ♥
- ✓ Near Pioneer Hall, Fort Wilderness
- ✓ Table service, dinner
- ✓ Full-service bar
- ✓ Reservations not required

✓ Tips: Crockett's Tavern serves wines from Fess Parker's Winery. Our favorite is the Johannesburg Riesling.

We're not sure why we feel so comfortable here. Granted, one of us, in our youth, absolutely lived and breathed Davy Crockett. But the place definitely feels good. The food is interesting but not outstanding. Crockett's Smoked Prime Rib, Georgie Russell's Bourbon Tenderloin, and Davy's Fresh Catch are a few of the offerings. It all has, as you would expect, a touch of the frontier.

DOLPHIN FOUNTAIN
$ ★★★
✓ The Dolphin
✓ Table service, fifties soda shop, open 11 A.M. to 11 P.M.
✓ Atmosphere is loud, bright, and fun.
✓ Tip: Good fries. Also serves espresso and cappuccino.

"The Golden Oldies" here refer more to the fried foods than to the fifties rock 'n roll background music. Hot dogs, hamburgers, grilled chicken sandwich, and BLT about sum it up. Toss in a salad, some nachos and fries, and a large selection of soda fountain sweets, and you've pretty much described this fun place. This is the Beaches and Cream of the Dolphin. Every resort should have one!

THE *EMPRESS LILY* CRABHOUSE RESTAURANT
We don't have much to tell you about this place except it doesn't even have a name yet. Levy's Restaurants of Chicago, which operates both the Fireworks Factory and the Portobello Yacht Club, will be managing this new restaurant located on the *Empress Lily* riverboat at Pleasure Island. The Disney character breakfast will resume here when the restaurant opens in early 1996. No other details have been released.

EVERGREEN'S
$ ★★
✓ Poolside at Shades of Green
✓ Table service, lunch and dinner
✓ Full-service bar, including draught beer
✓ No reservations
✓ Atmosphere is pleasant.
✓ Tip: Try the Angus Beef Burger.

This is basically a lunch place, but it is a good one. The menu is small, including pizza, rotisserie chicken, a very good hamburger, and a variety of sandwiches and salads. The atmosphere is pleasant and restaurant-like except for the upside-down tennis court (with players) on the ceiling. Antique golf and tennis equipment adorn the walls. This is a popular lunching place for golfers.

50's PRIME TIME CAFE
$$ ★★
✓ Disney–MGM Studios
✓ Table service, lunch and dinner
✓ Full-service bar
✓ Reservations suggested
✓ Atmosphere, though not romantic, is really Disney and a riot.

There is more about this place that is standard Americana than simply the menu. Prime Time looks like the average American kitchen of the 1950s. Each table has its own TV that plays snippets of *I Love Lucy, I Married Joan,* and other 50s sitcoms. There are old appliances, cupboards, and decorations that are the authentic stuff. Waiters and waitresses are Mom and Pop, and you'd better finish your food if you expect to get dessert. The food is good, but the experience, especially if you lived through this period, is worth the price. (It is a bit disconcerting to see that things from our youth are now antiques.)

The menu features burgers, meat loaf, grilled chicken, salads, soups, and other American classics.

FIREWORKS FACTORY
$$ ★★
✓ Pleasure Island (admission not required)
✓ Table service, lunch and dinner
✓ Full-service bar, outstanding selection of brew
✓ Reservations not required
✓ Atmosphere is interesting, colorful, and fun. Can be noisy.
✓ Tip: A good place to have dinner before a night out at Pleasure Island.

The Fireworks Factory is run by Levy's Restaurants of Chicago. It is basically a barbecue place with above-average barbecue. It offers a large menu for both lunch and dinner as well as one of the biggest selections of beers at Disney. The food is quite good, and we frequently dine here on appetizers. Entrees include mesquite-smoked chicken, shrimp quesadillas, applewood-smoked baby back ribs, and barbecued shrimp. The bread basket features cornbread, and the barbecued beans are the best that we've ever had out.

The "story" of this restaurant is that it was once a fireworks factory, *before* the explosion. You can just imagine the decor. A sort of post-incendiary motif, with lots of fun details. The bases of the tables look like manhole covers.

Flagler's

$$ ★★★ ♥♥♥
- ✓ The Grand Floridian
- ✓ Table service, dinner only
- ✓ Full-service bar
- ✓ Reservations suggested
- ✓ The atmosphere is romantic and elegant.
- ✓ Tip: Servings are large. Order an extra salad and share an entree and dessert.

Flagler's is a fancy eatery that offers fine foods and impeccable service. Singing waiters and waitresses and strolling musicians lend this restaurant more than just a touch of romance. Seafood, steaks, and pastas are the specialties. The food here is delicious and well prepared but leans a bit towards the rich and creamy end of the spectrum. Flagler's is fine dining and, for a special night out, we recommend it.

Garden Grill

$$ ★
- ✓ The Land Pavilion, Future World, Epcot
- ✓ Table service, family-style, lunch and dinner
- ✓ Beer and wine
- ✓ Reservations strongly suggested
- ✓ Atmosphere is pleasant, although part of the trip is noisy.

This restaurant is built on a revolving deck. The journey takes diners through a small and beautiful section of this pavilion. Character meals are featured all day with Farmer Mickey and Minnie. Service is family-style, which means they'll keep bringing you food until you have had all that you care to eat. For us, this didn't take long. We found the food here to be merely adequate. Entrees include Rotisserie Chicken with Rocky Top Seasoning, fish, and hickory-smoked steak. The theme here is fresh food, but cooking for these kinds of numbers has taken its toll on the cuisine.

GRAND FLORIDIAN CAFE

$$ ★★★ ♥♥
- ✓ The Grand Floridian
- ✓ Table service, breakfast, lunch, and dinner
- ✓ Full-service bar
- ✓ Reservations suggested during peak hours

This is the Grand Floridian's all-purpose restaurant, and as you might expect it is an outstanding place to eat. It is also a very good value. The menus for each meal are large and interesting. While the Grand Floridian Cafe is not fine dining, it is an excellent place to get a very good meal. Linen tablecloths, beautiful table service, and a splendid view make this a good choice for any meal. The Grand Floridian Cafe is beautiful and pleasant.

Breakfasts include everything from a muffin to Mexican-style eggs served on a tortilla. Lunches include an impressive array of sandwiches, salads, and a few entrees. For dinner, the Cafe offers everything from an outstanding burger to prime rib. There is also chicken pot pie, Maine lobster, and meat loaf. This is one of those restaurants that has something for everyone.

GRILL AT THE GARDEN GROVE

$$ ★★
- ✓ The Swan
- ✓ Table service, breakfast, lunch, and dinner
- ✓ Wines, beers, and full-service bar
- ✓ Reservations suggested for character breakfasts and dinner
- ✓ Atmosphere is pleasant but fairly noisy.

It is easy to think that this is actually two restaurants. When open for lunch and breakfast, it is called the Garden Grove Cafe. It takes on a more elegant incarnation in the evenings as it gears up for dinner and becomes the Grill at the Garden Grove. We found either place a bit noisy, due largely to the gazebo shape.

This is the Swan's all-purpose eatery. The food is good, and dinners are even a bit better. On Tuesday, Wednesday, and Saturday, there is live entertainment during dinner. The Cafe features character breakfasts on Wednesday and Saturday, and character dinners on Monday, Thursday, and Friday.

The Grill is pretty fancy dining, with the emphasis on "grill." Steaks and fresh seafood are the specialties. Entrees include salad and side dishes, and prices begin at around $20.

HARRY'S SAFARI BAR AND GRILL

$$$ ★★★   ♥♥

✓ The Dolphin
✓ Table service, dinner only
✓ Full-service bar, excellent wine list, many imported beers
✓ Reservations recommended

Harry's is a fun place to dine, especially if you have your children with you. You and your kids will arrive at your table to find a giant stuffed gorilla already seated and waiting for you. The restaurant is safari-themed and memorable. Service is outstanding and the food is wonderful. In short, Harry's is worth the trip. Lots of great appetizers and outstanding entrees are offered, such as prime beef, shrimp and crab cakes, and a vegetable feast.

A variety of fresh fish comes prepared in one of four delectable ways: hickory-smoked; pan-grilled with pistachios, pecans, and citrus; key lime barbecued served with black bean salsa; or jerk-blackened with plantains and tropical salsa. It's your choice. Portions are not overly large.

Harry's is beautiful, well-themed, and fun.

HOLLYWOOD BROWN DERBY

$$$$ ★★★   ♥

✓ Disney–MGM Studios
✓ Table service, lunch and dinner
✓ Full-service bar
✓ Reservations suggested
✓ Tip: The Derby features an early bird value meal from 4 to 5:30 P.M. daily.

This is a re-creation of the famous Brown Derby of Hollywood. Potted palms, elegant carpets, and a large, sunken dining area work to create a memorable dining experience. There are a lot of small touches here, such as lamps made from the pattern of Rudy Vallee's derby hat and copies of the restaurant's sketches. The Derby has a beautiful dining room featuring a live pianist.

The food here is better than that served in most of the theme parks, although it is fairly expensive. Lunches include pasta with garlic basil sauce, quiche, roast chicken, and a daily chef's special. The dinner menu is larger, adding such entrees as porterhouse steak, Fettuccine Derby, and pan-seared salmon. The Cobb salad is this restaurant's signature dish.

JUAN AND ONLY'S CANTINA AND BAR
$$ ★★★
- ✓ The Dolphin
- ✓ Table service, dinner only
- ✓ Full-service bar
- ✓ Reservations not required
- ✓ Tip: Try a light meal of appetizers in the bar.

We think that Juan's offers Disney's best Mexican food. Granted, the romantic atmosphere of Epcot's San Angel Inn is hard to beat, but the food at Juan's is simply better. Entrees here run the gamut from the usual to the gourmet. Entrees include fajitas, excellent chili rellenos, Red Snapper Vera Cruz, Roast Pork Adobado, and a large selection of combination platters.

The atmosphere is cute and south-of-the-border. This place has a story, and the decor (the bar is actually a jail) and menu tell the tale. This is a nice, colorful place to eat and frequently offers live entertainment.

KING STEFAN'S BANQUET HALL
$$$ ★★ ♥♥♥
- ✓ Fantasyland, Magic Kingdom
- ✓ Table service, breakfast, lunch, and dinner
- ✓ No bar (this is the Magic Kingdom!)
- ✓ Reservations a must
- ✓ Atmosphere is beautiful and memorable.
- ✓ Tip: Drop in for a dessert and a cappuccino.

King Stefan's is located inside Cinderella's Castle, and the atmosphere is regal. Unfortunately, the food does not equal the beautiful surroundings. The menu would have you think that this is going to be an experience in fine dining, but this is a wish not to be granted here. Basically, you are paying for the ambience. Entrees such as prime rib, grilled swordfish with smoked pepper butter, and seafood and vegetable pasta simply don't taste as good as they sound. While the castle banquet hall is charming and memorable, we wait for the food at King Stefan's to improve. We are still waiting.

L'ORIGINALE ALFREDO DI ROMA RESTAURANT
$$ ★★
✓ Italy Pavilion, Epcot
✓ Table service, lunch and dinner
✓ Beer and Italian wines only
✓ Reservations suggested during mealtimes
✓ Restaurant is attractive but crowded and noisy.

With a band of entertainers singing and playing during dinner, Alfredo's can be a fun place to eat if you don't mind the noise. Featured dishes here are the standards that have become known as Italian cuisine. Fettucini Alfredo, of course, is the signature dish. Pasta is made fresh.

LE CELLIER
$$ ★
✓ Canada Pavilion, Epcot
✓ Cafeteria, lunch and dinner
✓ Beer and wine
✓ Reservations not accepted
✓ Atmosphere is not memorable.

That Le Cellier is open only during the very busiest times of year should tell you something. Pork pie, seafood stew, and fried chicken are featured here, and none of it is memorable. With a number of other choices nearby (including the restaurants at the nearby Yacht and Beach Clubs), we see no reason to eat here.

LES CHEFS DE FRANCE
$$$ ★★★ ♥
✓ France Pavilion, Epcot
✓ Table service, lunch and dinner
✓ Full-service bar with French wines
✓ Reservations are a must, unless you arrive before 12:30 P.M. for lunch and 6 P.M. for dinner
✓ Atmosphere is pleasant, especially in the evening.

The kitchen and menu at Les Chefs are supervised by three of France's most famous chefs: Roger Verdé, Paul Bocuse, and Gaston LeNôtre. The restaurant itself is fancy, with paneled walls, exquisite fixtures, and works of French impressionist art. Service is impeccable, and tables are dressed with white linens. It is a delightful re-creation of a Parisian restaurant.

We like the food here. It is well prepared and imaginative, though a bit rich and creamy for our tastes. Still, Chefs de France does have its light offerings: a vegetable plate and a salmon tartare. Menus for lunch and dinner differ greatly, with only a few shared entrees. Dinner, naturally, is considerably more expensive. Some of the lunch entrees: brochettes of prawns with rice and basil butter, chicken breast in puff pastry with cream sauce, and braised beef in Burgundy with pasta. Dinner entrees include beef tenderloin with brandy sauce, broiled salmon with sorrel cream sauce and fresh vegetables, and filet of snapper and spinach baked in puff pastry. Both menus include an ample wine list as well as a good selection of soups, salads, and desserts.

Liberty Tree Tavern
$$ ★★
✓ Liberty Square, Magic Kingdom
✓ Table service, lunch and buffet dinner
✓ Reservations strongly suggested
✓ Atmosphere is pleasant and comfortable.
✓ Tips: Try the Liberty Tree for lunch. If you are looking for a light meal, try splitting one of the large sandwiches.

We think this is the best sit-down restaurant in the Magic Kingdom. That, unfortunately, is not saying a lot. Decor is Colonial American and it is done quite well, down to the "hand-hewn" ceiling of the waiting area. The Liberty Tree Tavern is a pleasant and restful place to eat. The food is well prepared but not great. The lunch menu offers a variety of large sandwiches and such entrees as fresh fish, turkey dinner, pot roast, and shrimp and vegetable pasta. The strawberry vinaigrette salad dressing is quite good. The Liberty Tree Tavern is sponsored by Stouffers.

The Character dinner buffet (at $20 for adults and $10 for children) features roasted chicken, flank steak, and several accompaniments.

MAMA MELROSE'S RISTORANTE ITALIANO
$$ ★★
✓ Disney–MGM Studios
✓ Table service, lunch and dinner
✓ Full-service bar
✓ Reservations strongly suggested
✓ Atmosphere is cute and interesting.

This neighborhood-style Italian eatery features a pleasant atmosphere that is crammed with an eclectic collection of entertaining props. Where else but at Disney World could you eat under a stuffed swordfish wearing sunglasses? Mama Melrose's is comfortable and fun.

The pizzas outshine any of those sold at the counter-service restaurants. Such entrees as vegetable lasagna, breaded chicken breasts, and an assortment of pasta dishes are all well prepared. This is by no means fine dining, but, at these prices, you get good food. The Mega Deal pasta entree features all-you-can-eat pasta served four different ways. Try them all. Other entrees include chicken Marsala, seafood pasta, and veal piccata. Mama's is popular. Even with reservations, we had to wait a few minutes.

MARRAKESH
$$ ★★★ ♥♥
✓ Morocco Pavilion, Epcot
✓ Table service, lunch and dinner
✓ Full-service bar
✓ Reservations suggested
✓ The atmosphere here is exotic.
✓ Tips: The Moroccan Diffa for Two provides a real assortment of tastes. There are other combination platters, too.

Marrakesh is one of Epcot's most exotic restaurants. Featuring a live belly dancer and musicians at both lunch and dinner, it is one of our favorites here. From a selection of couscous dishes to tagine of chicken, shish kebab, and Cornish Hen Emrouzia, Marrakesh delivers what so many other World Showcase restaurants merely promise: the exotic and the unique. If you are looking for a dining adventure beyond the usual, don't miss it.

MINNIE MIA'S ITALIAN EATERY
$ ★★
- ✓ The Village Marketplace
- ✓ Counter service, lunch and dinner
- ✓ No reservations

If you are looking for a quick bite while you're shopping at the Village Marketplace, this little place may be just the thing. The pizza is more like real pizza than that served at any fast-food outlet at WDW. There is also a selection of salads and other Italian entrees. Nothing great, but the food is inexpensive and fairly good.

NARCOOSSEE'S
$$$ ★★★★ ♥
- ✓ The Grand Floridian
- ✓ Table service, lunch and dinner
- ✓ Full-service bar
- ✓ Reservations suggested for dinner
- ✓ Atmosphere is memorable.
- ✓ Tip: For an outstanding bargain lunch, try splitting an order of seafood nachos. This is a great alternative to a mediocre meal elsewhere.

This is Disney's premier seafood restaurant. Right on the Seven Seas Lagoon, Narcoossee's is a beautiful place to dine, particularly after dark. Lunches feature some inexpensive sandwiches, but entrees are all moderately priced. Dinner at Narcoossee's is expensive. The food is all carefully prepared, and we would be surprised if you are disappointed.

Dinner entrees include an alligator steak, prime rib, Maine lobster, and grilled fish. Narcoossee's features a large and inviting menu of both seafood and meats. From the bar come yards of Tennant's ale. The bread basket is exceptional, and the smoked gator spread is unusual.

NINE DRAGONS
$$ ★★ ♥
- ✓ China Pavilion, Epcot
- ✓ Table service, lunch and dinner
- ✓ Full-service bar
- ✓ Reservations suggested
- ✓ A beautiful dining room. Quiet and pleasant.
- ✓ Tip: Try snacking here on dumplings, if you wish to enjoy the atmosphere.

With all of its carved furnishings and beautiful Chinese artwork, Nine Dragons is a lovely place to dine. The food is well prepared but just not exciting enough for our tastes. Offerings include Mu Shu Pork and Kung Pao Chicken. Dinners here are served as entrees, not the usual family-style Chinese. Add the high cost, and we have a hard time recommending it. We have stopped here for hors d'oeuvres, however, and have enjoyed them.

1900 PARK FARE
$$ ★★★
✓ The Grand Floridian
✓ Table service, character buffets, breakfast, and dinner
✓ Reservations recommended (this place is popular)
✓ Atmosphere is noisy and gay.
✓ Tip: Bring your camera for some terrific pictures. Ask your server to snap a photo of the two of you with some of the Disney characters.

We think that this is Disney's best buffet. Offerings for both breakfast and dinner are large and the quality is surprisingly good. The only drawback is that Park Fare is noisy. First there's all of the children and characters and then there is the giant mechanical organ. If you are looking for peace and quiet, this isn't it. If you are looking for fun and a character meal, we doubt that you'll find a better one than this.

OLIVIA'S
$$ ★★★ ♥
✓ The Vacation Club
✓ Table service, breakfast, lunch, and dinner
✓ Full-service bar
✓ Reservations suggested for character breakfasts

This is high on our list of hidden gems. Key West is the theme, and Olivia's ambience is airy and casual. This is a very pleasant place to dine. The menus for each meal are large, and the food is fresh and tasty. The conch fritters are some of the best we've ever had (and that includes the Bahamas). Breakfasts run the course from fresh fruit to steak and eggs. You can also choose muffins, bagels, and some interesting egg dishes, such as the Sounds of Sunset Omelette. For lunches and dinners, enjoy a great assortment of munchies, sandwiches, and even a turkey pot pie. Other specialties include Blackened Gator, Boot Key Chicken and Rib

Platter, and grilled shrimp. Olivia's is also home to an outstanding meatless burger.

The only drawback to Olivia's is getting there. You'll need a car or some fancy busing. Try busing from the Village Marketplace or one of the theme parks.

'OHANA AT PAPEETE BAY

$$ ★★★   ♥

✓ Great Ceremonial House, the Polynesian
✓ Table-service buffet, breakfast, and dinner
✓ Full-service bar, Polynesian specialty drinks
✓ Reservations required for the King's Table
✓ Atmosphere is beautiful.
✓ Tip: If you're at the King's Table, don't forget your Polynesian name.

'Ohana at Papeete Bay is beautiful, and everything here is steeped in the flavor of the South Seas. From the "thatched roof" and stone floor to the fire-pit grill, 'Ohana has the feel of a Polynesian longhouse. Costumed servers bring you course after course of roasted meats and seafood on sword-like skewers. It is a South Seas feast, fit for a Polynesian king.

There is a show twice nightly, with seatings at 5:15 and 7:30 P.M. Reservations for the King's Table are taken for these times, and we suggest that you make yours and be part of this fun show. Otherwise, you may dine anytime. The food here is surprisingly good. Grilled shrimp, chicken, and sausage as well as a wonderful vegetable lo mein make 'Ohana a good choice for fun dining entertainment.

PALIO

$$ ★★★★   ♥♥♥

✓ The Swan
✓ Table service, dinner only
✓ Full-service bar
✓ Reservations suggested
✓ Tips: If you want to make a budget meal out of it, order one pizza and one of the more moderately priced entrees. Drop by later in the evening for an espresso or cappuccino and your choice of desserts.

Your meal at Palio will begin with a Boccalino, the traditional "little jug" of wine. This restaurant is easily Disney World's finest in Italian cuisine. It is, we think, one of the very best places to dine at Walt

Disney World. If you are dining as a couple, let us suggest one of the comfortable booths where you may sit next to each other. Once the strolling violinist (or guitarist) begins, you'll begin to see why we rate this place as an outstanding romantic dining experience. Musicians play Tuesday through Saturday.

Palio is not a spaghetti-and-meatballs Italian restaurant. It is not difficult to eat here for about the same price as most of the Epcot restaurants. The food at Palio is incomparably superior. Entrees include seafood and spaghetti baked in parchment, ragout of lobster and tortellini, and pork alla Milanese. The osso buco was extraordinary, and we still long for the Risotto con Vongole. The specialty pizzas are small but exceptional. The dessert counter at Palio is Disney's finest, featurings about 20 incredible creations. The best of Disney.

PLANET HOLLYWOOD

$$ ★★★
✓ Pleasure Island (admission not required)
✓ Table service, lunch and dinner
✓ Full-service bar
✓ No reservations accepted
✓ Atmosphere is very interesting, not at all romantic.
✓ Tips: Ask for seating on the third floor. To avoid waiting in long lines at the door, try eating during the off-hours.

If this isn't the world's most outrageous Planet Hollywood, we would like to see the one that is. Built in a planet-shaped sphere, this restaurant is crammed full of real movie props and costumes. Loud and night-club-like, it is also interesting and fun. Some of the food is quite good, but some is average. In our quest for the best burger of Disney, this one was a real disappointment. The Thai shrimp, however, was excellent.

PLAZA RESTAURANT

$ ★
✓ Main Street USA, the Magic Kingdom
✓ Table service, lunch and dinner
✓ Reservations suggested
✓ Atmosphere is quaint.

This turn-of-the-century, art nouveau eatery is located at the end of Main Street, just as you round the corner towards Tomorrowland.

Nothing extraordinary here. A selection of sandwiches include Reuben, double-decker roast beef, Southwest chicken salad, and the usual burgers and hot dogs. Most are just under $10.

PORTOBELLO YACHT CLUB

$$ ★★★★ ♥

✓ Pleasure Island (admission not required)
✓ Table service, lunch and dinner
✓ Full-service bar, good wine list
✓ No reservations accepted
✓ Atmosphere is casual. Can be noisy at peak hours.
✓ Tips: If the weather is pleasant, try sitting in the beautiful garden area outside.

Portobello is one of our favorite places to eat at Walt Disney World. The menu features a large array of Northern Italian foods, all elegantly prepared. We've never had anything here that we didn't like a lot. One of our very favorites is Paglia e Fino con Salmone Affumicato (smoked salmon pasta). We have too many other favorites to list them all. However, the gelato cappuccino is one of our very favorite desserts, here or anywhere.

Don't miss eating here. For a moderately priced restaurant at Disney World, this place is one of the best. We like to share an entree along with several appetizers.

RAINFOREST RESTAURANT

$$

✓ The Village Marketplace
✓ Table service, lunch and dinner

This amazing restaurant replaces Chef Mickey's and is scheduled to open in the spring of 1996. Theming here may even out-Disney Disney itself. This eatery is destined to become extremely popular. Created to look, feel, smell, and sound like a tropical rainforest, it features periodic "thundershowers," a variety of live tropical birds, and a jungle of plants. The menu is simple with well-prepared meats, poultry, and seafood. Strong on fresh and natural, the Rainforest promises good, healthy food with an emphasis on delicious.

Since we have been unable to eat in the one other Rainforest Restaurant (in Minneapolis), we will wait to pass judgment on the food.

Having seen photographs of the original, however, we can promise that dining here will be unforgettable.

ROSE AND CROWN PUB AND DINING ROOM
$$ ★★   ♥
- ✓ United Kingdom, Epcot
- ✓ Table service, lunch and dinner
- ✓ Full-service bar with English ales and beers
- ✓ Reservations suggested
- ✓ Atmosphere in the patio is memorable, especially during pleasant weather or during IllumiNations.

A pleasant enough place to eat, especially if the weather is cool enough to dine on the patio overlooking the lagoon. The food here is well prepared and tasty, although nothing here seems particularly memorable (much like real British cuisine).

Fish and chips, roast lamb, steak and kidney pie, and a chicken and leek pie are among the many offerings. The restaurant is divided into three sections; each has a distinctly different decor, and each is comfortable and quiet.

SAN ANGEL INN
$$ ★   ♥♥♥
- ✓ Mexico Pavilion, Epcot
- ✓ Table service, lunch and dinner
- ✓ Full-service bar with Mexican beer
- ✓ Reservations suggested during busy mealtimes
- ✓ Tip: Try having a cold Mexican beer and some nachos or other appetizer. This way, you'll get to enjoy the atmosphere without having to eat an entire meal.

What a beautiful place this is. It's always nighttime at the San Angel Inn, which is set amidst the facade of a quaint Mexican village. The restaurant overlooks the most scenic part of the pavilion's boat ride, where the River of Time passes through a dense and mountainous jungle. Enjoy your meal on the lovely plaza at the river's edge, while a volcano smolders in the distance. It is truly memorable; a charming and romantic spot.

While the food claims to be authentic Mexican, we do not find it to our liking. It is no match for the lovely surroundings.

The Sand Trap

$ ★★

✓ The Bonnet Creek Golf Club at Osprey Ridge and Eagle Pines courses
✓ Table service, breakfast and lunch
✓ Full-service bar
✓ Reservations not accepted
✓ Atmosphere is pleasant.

This pleasant restaurant enjoys a country club setting. It would be just the place after a round on one of the Bonnet Creek courses. The menu includes the usual breakfast offerings and a selection of sandwiches, salads, and soups. The Sand Trap even makes its own potato chips.

Sci-Fi Dine-In Theater

$$ ★

✓ Disney–MGM Studios
✓ Table service, lunch and dinner
✓ Beer and wine
✓ Reservations a must—this place is popular (don't ask us why)
✓ Atmosphere is unique and interesting but noisy.
✓ Tip: If you are simply dying to see the inside of this place, drop in during the late afternoon hours and order a single dessert.

This is one of those places that you eat in to enjoy the theming rather than the food. We didn't even like the atmosphere all that much, but it obviously appeals to lots of other people. You'll eat in a "convertible" at a drive-in theater that shows nonstop 1950s sci-fi movie previews. Waiters and waitresses arrive on roller skates, and the menu is standard American fare: hot dogs, burgers, baked chicken, fried shrimp, and a few pasta dishes. It's all great fun, and you may really love this place.

We found the food barely acceptable, however. We are not comparing this to a fine dining establishment, either—the food was simply mediocre. We enjoy the food at 50's Prime Time much more.

Sum Chows

$$$ ★★★★ ♥♥♥

✓ The Dolphin
✓ Table service, dinner only
✓ Full-service bar, excellent wine list

✓ Reservations required
✓ Tip: Don't eat here without trying the Flash Fried Spinach.

Don't confuse this place with a Chinese restaurant. It is much, much more. Make no mistake about it, Sum Chows is one of the finest restaurants on Disney property. Poem of the Sea is tender chunks of Maine lobster with sweet peppers and black truffles in an herbed, white garlic sauce. Chen-Pi Chicken is an organic chicken breast with spicy orange sauce, served with lo mein. From rack of lamb to grilled salmon with Szechuan sauce, the entrees each reflect a different Asian culture. Each comes with a heavenly tofu and an aromatic jasmine tea.

Sum Chows is memorably elegant. The interior has been designed by the Dolphin's architect, Michael Graves. Red linen table cloths and classic Japanese flower arrangements create a serene and enchanting atmosphere. Service is as good as it gets. Add to this the first-class food, and Sum Chows is one of only several restaurants of this caliber here at Walt Disney World. This is a beautiful dining experience.

A special table is located in the kitchen for diners interested in a behind-the-scenes look at Sum Chows. Chat with renowned chef Christopher Salansky and his staff and watch your meal (and everyone else's) being prepared before your very eyes.

TANGAROA TERRACE

$ ★
✓ The Polynesian
✓ Table service, breakfast and dinner
✓ Full-service bar
✓ Reservations not required
✓ Atmosphere is pleasant. Can get noisy.

The Tangaroa Terrace seems to be having a hard time finding an identity. Every time we drop by, it has assumed a new style or cuisine. Currently, it features either an a la carte or buffet breakfast and an Oriental dinner, either buffet or a la carte. Before that, it was Italian. We can't make any guarantees what it will be by the time you get there, but it might be interesting.

The current breakfast buffet is about average for this sort of thing. Being able to order a la carte is a sensible option for those who eat small breakfasts and don't wish to spend $10 on a muffin, a bagel, or a bowl of cereal. The Oriental dinner buffet was competently prepared and a bargain at $12.

Tangaroa Terrace enjoys a tropical garden theme. It is comfortable without being particularly memorable. It is an acceptable place to eat, but not a dining experience.

TEMPURA KIKU
$$ ★★★

✓ Japan Pavilion, Epcot
✓ Table service, lunch and dinner
✓ Full-service bar
✓ Reservations suggested
✓ Atmosphere is unusual and interesting.

Not really a restaurant, Tempura Kiku is a fairly authentic tempura bar. With a few exceptions, most items on the menu are lightly battered and deep-fried, known in Japan as tempura. These include seafood, vegetables, and meats. There are tasty dipping sauces and a small selection of sushi and sashimi. The atmosphere is very Japanese: crowded yet comfortable. The quality of the tempura is very good.

Reservations are suggested, as there fewer than 30 seats at Tempura Kiku.

TEPPANYAKI DINING ROOM
$$ ★★★ ♥

✓ Japan Pavilion, Epcot
✓ Table service, lunch and dinner
✓ Full-service bar, Kirin beer and sake
✓ Reservations suggested during mealtimes
✓ Atmosphere is Japanese: pleasant and themed.

If you have ever eaten at a Benihana's restaurant, then you will know what this experience is all about. Here at Teppanyaki, you sit at tables with other Disney guests. The center of each table is actually a cooking surface, where a Japanese chef will "perform." The chef's deft chopping and slicing skills and some knife-acrobatics are quite impressive. Entrees include shrimp, chicken, beef, and lobster, each sliced or cubed and grilled right in front of you. There are also grilled vegetables and several dipping sauces. The food is quite good, and the show is fairly entertaining.

TONY'S TOWN SQUARE
$$ ★
✓ Main Street USA, Magic Kingdom
✓ Table service, breakfast, lunch, and dinner
✓ Reservations a must
✓ Atmosphere is pleasant, though noisy when crowded (nearly always).

The theme here is from *Lady and the Tramp*, Disney's classic animated film. Cuisine is Italian with few surprises. The atmosphere is pleasant, especially in the glassed-in garden area. The breakfast menu offers several good frittatas, but we would suggest having them serve the tomato sauce on the side. Lunches and dinners include the usual spaghetti, lasagna, and Joe's Fettucini. Pleasant enough, but Tony's simply doesn't excel at anything.

VICTORIA AND ALBERT'S
$$$ ★★★★ ♥♥♥♥
✓ The Grand Floridian
✓ Table service, dinner only, two seatings: 6 P.M. and 9 P.M.
✓ Full-service bar, outstanding wine list
✓ Reservation required (make them when you book your room)
✓ Charming and elegant decor, a real romantic experience
✓ Tips: We suggest wine pairing. It is a bargain, considering how much wine you will be served. If you are celebrating your anniversary or honeymoon, be sure to mention it when you make your reservation; they will do something special for you. Ask to be seated in the small dining room on the side, which has a lovely fireplace and is even more intimate.

For those of you celebrating something special at Walt Disney World, whether a honeymoon, an anniversary, or simply being in love, listen to this: Victoria and Albert's is the most memorable dining experience that we have ever had. The food was outstanding, the ambience was elegant and unforgettably romantic, and the service was impeccable and white-glove; the sum of the parts of this package added up to something so extraordinary that we still gush about it. Quite literally, we have experienced nothing like it. It is not your everyday extraordinary dining experience.

The menu at Victoria and Albert's changes to accommodate what is freshest and available. Generally, you will find a selection of three or four entrees, several soups, and a handful of appetizers. During our visit, the first course included yucca-crusted julienne of chicken with spicy Caribbean scotch bonnet sauce and Maine lobster salad with peppercorn mayonnaise and chilled asparagus. The soup course featured a heavenly consommé of duck. Entrees featured seared Atlantic swordfish dusted with five spices over braised Tat Soi, hoisin cream sauce and beef tenderloin with forest mushrooms and sweet vermouth demi-glace. There was even a mixed grill of South Texas wild boar, served over sautéed leeks with a blueberry thyme au jus. From salad to the memorable chocolate soufflé, everything was outstanding. And of course, each course was accompanied by a different wine. We never felt the slightest bit hurried and, we confess, it took us three hours to make our way through this sumptuous feast.

This is a formal dining experience, make no mistake about it. The dining room is small and intimate, with only fifty-six chairs. Table service includes real china, and accessories are all worthy of this first-class establishment: silverware and crystal.

If this romantic trip to Disney is for a special occasion, we urge you to consider this unforgettable and sublime dining experience. Expensive, no doubt, but worth the price. What better thing can lovers do to have such memories? Evening dress is required.

Whispering Canyon Cafe

$$ ★★★
- ✓ The Wilderness Lodge
- ✓ Table service, family-style, breakfast, lunch, and dinner
- ✓ Full-service bar
- ✓ Reservations suggested
- ✓ Atmosphere is charming and entertaining.
- ✓ Tip: There is a cozy little room by the fireplace. Request it when you make your reservations.

The Whispering Canyon serves its meals family-style. What this means is that the food arrives in large pans and is placed on a barrel-top lazy Susan on your table. It's all-you-can-eat, and the food will keep on coming as long as you are willing.

The food is surprisingly good, especially the grilled meats and vegetables. The strawberry shortcake was so good that we still yearn for more. Breakfasts feature the usual, while both lunches and dinners offer real, hardwood-grilled chicken, ribs, and sausage. Dinner features marvelous grilled vegetables.

Decor is the Wild West, and cast members are dressed in cowboy and cowgirl outfits. The furniture looks like full-size versions of a child's cowboy furniture of the 1950s. It is all quite charming and entertaining, too.

YACHT CLUB GALLEY

$$ ★★★
- ✓ The Yacht Club
- ✓ Table service, breakfast, lunch, and dinner
- ✓ Full-service bar
- ✓ Reservations not required
- ✓ Atmosphere is themed and pleasant.
- ✓ Tip: A nice place for lunch if you are over at Epcot. Simply stroll over from the International Gateway.

As we have mentioned, most of the premium resorts feature one all-purpose restaurant, which offers an assortment of dishes for each of the day's meals. We usually find ourselves comparing them all to the Yacht Club Galley. This is one of the best eating places around. Not a fine dining spot, the Galley serves food that is well prepared, tasty, and reasonably priced. Breakfasts are either a la carte or buffet. Lunches feature a large selection of soups, salads, and sandwiches, and dinner adds a number of New England–style entrees. In our many stays at the Yacht or the Beach, we have never been disappointed here.

Decor is yachty, with framed displays of knots and glass-encased models of the beautiful old J-Boats of last century's America's Cup races. Salt and pepper shakers resemble small lighthouses. This is a pleasant place to eat—not particularly memorable, but simply nice.

YACHTSMAN STEAKHOUSE

$$$ ★★★★ ♥♥
- ✓ The Yacht Club
- ✓ Table service, dinner only
- ✓ Full-service bar
- ✓ Reservations suggested after 6:30 P.M.
- ✓ Atmosphere is simple and beautiful.
- ✓ Tip: Try the Chateaubriand for Two at less than $40.

If you are looking for the best steak at Walt Disney World, look no further. The Yachtsman Steakhouse features the finest in aged, grain-fed cuts of beef. The variety is large. From Kansas City strips to Chateaubriand, there is the perfect cut for every taste. And if steak is not your thing, the Yachtsman offers a full menu of lamb, pork chops, poultry, and a seafood steak of the day. All of it is excellent.

The Yachtsman Steakhouse is a charming, quiet, and woody restaurant. Like the menu itself, the decor here is simple yet elegant. We highly recommend this restaurant.

YAKITORI HOUSE

$ ★★

✓ Japan Pavilion, Epcot
✓ Counter service, lunch and dinner
✓ Kirin beer
✓ No reservations
✓ Garden atmosphere is charming and restful.

When we eat in a foreign country, we always like to find restaurants where the locals eat. We guess that this same principle applies to Disney World. The first time we peeked in the Yakitori House, we were surprised to see that nearly every patron was Japanese. That it attracts so many visitors from Japan attests to its authenticity.

The menu here includes teriyaki sandwiches and Kushi-Yaki: skewered chicken, shrimp, or beef that has been basted in soy sauce and sesame oil. Yakitori also features a selection of Japanese sweets and beverages.

The restaurant itself is a bamboo-like structure. In good weather, we suggest eating outside in the lovely garden area.

$\mathcal{R}$ecreation and Other Pastimes

There is so much to do at Walt Disney World that it would probably still be the Vacation Capital of the World even without its themed attractions. Boating, biking, tennis, golf, horseback riding, fishing, waterskiing, and parasailing are just a few possibilities when it comes to recreational activities. And Walt Disney World is also home to a number of world-class fitness centers that offer massage therapy, saunas, spas, and personal training. To round out your activities, the World also features a village of unique and interesting shops, just the place to browse away a lazy afternoon.

Mixing your theme park adventures with plenty of recreation and relaxation will make for a leisurely and more memorable romance holiday. These activities will get the two of you out of the mobs and into more intimate settings. So, open yourselves up to a delightfully different kind of Disney experience. Take a sail or a cruise. Ride a bike or ride a horse. Get massaged or get out and go shopping. Be adventurous: go waterskiing or parasailing. Or both. Take advantage of a World of fun together.

Golf

No matter how you slice it, Walt Disney World is a golfer's paradise. With 99 holes of championship PGA-level golf and over 20,000 resort rooms, Disney World is the largest golf resort in the world. The six courses each present unique challenges to both the amateur and the professional. There are five, 18-hole championship courses and one, 9-hole executive course. All are open to the public and, as Disney resort guests, you'll get discounted green fees and preferential tee times. Green fees are $95 per round ($85 for resort guests) at each of the regular courses, cart included, and $25 at Oak Trail, the executive course. If this sounds a bit expensive, there is always play after 3 P.M. for $45 per round. If you are planning a Disney golf vacation, you might wish to pick up a Disney Golf Season Badge. This badge costs $50 and gives you unlimited play after 10 A.M. on any of the five 18-hole Disney courses, for only $35 a round. Good for a year and available at any of the Disney pro shops, this badge is a great deal if you plan to play even twice.

The six courses are located at three different locations around Walt Disney World. Both Osprey Ridge and Eagle Pines can be found at the Bonnet Creek Golf Club while the Palm and the Magnolia are located at Shades of Green. Oak Trail and the Lake Buena Vista courses are both near the Disney Institute. Here are the links, rated in order of difficulty by pros of the PGA:

- Osprey Ridge (6,680 yards, designed by Tom Fazio): Rated by the Pros as the toughest course here at Disney, this course has elevations that are not at all typical of central Florida. Osprey Ridge does not double-back on itself. It just takes off into the woods. Tom Fazio himself considers this one of his best courses.
- The Palm (6,461 yards, designed by Joe Lee): The eighteenth hole here has been rated the fourth toughest on the PGA Tour.
- The Magnolia (6,642 yards, designed by Joe Lee): This course has the Disney signature "Mousetrap" on its sixth hole. The final round of the Oldsmobile Classic is played here.
- Eagle Pines (6,309 yards, designed by Pete Dye): This low-profile course features dished instead of crowned fairways. Relatively flat, this course has no grass for rough.
- Lake Buena Vista (6,268 yards, designed by Joe Lee): This is a fairly short, wide-open course. Hole 16 is called the "Intimidator."
- Oak Trail (executive course, 2,913 yards, designed by Joe Lee): Green fees are $25 for nine holes, $35 for two rounds. No electric carts are allowed on this course, and golfers are allowed to carry their own bags.

Logistics

Tee times may be reserved up to 30 days in advance by Disney resort guests and seven days ahead by day guests. These courses are busy during the peak seasons, and we strongly suggest that you arrange your tee times if you want to play early in the day. For tee times at any of the six courses, call (407) 824-2270.

Club and shoe rentals are available at all six courses and are $20 per round for men's or women's clubs and $6 a round for shoes. Rental clubs here are Titleist.

Transportation

Complimentary transportation to any of the Disney golf courses is furnished at any of the Disney resorts. This does not include the Swan, the Dolphin, and all of the hotels at Hotel Plaza. To arrange your transportation at a Disney resort, notify Bell Services of your tee times. Try to give them a day's notice.

OUR RECOMMENDATIONS FOR GOLF

- The Disney/Oldsmobile Classic takes place in October. Guests are advised not to schedule play during this week.
- Shirts with collars are required at all Disney courses.

Tennis

There are so many tennis courts around Walt Disney World that you might think it's a tennis resort. Located in a variety of places, you'll have little trouble finding a convenient court. Most feature full-service pro shops.

- The Contemporary features six lighted, hydrogrid clay courts. Open 8 A.M. to 8 P.M., reservations are recommended. The cost is $12 per hour or $40 for length of stay. Ball machines, practice lanes, and a pro shop are available. For reservations, call (407) 824-3578.
- The Grand Floridian has two clay courts. Open 8 A.M. to 8 P.M. Play costs $12 per hour or $35 to play against the pro. Ball machines and pro shop are available. Reservations are recommended. Call (407) 824-2433.
- The Yacht and the Beach Clubs have two lighted courts, use of which is complimentary to all guests of these resorts. The courts are adjacent to the Beach Club. Open 7 A.M. to 10 P.M. No pro shop, no reservations. Equipment is available at the resort's health club at no charge.

- Fort Wilderness has two lighted courts. Open 8 A.M. to 6 P.M., there is no charge for their use. Open to all Disney resort guests. Rental racquets are available at the Bike Barn. No reservations.
- The Vacation Club has two lighted courts, open 7 A.M. to 11 P.M. Use is complimentary for registered guests of the Vacation Club on a first-come, first-serve basis. Rental equipment is available at Hank's.
- The Swan and the Dolphin share eight lighted tennis courts. Open from 8 A.M. to 11 P.M., cost is $12 per hour and is complimentary after 7 P.M. A full-service tennis club and pro shop are adjacent to the courts. Reservations only from 8 A.M. to 7 P.M.
- Shades of Green has two lighted tennis courts. Open from dawn until 10 P.M., use is complimentary for guests of the resort. No reservations.

OUR RECOMMENDATIONS FOR TENNIS

- Disney resort guests may make tennis reservations up to 30 days in advance. Call (407) W-DISNEY (934-7639).
- Tennis attire is required at all courts. Rental equipment is available everywhere.

Boating Around the World

One of our favorite things to do at Walt Disney World is to go boating. Despite the fact that we live on our own sailboat and have our own little fleet, we simply love boating around Disney. It is fun and gives an interesting perspective on this fabulous place.

A variety of craft are available nearly anywhere there's a body of water. Most marina rental areas open at 10 A.M. and stay open until dusk, usually 6 P.M.

Marina rental locations are listed following.

- The Seven Seas Lagoon and Bay Lake
    The Contemporary
    The Polynesian
    The Grand Floridian
    The Wilderness Lodge
    Fort Wilderness

- Lake Buena Vista and the Village Waterways
  The Village Marketplace
  The Vacation Club
  Port Orleans
  Dixie Landings
- Crescent Lake
  The Yacht and the Beach Clubs
  The Swan and the Dolphin
  Disney's BoardWalk
- Barefoot Bay at the Caribbean Beach

Watercraft

All boats are not available at all locations. While prices and hourly minimums vary a little from marina to marina, the following should give you a good idea of what you will spend to rent a watercraft:

- Pedal boats, rowboats, and canoes: about $5 per half-hour
- Sailboats: most about $6 per half-hour
- Sunfish: $10 hourly
- Capri sailboats: $12 hourly
- Hobie Cats (for experienced sailors only): $15 hourly
- Aqua Cats, Aqua Fins: $10–14 hourly
- Water sprites (two-person mini "speed" boats): $17 per half-hour
- Canopy boats: $18 per half-hour
- Pontoon boats (Flote boats), 20 or 24 feet: $40 or $50 hourly
  20-foot pontoon boats can accommodate a maximum of
  10 people.
  24-foot pontoon boats come with a driver.
- SeaRayder speedboats (the Contemporary only): $26 per half-hour

OUR RECOMMENDATIONS FOR BOAT RENTALS

- The Seven Seas Lagoon and Bay Lake are the best places to rent a boat. Since these two bodies of water connect, this makes for the largest area to explore. There is more to see, as well. If you are not staying in one of the resorts here, simply go and rent the boat of your choice at any of the marinas listed at the Seven Seas Lagoon or Bay Lake.

- The best selection of sailboats is at the Polynesian. We think that the Seven Seas Lagoon makes for the best sailing, too.

Other Boating Adventures

There are a few really special things that you can do on the waters of Disney. The most enchanting is to take a ride aboard *Breathless,* Disney's 1934 vintage, Chris Craft speedboat. Located at the Yacht and the Beach, this handsome wooden craft is a boat lover's dream. With perfect varnish-work and shiny chrome fittings, *Breathless* is available only with a driver. A half-hour cruise will cost $50 with up to five passengers.

For $75, this elegant yacht ♥♥♥♥ will take the two of you over to Epcot to watch IllumiNations. Truly romantic and unforgettable, this is the perfect experience for a special occasion.

Also, Flote boat fireworks cruises are available at either the Polynesian, the Grand Floridian, or the Contemporary. Any of these will take out a small group to view the Fantasy in the Sky fireworks and the Electric Water Pageant. Cost is $26 per person or $150 for the exclusive use of the boat for the two of you, driver included.

Waterskiing is also available at Walt Disney World. The ski boats are all located at Fort Wilderness, and the cost for waterskiing is $75 per hour. You can be picked up for free, by boat, at any of the Magic Kingdom resorts. Reservations with deposit are required and can be made up to two weeks in advance by calling (407) 824-2621. If waterskiing isn't enough of a kick for you, there's always parasailing. This is available only at the Contemporary. For 8 to 10 minutes of flight time, the cost is $40 per rider. Observers can go along in the boat for $15.

Biking

If you are looking for a pleasant way to do some sightseeing and get a bit of exercise, you can rent bikes at several places. Rentals can be found at Fort Wilderness, the Wilderness Lodge, the Vacation Club, Dixie Landings, Port Orleans, or the Caribbean Beach. The variety of bikes is large and includes men's, women's, and children's, as well as tandem bikes and bikes with child carriers. Rates are pretty uniform, usually around $3 per hour or $7 to $8 per day. Most rental shops open around 10 A.M. and require returns by closing, usually before sunset.

OUR RECOMMENDATIONS FOR CYCLING

- The best place to ride is Fort Wilderness. Try renting your bikes at the Wilderness Lodge and taking the path through the woods and around the lake to Fort Wilderness. There are nearly 10 miles of paths and roads there, much of it is shaded and all of it is interesting. There is lots to do over there as well.

Fishing Excursions

Guided fishing trips are available both on Bay Lake and at Lake Buena Vista. Hotel guests are not allowed to keep the fish, although exceptions are made for guests of Fort Wilderness and other areas that have kitchens, including the Vacation Club and the Village at the Institute.

Bay Lake has only recently been opened to fishing. Having been stocked in the 1970s with thousands of fingerling bass, this lake now offers anglers the opportunity to sample central Florida's world-famous bass fishing. A two-hour excursion costs $125 for up to five people and includes boat, guide, fishing gear, and refreshments. Live bait is extra. Reservations may be made up to two weeks in advance, and trips may be canceled due to inclement weather. For reservations, call (407) 824-2621. These excursions depart daily from both Fort Wilderness and the Polynesian. Hours are 8 to 10 A.M., 12 to 2 P.M., and 3 to 5 P.M.

Another guided fishing trip can be found at the Village Marketplace marina. Basically the same deal, this one is only $120. Longer excursions can be arranged for about $25 per extra hour. Again, reservations may be made up to two weeks in advance by calling (407) 828-2204. Rules for keeping fish remain the same.

For a less extravagant fishing experience, try the fishing pond near Ol' Man Island at Dixie Landings. Poles are available for rent at $3 per hour. Your catch must be returned. Dixie Landings also offers a two-hour excursion along the Sassagoula Waterway and on down to Lake Buena Vista. This guided catch-and-release trip costs $40 per person. This is a good trip and a real bargain for the money.

Another budget option is fishing the many waterways that run through Fort Wilderness. Here you can rent a pole at the Bike Barn for $3 per hour or you can use your own gear. You can even rent a canoe for $10 a day and make a real trip out of it. If you are staying out there, keep your catch and have it for dinner.

Jogging and Walking

Nearly every resort offers a jogging or walking path. Check with the Guest Services at your resort for a map. Some of our favorite paths include the ones in the Yacht and the Beach/the Swan and the Dolphin area, the Wilderness Lodge to Fort Wilderness area, Dixie Landings and Port Orleans, and a long circuit around the Polynesian and the Grand Floridian. There are also especially nice paths at the Vacation Club, the Village at the Institute, and the Caribbean Beach, as well. Walking and jogging have become national pastimes, and the folks at Disney have been paying attention.

Nature Walks

There are two pleasant nature walks at Walt Disney World. One is Discovery Island, Disney's own wildlife preserve. Admission is charged, but there is much more here than simply a walk. The other walk is on the north end of Fort Wilderness, which is open to anyone interested. The Wilderness Swamp trail runs for nearly two miles along the shores of Bay Lake and through some heavily forested areas. It is beautiful and quiet. This trail can be most easily reached by taking a boat to Fort Wilderness from the dock at the front of the Magic Kingdom. Pick up a map of the trail at Guest Services in nearby Pioneer Hall.

Horseback Riding

The Fort Wilderness Trail Ride departs daily from the Tri-Circle-D Ranch Livery and Trail Blaze Corral, located near the parking area to Fort Wilderness. The horses are good ones (Arabians and Appaloosas), and the pace is very slow. It is more of a horseback walk. No galloping is allowed. If you are not an experienced rider, you may find this to be something special. It is scenic and fun.

Cost is about $16 per person. Children under 9 years of age are not permitted, and there is a 250-pound weight limit. Reservations are a good idea here, as this is a popular pursuit. For reservations up to five days in advance, call (407) 824-2832.

HORSEBACK RIDING TIPS

- Wear long pants and don't bring along a lot of stuff such as cameras and pocketbooks. Horses don't have back seats or glove compartments.

- Trips begin at 9 A.M., 10:30 A.M., 12 P.M., and 2 P.M. The ride lasts about 45 minutes.
- For experienced riders, this isn't much of a ride. But novices will enjoy it, perhaps even catching a glimpse of the Fort Wilderness wildlife population: deer, wild birds, and maybe even a gator.

Health Clubs

Most of the full-amenities resorts feature health and fitness centers. Some are open to any Disney resort guest, and some are available only to their own guests.

- Body by Jake is the Dolphin's health club. We think that it is the best on property and offers the widest variety of services. This large and modern facility includes a complete assortment of Polaris equipment, aerobic room, co-ed Jacuzzi, saunas, and locker rooms with showers. Jake's offers an impressive array of personal training, massage therapy, body wraps, and aerobics. Guests of the Dolphin may enjoy unlimited use of this marvelous facility for $16 per person for the entire length of stay. For a family of four, the rate is only $26. Body by Jake is also open to guests of any Disney resort for $8 per visit. Hours vary seasonally. Basic price does not include massages, personal training, or body wraps.
- St. John's Health Club at the Grand Floridian is located adjacent to the swimming area. It may be used by the registered guests of this resort only. This health and fitness center is equipped with the latest Nautilus machines and a sauna and features a staff of accredited exercise physiologists and licensed massage therapists. Visits cost $5 each. A Length of Stay Pass is available for $10 for individuals, $15 for families.
- The Ship Shape Health Club is the fitness center at the Yacht and the Beach Clubs. This is a very nice place and features a large indoor, co-ed Jacuzzi, Nautilus machines, sauna, and massage therapy. Adjacent to the pool complex, Ship Shape is available to all Disney resort guests. Personal training is also offered. Individual visits are $7 per day and Length of Stay Passes cost about $10 per person, $20 for families.
- The Olympiad Health Club is located at the Contemporary and is open to all Disney resort guests for $5 per visit or $10 for length of stay. This well-equipped facility features the only tanning salon on property, as well as massage therapy, aerobics, Nautilus equipment,

and sauna. Personal training is available by appointment. The Olympiad is located on the third floor of the resort.

- Muscles and Bustles at the BoardWalk features a complete health club with state-of-the-art exercise equipment, massage therapy, and sauna.
- The Swan Health Club provides a modern facility for guests of its resort. This fitness center is located adjacent to the resort's lap pool and features exercise equipment, Sprint weight system, stair machines, treadmills, and free weights. Men's and women's locker rooms each feature showers and a dry sauna. Use of this facility is complimentary with a visit to the Swan.
- R.E.S.T. Fitness Center at the Vacation Club offers a fully equipped health club. This one is available only to guests or members of the Vacation Club, and use of it is complimentary. This facility includes massage and personal training, Nautilus equipment, co-ed steam room, and whirlpool bath.
- Shades of Green has a fairly well-equipped health club, which is free for guests of that resort. All of the hotels along Hotel Plaza Boulevard except the Travelodge also have fitness rooms or health clubs. The Buena Vista Palace has announced plans for a European-style health spa to be built sometime in 1997.
- When it opens in February of 1996, the Disney Institute will very likely have the most complete health and fitness center at Walt Disney World. We were shown the building under construction. This facility includes every conceivable piece of equipment, including a specially designed water aerobics pool. With health and fitness programs to go along with it, the Institute promises to be something truly unique.

Miscellaneous Sports

Some of the Disney resorts feature special sports that are not found elsewhere. Here is a brief list of them.

- Basketball: the Vacation Club
- Croquet: the Yacht and Beach Clubs, Disney's BoardWalk, Port Orleans
- Volleyball: the Beach Club, the Contemporary
- Bocci ball (lawn bowling): the Yacht and Beach Clubs

Shopping at the Disney Village Marketplace

While we don't expect shopping to be one of the major activities of your romance vacation, we are sure that you'll want to pick up at least a few mementos of your time together at Disney World. Shopping, we can tell you, is very good. In fact, an entire area is dedicated to it, called the Disney Village Marketplace.

With 18 shops and more than just a few restaurants, the Village Marketplace definitely deserves a place on your not-to-be-missed list. From imported handicrafts to gourmet cooking gear, the Marketplace offers a wide variety of browsing. We suggest that you set aside some time to explore this area. It will be relaxing and fun.

The Village Marketplace is not a Disney strip-mall. It is an attractive village of shops located on the shores of Lake Buena Vista and right next door to Pleasure Island. It's the perfect spot to browse before an evening of excitement. The 18 shops of the Marketplace are open from 9:30 A.M. to 11 P.M. While these stores do not specialize in bargains, they do offer a large assortment of quality merchandise, much of which you will not see elsewhere.

Here are some of our favorite shops at the Village Marketplace.

- Mickey's Character Shop is the place to go for your Disney logo clothing or accessories. This is definitely the largest and the best selection of Disney character merchandise at Walt Disney World.
- The Gourmet Pantry offers a combination of beautiful cookware and accessories as well as gourmet foods and wines. It also has a wonderful little bakery and deli, as well as a large selection of coffee, wines, candy, and condiments. There is even a small grocery section. This is just the place to go for in-room snacks or breakfasts.
- Team Mickey's Athletic Club features everything from Mouse-logo golf shirts to tennis shoes.
- The Christmas Chalet has an outstanding selection of Christmas decorations year-round. Pick-up a little something special for your tree. This is very nice stuff.
- You and Me Kid features children's clothing and toys.
- Discover has "nature" as its theme, and here you will find an assortment of clothing and ecological artifacts. This is an interesting store.
- The Art of Disney is a great place simply to browse. Here you'll find original and limited-edition animation cels as well as other Disney art.

Besides these few shops, a number of men's and women's clothing stores offer some very nice things. There is also a jewelry store, a glass shop, a photo store, and a book store. There's even a Guest Services.

You'll also find some fine eating places in the neighborhood. Cap'n Jack's Oyster Bar, the Rainforest Restaurant (opening spring of 1996), and Minnie Mia's each have something interesting to offer.

Bargain Hunting for Character Merchandise

If you have access to a car, you might be interested in the Character Warehouse. This large store is located in Belz Outlet Center in Orlando and sells last year's Disney character merchandise at bargain prices. Items that sold last year for $36 might be found here for $15. You never know what you'll find, but at these prices you're certain to see something.

To get there, take I-4 East (to Orlando) to International Drive. Take a left at the light and follow International Drive to the end. Look for Mall #2, with two towers. The Character Warehouse is inside.

The Ultimate Romance at Walt Disney World

$\mathcal{D}$isney Fairy Tale Weddings

We must confess, when we first heard that Disney was doing weddings, even we were a bit skeptical. "Why," we wondered, "would anybody want to get married at Disney World?"

A wedding, we reflected, was something between a celebration and a theatrical performance, with the ceremony, reception, rehearsal dinner, and lots of organization and transportation. There would also be accommodations, catering, and entertainment. Who better to create such an event than the imaginative and resourceful people at Walt Disney World? And in what more enchanting a place could one imagine a wedding so rich with possibilities?

On we went, realizing that the choice of locations, accommodations, cuisines, and entertainment was not only superb but virtually limitless. Have the ceremony at the Wedding Gazebo on the garden lawn of the Yacht Club or in the Magic Kingdom after closing. Or be married in the new Disney Wedding Pavilion, on its own tropical isle on the Seven Seas Lagoon. Guests could stay in any of the wonderful Walt Disney World resorts. How about, we wondered, a rehearsal beach-party dinner, calypso-style? Or a South Seas Banquet at 'Ohana at the Polynesian? Or have Mickey and Minnie drop by for the reception at the California Grill, high atop the Contemporary?

That a Disney wedding could be an extraordinary and memorable affair was beginning to make sense to us. A lot of sense. But who could possibly afford such an extravagant event besides the rich and famous? And so we began our exploration of Disney's Fairy Tale Weddings. Our interest had been piqued, and we did not cease until we had discovered that, from the intimate to the magnificent, there is a Fairy Tale Wedding to suit any taste and virtually any pocketbook.

You may not feel that a Disney wedding is right for the two of you. Take a careful look at what Disney Fairy Tale Weddings has to offer, and then make up your minds. Remember, your wedding will only happen once. At Walt Disney World, you can make it a once-in-a-lifetime experience as well.

Types of Fairy Tale Weddings

There are two basic varieties of Disney Fairy Tale Weddings: Intimate Weddings and Destination Weddings. Intimate Weddings are small. With a maximum of eight guests, these lovely affairs are beautiful and private. Larger weddings fall into the next category. Facilities, reception, and accommodations all become factors in an affair that includes more people and more planning. Of course, the bigger and grander the wedding, the greater the cost. Destination Weddings can be either Traditional, Themed, or Theme Park Weddings. This last category takes considerations into yet another arena: private, after-hours use of one of the Walt Disney World theme parks, which means significantly greater expenses.

With the Intimate Wedding costing around $2,100, fabulous honeymoon included, we hope that you are beginning to see the possibilities in a new light. If price is no object, then you may be viewing all of this with great interest. The potential for your Disney wedding and honeymoon will be without limit.

Most weddings do have a budget, though, and reality will very likely demand something more down-to-earth than a Cinderella fantasy in the Magic Kingdom. Between the intimate and the extravagant lies a great deal of territory. Somewhere in this area lies the special Disney wedding for you.

Disney Intimate Weddings

If the two of you are planning a small wedding, the Intimate Wedding may be perfect. Each of these weddings is really a package. For one price, you get a lovely ceremony at one of a variety of beautiful and romantic Disney locations and an unforgettable Disney honeymoon with your choice of luxurious Disney resort accommodations. The Intimate Wedding ceremony includes an official to perform the service, a bouquet for the bride and a boutonniere for the groom, a wedding cake and champagne toast, a solo musician during the ceremony, and a special wedding gift for the bride and groom. You even get your own wedding consultant, who not only will help you make the decisions but will also make all of the arrangements.

And, with the two of you already at Walt Disney World, your honeymoon will begin at once. You'll both be the pampered guests of either the Yacht or the Beach Clubs, the Polynesian, the Wilderness Lodge, or the Grand Floridian. Any one of these luxurious resorts is guaranteed to provide an exciting and unforgettably romantic atmosphere. You'll also have, for the length of your stay, unlimited admission to all of the Disney attractions. You'll even have the use of bicycles, canoes, sailboats, and pedal boats at your resort. Also included in this package is a dinner for two at your choice of select Disney restaurants or one Disney character breakfast. You will even receive a specially delivered Romance Basket filled with special treats such as bubble bath, chocolates, wine, and souvenir wine glasses. The World will be yours.

Limited to eight guests, the locations for these Intimate Weddings are varied. The Wedding Gazebo at the Yacht Club is one. Set in a lovely rose garden, it has been designed especially for Disney Fairy Tale Weddings. The stately elegance of this setting provides more than just a touch of romance.

You will approach along a cobbled path that leads through the garden gate and up to the Victorian gazebo. With its carved wooden hearts and Cupid weather vane, this beautiful creation is the quintessential setting for love. Wedding planners have been hard at work before you arrive, and champagne and wedding cake await. This is a white-glove affair. Guests are seated in the rose garden, and the violinist begins to play. After the ceremony, everyone enjoys a champagne toast, all set to the music that you have selected. The cake is cut, the magic begins.

Variations of this theme are what Disney Fairy Tale Wedding specialists do best. We stayed at the Yacht Club and watched as several of these memorable events unfolded. Believe us when we tell you that, time after time, we were moved. These charming affairs are most definitely not performed on an assembly line. Each reflected careful planning as well as the personal touches of both bride and groom. In two days, we witnessed five of these touching ceremonies. Each was unique. All were enchanting.

One ceremony was in the morning, three were in the afternoon, and another was late in the day, near sunset. One couple arrived by horse-drawn coach, another in Disney's vintage white Cadillac motor-car. Others simply arrived on foot. One wedding had a handful of guests, three others had eight, and one simply involved the bride and groom, an officiant, and several attendants.

Music at one wedding featured a singer; at the others, a violinist performed. Tunes varied from "Wish upon a Star" to the more traditional. Mickey, in top hat and tails, and Minnie, in a sparkling evening gown, appeared at several ceremonies. Some were videotaped, and each was well-photographed. The guests were thrilled at the perfection of the event, and so were we.

Each of these wedding ceremonies was definitely traditional. Dress ranged from formal to casually elegant. Even the presence of Disney characters during the champagne toast and cake cutting brought only a touch of Disney to the affairs.

There are other beautiful locations available for Intimate Weddings, and each offers a special and romantic vista of Walt Disney World. Among them are Sunset Point at the Polynesian, the fourth floor overlook at the Wilderness Lodge, and Picture Point at the Disney Wedding Pavilion. Packages for an Intimate Wedding begin around $2,100, with a minimum honeymoon of four days at the Wilderness Lodge. Choosing one of the other resorts will add to the cost of your package. The Intimate Wedding Package is very attractive, even in its most basic form. "No frills" at Disney still means outstanding. We are confident that your Intimate Wedding will exceed your expectations.

Value-wise, the Intimate Wedding seems equally attractive. Disney figures that the ceremony itself accounts for about $500 of the package, which is exceptional, considering that it includes wedding officiant, location, flowers, musician, cake, champagne, and more. Special resort rates at a wide variety of Disney resorts are even available for your wedding party.

While Intimate Wedding packages do not include a reception, your wedding specialist will be happy to help you arrange something. Or you can simply make your own arrangements for a dinner party at one of the many fine Disney restaurants.

Packages can be elaborated upon to nearly any degree. Additional resort nights may simply be added on. Stepping up to an even more lovely and expensive resort will, of course, cost more. For a four-day stay at the Polynesian, add about $300. Add an additional $600 to the basic package for a stay at the Yacht or the Beach Clubs. Use of the magnificent Wedding Pavilion will cost an additional $500.

The Food 'n Fun Plan can be added to the Intimate Wedding Package. For about $450 for a four-day stay, this plan gives you both two meals a day in a variety of Disney restaurants. With gratuities included, this means no spending limits on meals. Alcoholic beverages are not part of this plan, however. Food 'n Fun will also give you use of a few more forms of Disney recreation, including water sprites, canopy boats, and pontoon boats.

There are other Intimate Wedding options too. Choices for music are either a single flutist, violinist, or guitarist. Any other type of performer or additional musicians will be extra. Adding Disney characters to your Intimate Wedding can get expensive. For both Mickey and Minnie, expect to pay $600.

Your Intimate Wedding coordinator will be happy to work out all of the plans with you. Pricing for transportation, Disney characters, entertainment, and other extras are the same as those for Destination Weddings, and we'll give you some of these figures later. Remember, though, that a Disney Fairy Tale Intimate Wedding is limited to eight people, including the bride and groom. If you simply cannot keep your numbers down to this figure, you'll have to step up to the next level.

Planning Your Intimate Wedding

Your Intimate Wedding will begin with a phone call: Walt Disney Fairy Tale Weddings at (407) 828-3400.

If you are calling to reserve your ceremony, a wedding coordinator will return your call within 48 hours. Remember, Disney Fairy Tale Intimate Weddings require a minimum 10-day notice. If you are not in a hurry, a wedding representative will get back to you within a few days. This person will have all of the latest information and, if you two have already made the big decisions, you'll find that everything else will go smoothly. Once your plans are finalized and details are worked out, you will be expected to make a deposit equal to the first night's lodging at the resort of your choice. After that, you simply have to show up.

Destination Weddings

One of the most important things to know when it comes to a Destination Wedding is that it is not a product. You will not be shown Package A, Package B, and Package C. Far from it. Disney Fairy Tale

Weddings is a service, one that has been created to help you design your very own and very special wedding.

Since a Destination Wedding involves more people, there will be many more elements to consider. Even a modest wedding will entail such considerations as catering, guest accommodations, floral arrangements, and dozens of other important details. Overseeing, organizing, and orchestrating your entire Disney wedding will be your very own wedding specialist. Throughout the entire process, this specialist will be there to answer your questions, to find solutions to your problems, and to make your every dream come true.

While each Fairy Tale Wedding is a unique interpretation of your wishes, there are three general styles: Traditional, Themed, and Theme Park. You can decide whether to have your traditional ceremony with Walt Disney World as the backdrop or to make your wedding a celebration complete with Disney characters and themed decorations. The choice will also be yours whether to have your wedding at the beautiful Disney Wedding Pavilion or in one of the many other unforgettable Disney locations. Choose the romantic and Victorian elegance of the Grand Floridian, or enjoy the casual, seaside splendor of the Beach Club. Whatever location you select, you will be free to make your wedding as "Disney" as you want it to be.

The use of characters is only one way to make your wedding a themed affair. Props, scenery, landscaping, and special effects can also be used to fashion the ultimate fantasy for any or all of your wedding plans. Such motifs as Beauty and the Beast, Cinderella's Ball, and Aladdin are but a few of the hundreds of themes that can be created. Have a Wild West Wedding at Fort Wilderness, a moonlight wedding cruise on the *Kingdom Queen* stern-wheeler, or let Disney create a storybook Alice in Wonderland setting. There are no limits to the magic at hand.

Of the Destination Weddings, Theme Park Weddings are the grandest of all. Each of these is staged after-hours at either Epcot, Disney–MGM Studios, or the Magic Kingdom. These weddings tend towards the spectacular, with prices to match.

A fantasy wedding at Disney–MGM Studios might be the perfect marriage for two film buffs. It begins with the bride's arrival by motorcade down Hollywood Boulevard. Vintage vehicles, fireworks, and cheering crowds set the scene. The wedding ceremony takes place in the courtyard of the Chinese Theater, finalized with the traditional Hollywood handprint in cement. The wedding party then boards the

Great Movie Ride for a trip through the most memorable cinematic scenes of all time. The ride ends as the wedding party arrives in the soundstage, where a glittering and lavish sit-down dinner and dance await. Potted palms, sparkling lights, and a champagne toast begin the evening's festivities. The movie screen backdrop of silent film clips and a small orchestra craft the magical atmosphere for this unforgettable event.

This is but one of countless such scenarios. Have an Under the Sea Wedding at the Living Seas Lounge in Epcot or enjoy something more traditional in the formal English garden of the United Kingdom Pavilion. For something a bit offbeat, there's always the unusual atmosphere of the Twilight Zone Tower of Terror courtyard. The possibilities for Theme Park Weddings are limited only by your imagination.

Planning Your Destination Wedding

Having compared Disney weddings to those that can be arranged outside of Walt Disney World, we must tell you that these weddings are, indeed, expensive. We are talking Disney World here, and, for such a setting and such quality, you must expect to pay more. Exactly how much more will depend on your choices and just how large a wedding you are planning. We suggest that you shop around wherever you live in order to give yourselves an idea of just how much a wedding will cost in your home town. Take into consideration the difference between having your reception at a local restaurant or country club and having it in the Grand Floridian Ballroom.

The Guidelines

Because Disney Fairy Tale Weddings does not charge for the use of private banquet rooms, a $7,500 minimum expenditure applies to all wedding groups that exceed 8 persons. This minimum applies only to what is spent on the actual day of your wedding. It includes food and beverages, entertainment, flowers, transportation, and, if you wish to use it, the cost of the Wedding Pavilion. It does not include guest accommodations or anything that occurs on previous days, such as the rehearsal dinner. It also does not include extras such as the officiant and photographic services.

Minimum food and beverage expenditures are $50 per person for brunches held before noon and $75 per person for luncheons and dinners held later. All include service staff in tuxedo attire with white glove service, head table, white linen, elegant place settings, tables for gifts, cake and guest book, and, of course, all include the traditional cake and champagne toast. Sales tax, 18% gratuity, and alcoholic beverages are additional.

Of course, the menu will be of your choosing. The "minimum" dinner will be a seven-course banquet created by Disney's award-winning culinary staff. A typical wedding dinner might include a one-hour pre-reception of fruits and cheeses followed by the sit-down dinner of shrimp cocktail, Caesar salad, and an entree and dessert. Your wedding cake will be a custom-designed, multitiered masterpiece.

Are you still with us? There is more. Both you and your guests will be expected to stay in Disney resorts. A minimum number of resort nights must be guaranteed based upon the size of your wedding party. It is a simple formula, one that you should have no difficulty satisfying. Know too that discounts are available for all wedding parties, with prices beginning at $69 per night. Having your entire wedding group along with you at Disney will enhance the affair, making it even more memorable for everyone. Transportation for your guests will be simpler, and they will be having their own Disney vacations.

A Sample Destination Wedding for One Hundred People

The enchanting Wedding Pavilion is the setting for this unforgettable ceremony. Floral decorations, four bridesmaids, ring bearer, and flower girl make this a charming and traditional affair. The bride and groom take their vows before a backdrop of Cinderella's Castle. After the ceremony, photographs are taken in the Picture Point rose garden overlooking the lagoon. Bride and groom then depart for the reception in a chauffeured and awning-covered boat.

The reception takes place at the Grand Floridian Ballroom, where a musical trio furnishes the atmosphere for this white-glove affair. The dazzling menu features platters of fresh fruits and assortments of cheese, crudites, and dip. An open bar begins the festive occasion.

Following this, an elegant and formal dinner is prepared by the master chefs of Disney. Table settings feature floral centerpieces, crisp linens, and crystal glassware. The menu includes shrimp cocktail with key lime cocktail sauce, Caesar salad, grilled chicken breast with pecan Amaretto sauce, confetti rice, fresh seasonal vegetables, oven-fresh breads, and strawberry Napoleon. Afterwards, everyone enjoys the wedding cake, a champagne toast to bride and groom, and a memorable evening of dancing and cocktails in the lovely ballroom.

Such a lavish wedding would cost about $13,500, including tax and gratuities. This includes floral arrangements for the ceremony and all participants, a four-hour open bar, three hours of entertainment with harp, flute, and violin, and three hours of entertainment with a disc jockey and sound system. A complimentary wedding night at the Grand Floridian for bride and groom would also be part of the package. Not included are the photography, wedding invitations, and favors. Considering that the average wedding in the U.S. costs $17,000, this affair, modest by Disney standards, seems reasonable, even attractive.

Destination Theme Park Weddings

A variety of considerably higher minimums applies to weddings in any of the three theme parks. To begin with, a $6,500 food and beverage minimum applies for any Theme Park Wedding. For a Magic Kingdom wedding, expect to spend no less than $35,000 for the total package, and for a wedding at either Epcot or Disney–MGM Studios, a minimum expenditure would be $18,000.

A Magic Kingdom wedding could take place in the lovely rose garden at the Swan Boat Landing near Cinderella's Castle. Guests arrive by horse-drawn trolleys down Main Street. The bride arrives in Cinderella's glass carriage, drawn by six white ponies and driven by two costumed footmen. Following the ceremony is a fantasy reception in the castle courtyard, after which guests ride on Cinderella's Golden Carousel. The new husband and wife appear on the castle parapet, heralded by costumed trumpeters, and guests enter King Stefan's Banquet Hall for a specially prepared meal and a magical evening of dancing.

This storybook wedding includes round-trip transportation for all guests to the Magic Kingdom entrance and private use of the theme park for the duration of the wedding. All setup services for landscaping, dance, reception, and ceremony would be included, as would the sound system, lighting, and a special bridal dressing area.

The food and beverage package would include a one-hour reception with a variety of hors d'oeuvres and a four-hour unlimited open bar. Dinner would feature a seven-course meal, the menu to be arranged with Disney catering services. Cake and a champagne toast cap off the dinner. Floral arrangements, photography, wedding officiant, invitations, and wedding favors are not included. The total cost for this would be about $35,000.

The Destination or Theme Park Wedding Process

A Destination Wedding or a Destination Theme Park Wedding takes a great deal of planning. On average, couples make their initial contact with Disney about one year before the anticipated day. Specific reservations may be made for Theme Park Weddings up to one year in advance, and plans may be finalized for non-theme park weddings up to eight months in advance. Again, the process begins with a phone call to Disney Fairy Tale Weddings. Request a full information kit and look it over carefully.

Once you have decided upon a date, you are ready to make your second call to Disney Fairy Tale Weddings. A sales manager will happily provide you with any information that you might wish. This person will be knowledgeable in helping you to sort out the many possibilities and to limit the selections to something that reflects your own unique personalities and expectations.

When the magical date arrives to make your reservations, you will both be prepared. This will be the real beginning of your Disney wedding adventure. You will receive a letter of agreement and be asked to make a deposit to secure your banquet hall and special hotel rates. This deposit will apply to your minimum expenditures. At this time, you will also meet your wedding services manager. This knowledgeable and dedicated specialist will be with you throughout the entire process of your Fairy Tale Wedding. Once you have locked in your locations and date, you will be asked to make an on-site inspection to ensure that everything meets your expectations. If you are unable to do this, your wedding services manager will see that you receive the proper information and photographs.

Now that the basics are out of the way, the real fun begins. You will need to make a lot of important decisions, and your wedding services manager will know the ins and outs of the entire process. Your specialist will work within the parameters of your budget to orchestrate every element of your wedding. Invitations, menus, china and place settings, floral designs, entertainment, photographic services, and guest accommodations are just a few of the considerations. Simply looking over locations, inspecting fabric swatches, and tasting sample menus will be a pleasure. Disney's famous and meticulous attention to detail will focus on every phase of your storybook wedding.

Once you have made the decisions, you will be free to enjoy yourselves right up until the traditional preceremonial jitters. All of the work and worry, all of the organization and implementation, will have been done by your wedding services manager and a team of dedicated experts. Disney Fairy Tales Weddings is dedicated to making the reality of your wedding exceed your expectations.

The Particulars

You have many options when it comes to Disney Fairy Tale Weddings. The following sections cover this information. Remember, though, that prices are subject to change and can only be guaranteed six months ahead of your wedding date.

The Walt Disney World Wedding Pavilion

Built on its own special island in the Seven Seas Lagoon, this marvelous creation's only purpose is to be the perfect location for your storybook wedding. Like a Victorian summer house, the charming glass-enclosed building sets the perfect stage. Gabled roofs and sloped turrets, intricate gingerbread of carved hearts and cupids, and arched windows and panoramic vistas of the lagoon create an atmosphere that is enchanting and unforgettable.

The location, the elegant pavilion itself, and Disney's unfaltering sense of landscaping come together in an island masterpiece. Quaint yet lavish, the Wedding Pavilion is yet another success for the Disney imagineers.

The spacious chapel is large enough to accommodate 250 guests. Attention has been focused on every detail, from the vaulted ceilings to state-of-the-art sound and video systems. Nothing has been overlooked. Behind the alter, a stained-glass window perfectly frames Cinderella's Castle. Sound, lighting, and every possible camera angle have been calculated into this formula for the perfect wedding.

The Pavilion's on-site florist ensures the freshest of wedding flowers. Outside, Picture Point has been placed to provide a picturesque backdrop both for the wedding and for the bridal portraits. Picture

Point's ornate trellis is set amidst a formal rose garden, overlooking the Seven Seas Lagoon and Cinderella's Castle.

The Wedding Pavilion also features Franck's Wedding Salon, borrowed from the Disney film *Father of the Bride*. It is in this elegant French Provincial setting that the two of you will meet with your wedding specialist to make your plans. Besides its ideal location and captivating charm, Disney's Wedding Pavilion offers every conceivable amenity for a memorable celebration.

The fee for use of the Wedding Pavilion is $1000, regardless of the size of your wedding. This flat fee includes an organist.

Invitations and Bridal Organizer

Fairy Tale Weddings offers a selection of specialty invitations with themes such as Cinderella and Snow White. Available too is a stylish leather accordion file, embossed with a Cupid Mickey Mouse, for collecting wedding mementos such as notes, photographs, and fabric swatches.

Beverage Options

For a two-hour, hosted open bar, expect to spend about $22 per person and $6 per person for each additional hour. For beer and wine, two hours per person costs about $14 and each additional hour costs $4. Other options are host-sponsored per drink or cash.

Special Transportation

Whether you are arriving in Cinderella's glass coach or departing in a vintage white Cadillac, Disney offers an assortment of memorable transportation. A horse and carriage costs around $750, and the charming glass coach, complete with 6 white ponies and costumed footman and driver, about $1500. The chauffeured Cadillac costs $350 and a flote boat, with driver, only $75.

Entertainment

Single performers such as harpist, flutist, or violinist are available from $225. For a duo, prices begin at $375 and for a trio of musicians, such as a jazz or calypso group, $550. Rock bands, orchestras, and country and western bands all cost around $2,000.

Disney Character Entertainers

For one Disney character, the cost is $400. For two, $600; for three, $800. A herald trumpeter in full regalia is $250, and the Dapper Dans barbershop quartet is $700.

THEME PARK WEDDING ADD-ONS

- Merlin the Magician and the Sorcery and the Stone show in Fantasyland: $500
- Magic Kingdom attractions: from $930
- Fantasy in the Sky fireworks show: $15,000

The Rehearsal Dinner

While it is not mandatory to have a rehearsal dinner, it is common. There is nothing common, however, about the possibilities of a rehearsal dinner at Walt Disney World. From a dinner in the library of the Adventurer's Club at Pleasure Island to a sumptuous meal in your own private room at the California Grill, the options are many. Have a cookout on the beach with a calypso band or a Polynesian banquet at 'Ohana. You can choose from any of the fine dining places, the clubs at Pleasure Island, or have a catered rehearsal dinner at nearly any Disney location.

A Fort Wilderness cookout with all the fixings would cost around $20 per person. Something a bit more upscale but still casual, such as a Grand Floridian Summerhouse cookout with grilled chicken and a more gourmet selection of accompaniments, would cost a bit more than $30 per person. Pull out all the stops at the California Grill for a truly sumptuous dinner, and the cost would be about $43 per person.

CHAPTER 9

$\mathscr{H}$oneymoon Packages

Honeymooning used to mean a trip to Niagara Falls. Then a cruise to the Caribbean became the rage. Nowadays, newlyweds are looking for a honeymoon adventure, and Walt Disney World has become one of the leading vacation places for newly married couples. Disney World combines nearly every element desired for a honeymoon: warm weather, luxurious and romantic resorts, great nightlife, and first-class dining. In a single visit, a couple can boat, swim, golf, play tennis, dance, go horseback riding, enjoy gourmet dining, and go out at night, *and* they can also enjoy the Disney attractions. It is easy to see why Walt Disney World has become the number one honeymoon destination in the U.S.

Newlyweds are also eager for all-inclusive packages. These package vacations include everything from resort accommodations and recreation to meals. With all the money paid up front, a packaged honeymoon allows the bride and groom to enjoy their time together without worrying about overspending. With an all-inclusive package, the only worry will be what to do next.

Disney offers a variety of all-inclusive packages. Some provide accommodations, tickets to all attractions, recreation, and several meals a day. Others provide even more, including golf, tennis, gourmet dining, and a personalized photo album. Some of these are regular packages, while others are designed especially for honeymooners. An all-inclusive Disney package is a particularly special experience. The grander the package, the more pampered and privileged you both will feel.

Of course, there is nothing that says you must get an all-inclusive package. If you are careful spenders, we know that you will be able to enjoy your Disney honeymoon with resort reservations and some planning. But you will do this at a cost, and that cost is the carefree and pampered feeling that you get from a package. Without a package, all of the possibilities remain, but you'll have to be careful. We'll give you some ideas later on getting the most out of your own honeymoon "package."

Walt Disney World Honeymoon Packages

Disney currently offers three vacation packages for newlyweds. Each includes resort accommodations and admission to all of the Disney attractions. The Honeymoon Escape is the most basic. It also includes limited recreational activities but does not include meals. The other two, the Honeymoon Enchantment and the Grand Honeymoon, are all-inclusive. Each provides meals and unlimited recreation. The Honeymoon Enchantment is simply lavish. The Grand Honeymoon goes right over the top. Each of the three offer these basic amenities:

- A minimum four-night stay in a choice of Walt Disney World resort accommodations
- Unlimited admission for length of stay to all Disney attractions (includes the Magic Kingdom, Epcot, Disney–MGM Studios, Pleasure Island, Blizzard Beach, Typhoon Lagoon, River Country, and Discovery Island)
- Hourly use of bicycles, canoes, sailboats, and pedal boats, at select Disney resorts
- A Romance Basket filled with special treats such as bubble bath, chocolates, wine, and souvenir wine glasses (contents may vary)

The Honeymoon Escape

A Honeymoon Escape package for two begins at just under $1,000 for a minimum of four nights and five days. This package, along with the basic amenities, also includes:

- Your choice of the following resorts:
    The Caribbean Beach
    Port Orleans ♥♥
    Dixie Landings
    The All-Star Resorts
- One breakfast for both of you at your choice of selected Disney dining locations (gratuities included)

The Honeymoon Escape is not an all-inclusive package, because it does not provide meals. What's more, the minimum figure is good only at the All-Star Resorts, which would not be our choice for a honeymoon destination. You will be able to upgrade to any other Disney resort, but it will cost more. For example, a four-night Honeymoon Escape at the Caribbean Beach, Port Orleans, or Dixie Landings is about $1,150, while a four-night Honeymoon Escape at the Wilderness Lodge is about $1,300.

If four nights doesn't sound like much of a honeymoon to you (it doesn't to us), then you could easily add more nights to this package. A seven-night Honeymoon Escape at the Caribbean Beach, Port Orleans, or Dixie Landings is about $1,700.

As a stand-alone package, the Honeymoon Escape is not an exceptional deal. Compare it to booking your own room with Length of Stay Passes, and you'll quickly see that you're paying several hundred dollars for the Romance Basket, a breakfast for each or you, and the limited use of recreational activities—a questionable value even if you make good use of the bicycles and boats. You'd be better off booking your own room, getting a couple of Length of Stay Passes, and paying for everything as you go.

The Food 'n Fun Plan can be added to the Honeymoon Escape. For around $120 per day for both of you, this plan provides two meals daily in a select assortment of Disney dining locations as well as use of more Disney recreation. While recreation would include most motorized watercraft, it would not include golf or fishing excursions. With recent cutbacks in the restaurants included in this package, we have a hard time recommending it. A four-night Honeymoon Escape at Port Orleans, Dixie Landings, or Caribbean Beach, with Food 'n Fun, costs about $1,500; seven nights, about $2,300. For what you would get, we think that you could do much better paying as you go.

The Honeymoon Enchantment

Prices for the Honeymoon Enchantment ♥♥♥ begin at around $2,200 per couple for the minimum four nights and five days. This package includes all of the basic amenities, plus:

- Your choice of one of the following resorts:
    The Grand Floridian ♥♥♥♥
    The Polynesian ♥♥♥
    The Yacht or the Beach Clubs ♥♥♥♥
    The Contemporary ♥
    The Wilderness Lodge ♥♥♥
    The Vacation Club Villa ♥♥

The Village at the Institute
Fort Wilderness Campsites
- Unlimited use of all recreational activities, including motorized watercraft, golf, tennis, and much more
- Breakfast, lunch, and dinner (gratuities included) in your choice of Walt Disney dining locations; does not include Victoria and Albert's or room service
- Honeymoon photo session with a keepsake album

The Grand Honeymoon

The Grand Honeymoon ♥♥♥♥ is an exceptionally elegant package. It is expensive, but it will have you feeling like Cinderella and Prince Charming. Four-night, five-day minimums begin at around $3,100 per couple. Including the basic amenities, your every wish will be granted with:

- Your choice of the following resorts:
     The Grand Floridian ♥♥♥♥
     The Yacht or Beach Club ♥♥♥♥
- Unlimited use of all recreational activities, including motorized watercraft, golf, tennis, and much more
- Breakfast, lunch, and dinner (gratuities included) at your choice of Walt Disney World dining locations, including the unforgettable Victoria and Albert's ♥♥♥♥ and room service
- Private dining ♥♥♥♥ with your personal chef preparing a meal right in your room or wherever you want it (does not include alcoholic beverages, specialty trays, or caviar)
- Private golf and tennis lessons
- Use of health club (does not include massage)
- Special room amenities, including fresh flowers daily, fruit basket, and nightly turndown service
- Use of video camera in theme parks
- Honeymoon photo session with keepsake album

Upgrading to a More Expensive Resort

The prices quoted for these packages are for the least expensive resort listed in the package. Upgrading to a more expensive resort adds to the cost. Here are two examples:

- Four-night Honeymoon Enchantment at the Beach or the Yacht Clubs: about $2,700
- Four-night Grand Honeymoon at the Grand Floridian: about $3,400

Adding Nights

Adding extra nights to these basic four-night packages is easy. For seven nights of bliss and eight days of fun, here are two examples:

- Seven-day Honeymoon Enchantment at the Beach Club: about $4,200
- Seven-day Grand Honeymoon at the Wilderness Lodge: about $4,000

As a comparison, at the Grand Floridian, the same package costs around $5,300.

Upgrading Your Package to a Suite

It is also possible to upgrade any of the honeymoon packages to either a suite or to concierge service. To do this, you'll have to arrange it with the "suite people," who handle all reservations involving suites. For more information, see "Upgrade Your Package to a Suite or Concierge Service" in Chapter 1.

Upgrading to a suite will be an expensive affair. Most suites begin at around $500 per night, and some cost considerably more. We recommend three honeymoon "rooms" that are relatively affordable. Two are at the Grand Floridian and enjoy concierge service: either the honeymoon room on the private Clarendon level or the Turret room, each cost about $500 nightly. The other honeymoon room is at the Wilderness Lodge and costs about $225 per night. (For more information about these rooms, see Chapter 2.) Here are examples of honeymoon package upgrades to these rooms:

- Seven-night Grand Honeymoon at the Grand Floridian, in either of the honeymoon rooms: about $6,800
- Seven-night Honeymoon Enchantment in one of the four honeymoon rooms at the Wilderness Lodge: about $3,700

Non-Honeymoon Packages

Each of the three honeymoon packages resembles one of Disney's regular vacation packages. The Classic, Deluxe, and Grand Plan packages include features similar to the Honeymoon Escape, Honeymoon Enchantment, and Grand Honeymoon packages.

Comparisons will show that the honeymoon packages cost about $300 more than their similar counterparts. With the Honeymoon Enchantment and Grand Honeymoon packages, you get both the Romance Basket and the photo session with the keepsake album. Is it worth the difference? We'd have to say yes.

While the Romance Basket is merely a nice touch, the photo session is something truly special. You get a two- to three-hour session with a photographer, who will follow you around the parks to your choice of locations. The result is a beautiful and personalized leather keepsake album filled with photographs of the two of you enjoying your honeymoon at your most memorable Disney places. Yes, this makes the package worth it. What better picture memories could you possibly get than this? And how difficult is it to get even a few good pictures of the two of you together?

As for the Honeymoon Escape, without the photo album it is not much of a deal, and there is no way to add the album. If this is all that you can afford, we would suggest that you opt either to pay as you go or to get a basic classic package instead.

Creating Your Own Honeymoon "Package"

Not all couples can afford an all-inclusive package. You can easily arrange your own honeymoon and still have a marvelous and carefree time. Here are some tips for getting the most out of your own honeymoon package:

- Make full use of all resort discounts: Magic Kingdom Club, Florida Resident Specials, Annual or Florida Resident's Seasonal Passport, AAA, or whatever you are able to get. Check out all of the sources for the best resort deal.
- Take advantage of value season. You'll save money, and you'll find that the World is a more pleasant and romantic place without mobs of people.

- When you make your reservation, be sure to have them note that it is your honeymoon. Each of the Disney resorts offers a gift to newlyweds. Most will deliver a rose and a split of champagne to your room. Free upgrades to nicer rooms are not unheard of, especially during value season, when those rooms may be vacant.
- The Length of Stay Pass is a good deal and will give you the freedom to hop parks and see whatever you'd like, whenever you want to see it.
- Have your own Romance Basket delivered right to your room. Call Walt Disney World Florists at (407) 827-3505 to make arrangements.
- Some reasonably priced and romantic rooms:
  A Honeymoon room at the Wilderness Lodge, about $225 per night ♥♥♥
  King bed with courtyard view at Port Orleans or the Caribbean Beach, about $125 per night ♥
  King bed with river view at Dixie Landings, about $125 per night ♥
- Concierge rooms are expensive, but they still cost less than the all-inclusive packages. They include upgraded room amenities, continental breakfasts, day-long snacking, and afternoon-to-evening wines and cordials. This is a level of pampering that you will truly appreciate. Disney World concierge services are offered at the following resorts:
  The Polynesian concierge, from $305 nightly
  The Yacht Club concierge, from $370 nightly
  The Grand Floridian concierge, from $470 nightly
  The Dolphin Towers Concierge, from $310 nightly
  The Royal Beach Club at the Swan, from $330 nightly

OUR HONEYMOON RECOMMENDATIONS

- If you can afford either the Honeymoon Enchantment or the Grand Honeymoon, go for it. Either will make a special and romantic experience that you will remember always. Honeymoon Packages are expensive, but remember this is your honeymoon. If you can't spoil yourselves now, when can you?
- For honeymoon package reservations, call (407) 828-3400.

- Most of the prices we have quoted are for standard-view rooms. Since this is your honeymoon, we urge you to get the best view that you can. The truth is that standard-view rooms just don't provide the magic of looking out on Cinderella's Castle or even onto the courtyard of Port Orleans. There is a time for a standard room, and there is a time for something special.
- Prices quoted here are regular-season prices. Value-season discounts apply to these packages.
- Don't forget to request a king-size bed when you make your reservations.
- For honeymooners, we especially recommend these romantic resorts:
  The Grand Floridian
  The Yacht and the Beach Clubs
  Port Orleans
  The Polynesian
  Alligator Bayou at Dixie Landings
  The Wilderness Lodge
  Disney's BoardWalk (opens summer 1996)
- Here are some of our favorite romantic resort rooms:
  Lagoon-view rooms at the Grand Floridian or the Polynesian
  Any concierge service room
  One of the four honeymoon rooms at the Wilderness Lodge
  Either of the two types of honeymoon rooms at the Grand Floridian
  The Premier King View room at the Dolphin
  Upper-floor Epcot-view room at the Beach Club
  One-bedroom Villa at the Vacation Club
  The suite at Shades of Green
  Lagoon-view at the BoardWalk (opens summer 1996)
- If money is no object, the following are absolutely lavish suites:
  The Yellowstone, Wilderness Lodge
  The Commodore, the Yacht Club
  The Captain's Deck, the Yacht Club
  Garden King suite, Bali, the Polynesian

Appendices

$\mathcal{T}$he Disney Phone Directory

Automotive Service

Disney Car Care Center: (407) 824-4813

Barber and Beauty Shops

Contemporary Hair Styling Salon: (407) 824-3411
Ivy Trellis Barber and Beauty Shop, the Grand Floridian: (407) 824-3000, ext. 2581
Periwigs Hair Salon, the Yacht and the Beach Clubs: (407) 934-3260

Birthday Parties

Cubs Den, the Wilderness Lodge: (407) 824-1083
Theme park: (407) 934-6411

Child Care

Cubs Den, the Wilderness Lodge: (407) 824-1083
KinderCare: (407) 827-5444
Mouseketeer Club House, the Contemporary: (407) 824-3038
Mouseketeer Club House, the Grand Floridian: (407) 824-3000
Neverland Club, the Polynesian: (407) 824-2000 ext. 2170
Sandcastle Club, the Yacht and the Beach Clubs: (407) 934-6290

Dining

Disney Dinning Experience: (407) 828-5792
Reservations, Buena Vista Palace, Arthur's 27: (407) 827-3450

Reservations, the Dolphin restaurants: (407) 934-4025
Reservations, the Swan restaurants: (407) 934-3000 ext. 2181
Reservations, theme park and Disney resort restaurants, dinner shows, and
special request meals: (407) WDW-DINE (939-3463)

Florist

Gooding's Florist: (407) 827-1206
Walt Disney World Florist: (407) 827-3505

Foreign Language Services

Foreign Language Center (407) 824-7900

Health Clubs

Body by Jake, the Dolphin: (407) 934-4264
Olympiad Health Club, the Contemporary: (407) 824-3410
Ship Shape Health Club, the Yacht and the Beach Clubs: (407) 934-3256
St. John's Health Club, the Grand Floridian: (407) 824-2433
Swan Health Club: (407) 934-1360

Information

Disney's Walk Around the World: (407) 272-6201
General WDW Information: (407) 824-4321
Guided Tour Information: (407) 824-4321
Hearing-Impaired Guest Information: (407) 827-5141
Magic Kingdom Club: (407) 824-2600
Magic Kingdom Club Gold Card: (800) 89-DISNEY (893-4763)

Kennel (Overnight)

Fort Wilderness Kennel: (407) 824-2735

Lost and Found

Central Lost and Found, TTC: (407) 824-4245

Medical Facilities

Buena Vista Medical Center Pharmacy: (407) 828-8125 (free delivery for WDW resort guests)
Buena Vista Walk-in Medical Center: (407) 828-3434
First Aid and Emergency Dental Referral: (407) 648-9234 or 846-2093
Gooding's Pharmacy: (407) 827-1207
HouseMed/Mediclinic: (407) 396-1195
Sand Lake Hospital: (407) 351-8500

Recreation

Fishing, Bay Lake, Wilderness Marina: (407) 824-2621
Fishing, Bayside Marina, the Yacht and the Beach Clubs: (407) 934-3256
Fishing, Dixie Landings: (407) 934-5409
Fishing, Lake Buena Vista, Village Marketplace: (407) 828-2204
Golf course, Bonnet Creek Pro Shop: (407) 824-2675
Golf course, Lake Buena Vista Pro Shop: (407) 828-3741
Golf course, Palm and Magnolia Pro Shop: (407) 824-2288
Golf studio, Advance Tee Times: (407) 824-2270
Parasailing: (407) 824-3586
Tennis reservations, the Contemporary: (407) 824-3578
Tennis reservations, the Grand Floridian: (407) 824-2433
Tennis reservations, the Swan and the Dolphin: (407) 934-4396
Trail ride, Fort Wilderness: (407) 834-2832
Waterskiing: (407) 824-2621

Resort Reservations

AT&T True Rewards: (800) 298-5061
Buena Vista Palace: (800) 327-2990
Central Reservations Office (CRO): (407) W-DISNEY (934-7639)
Courtyard Marriot, WDW Village: (800) 223-9930
Disney Institute: (800) 4-WONDER (496-6337)
DoubleTree Guest Suites: (800) 222-TREE (222-8733)
The Grosvenor: (800) 624-4109
The Hilton: (800) 782-4414
Hotel Royal Plaza: (800) 248-7890
Magic Kingdom Club: (407) 824-2600
Shades of Green: (407) 827-3600
Special Programs: (407) 827-7200
Travelodge: (800) 578-7878
WDW Travel Company: (407) 828-3232

Resorts, Hotel Plaza

Buena Vista Palace: (407) 827-2727
Courtyard Marriot, WDW Village: (407) 828-8888
DoubleTree Guest Suites: (407) 934-1000
The Grosvenor: (407) 828-4444
The Hilton: (407) 827-4000
Hotel Royal Plaza: (407) 828-2828
Travelodge: (407) 828-2424

Theaters

AMC, Pleasure Island: (407) 827-1300, 837-1303

Transportation

Florida Town Cars: (800) 525-7246, (407) 277-5466
Mears: (800) 759-5219, (407) 423-5566
Taxi services at WDW: (407) 824-3360

Travel Services

AAA Disney Travel Center in Orlando: (407) 854-0770
American Express Office, Epcot: (407) 827-7500
Delta Travel, the Contemporary: (800) 221-1212, (407) 849-6400

Weddings

Disney Fairy Tale Weddings: (407) 828-3400

APPENDIX B

$\mathcal{R}$omantic Adventures

Here are a few romantic things that you'll find waiting for you at Walt Disney World, although we're sure you won't have much trouble coming up with some of your own ideas.

- A private Illuminations cruise for two on *Breathless,* the Yacht Club's vintage 1934 speedboat: ♥♥♥♥
- High Tea at the Garden View Lounge of the Grand Floridian: ♥♥
- A "Wine Flight" at the Beach Club's romantic lounge, Martha's Vineyard: ♥♥♥
- A picnic lunch from a favorite restaurant to Discovery Island after a relaxing morning: ♥♥
- His and hers in-room massages: ♥♥♥
- The free Sassagoula River launch up to Port Orleans and dinner at Bonfamille's Cafe: ♥♥
- A special and unforgettable dinner at Victoria and Albert's: ♥♥♥♥
- Quiet, romantic moments for just the two of you: ♥♥♥
- Fantasy in the Sky or the Electric Water Pageant from the beach swings at the Grand Floridian or Polynesian resorts: ♥♥♥♥
- Breakfast in bed: ♥♥♥♥
- Private dining in your room or on your balcony: ♥♥♥
- A torchlit stroll on the Polynesian grounds: ♥♥
- A sketch of you at Epcot's France: ♥♥
- An espresso and a dessert in the evening at Au Petit Cafe: ♥♥
- The view from the fifteenth-floor observation deck at the Contemporary, or a nightcap at the California Grill Bar: ♥♥

- Send someone you love a rose (Disney Florist, 827-3505): ♥♥♥
- A light dinner at the Pleasure Island Jazz Club while you enjoy the music: ♥♥
- One of the Magic Kingdom fireworks cruises from the Grand Floridian, the Polynesian, or the Contemporary: ♥♥♥
- Drinks and hors d'oeuvres during IllumiNations at Japan's Matsu No Ma Lounge at Epcot: ♥♥♥
- A late-night hot tub: ♥♥♥

The Best of
Walt Disney World

Here, we hand out our "Best of Disney" awards. Of course, these are just *our* favorites.

- Best All-Around Resort: the Yacht and the Beach Clubs
- Most Romantic Resort: the Grand Floridian
- Most Romantic Room: the Turret room at the Grand Floridian
- Best Pool: Stormalong Bay, the Yacht and the Beach Clubs
- Best Hot Tub: the Yacht and the Beach Clubs
- Best In-Room Jacuzzi: the Vacation Club Villas
- Best Resort Lobby: the Wilderness Lodge
- Best Public Restroom: the lobby of the Beach Club
- Best Restaurants (sorry, we couldn't narrow this down any further): California Grill, Portobello Yacht Club, Sum Chows, Victoria and Albert's
- Most Romantic Dining Experience: Victoria and Albert's, the Grand Floridian
- Best Seafood: Narcoossee's, the Grand Floridian
- Best Steak: Yachtsman Steakhouse, the Yacht Club
- Best Char-Grilled Hamburger: Concourse Steakhouse, the Contemporary
- Best Grilled Hamburger: All-Star food courts
- Best Veggie Burger: Olivia's, the Vacation Club
- Best Hot Dog: Beaches and Cream, the Beach Club
- Best Dessert Selection: Palio, the Swan
- Best Cup of Coffee: Lobby Court Lounge, the Swan
- Best Thrill Ride: Splash Mountain
- Best 3-D Film: *Honey, I Shrunk the Audience*
- Most Romantic film: *Impressions de France,* Epcot
- Best Water Park: Blizzard Beach

The Real Tomorrowland: Future Development at Walt Disney World

Cranes and constructions crews are a common sight at Walt Disney World. This has been a decade of great growth, and it is beginning to look like it has just gotten started. A variety of projects are currently underway at Disney World; some are grand, and some are small. The end of the decade will unveil a lot of new things. Here are some of them.

Disney's Wild Animal Kingdom

After years of rumors regarding a fourth theme park, Disney has, at last, announced plans for the Wild Animal Kingdom. The largest of all Disney theme parks and five times the size of the Magic Kingdom, the new park will feature a combination of thrill rides, exotic landscapes, and encounters with live animals.

The centerpiece of this theme park will be the 14-story Tree of Life. Intricately carved and more than 50 feet wide at its trunk, it will serve as the symbol for this new land. The park will consist of three different areas that follow the themes of the real, the mythical, and the extinct.

In one area of the park, guests will take thrilling safaris among herds of live animals. Zebras, giraffes, hippos, lions, and elephants will be presented in exotic African landscapes. The land of mythical creatures will be created as only Disney can. Make-believe animals from legends and fairy tales will come alive in creative storytelling and theme park magic. The third area of Disney's Wild Animal Kingdom will focus on creatures long-extinct. Advanced audio-animatronics will bring the dinosaur era alive in Disney's most ambitious thrill attraction.

Disney plans to open the Wild Animal Kingdom in 1998. We wonder at the possibility of new resorts and attractions at this amazing park and, with the rest of the world, we will wait and see.

The Disney Village Marketplace Expansion

With an expected opening of 1997, Disney is planning to nearly double the size of the Village Marketplace and Pleasure Island. Plans include a 1,500-seat performing arts theater, two celebrity nightclubs, 14 more screens for the AMC movie complex, two "star-name" restaurants, and two Disney superstores. Included in this, the largest entertainment expansion of its kind at Disney, will be the House of Blues, partly owned by Dan Aykroyd, Gloria Estefan's Latin nightclub Lario's, and a Wolfgang Puck cafe. The World of Disney will be the largest Disney character merchandise store in the world. Team Mickey will be national headquarters for collectible merchandise for Disney sports franchises.

Disney Coronado Springs Resort

Opening in the fall of 1997 will be the Southwest-themed Coronado Springs Resort. This charming resort will feature palm-shaded courtyards, elegant haciendas, adobe walls, and Spanish-style tile roofs. It promises to embrace its guests with the traditional beauty of the Southwestern U.S. With nearly 2,000 rooms, this will be Disney's first moderately priced resort to feature a convention center. The resort will offer white sand beaches, watercraft rentals, four themed pools, specialty shops, dining court, and a full-service restaurant. The Coronado Springs will be located on 136 acres west of World Drive and north of the Disney-MGM interchange.

The Walt Disney World International Sports Complex

When this multimillion-dollar facility opens its doors in 1997, it will be able to accommodate professional-caliber training and sports competition, vacation-fitness activities, and tournament events in individual and team sports of nearly any type. With a large baseball stadium, fitness center, 5,000-seat field house with six basketball courts, 12 tennis courts, a track and field complex, and a host of other world-class sports facilities, the Disney Sports Complex will be ready to host virtually any sporting event: professional, collegiate, or amateur.

Sports include golf, tennis, football, basketball, gymnastics, fencing, volleyball, softball, and many more. The director of all of this will be ex-NFL linebacker Reggie Williams. There will be a staff of more than 100 coaches, counselors, and trainers.

From renderings that we have seen, we can tell you that this will be an architectural masterpiece. What else could we expect from Team Disney?

Disney Cruise Lines

This should come as no surprise to Disneyphiles: two brand new cruise ships with Mickey Mouse on the smoke stacks. The first of these specially designed and themed vessels is expected to begin operations in November of 1998. Setting sail from a homeport of Canaveral, Florida, both ships will feature popular Disney themes as an integral part of the decor. Of course, the emphasis on entertainment and activities will be for the family.

Disney Vision

This is a new attraction for Disney–MGM Studios, scheduled to open some time in 1998. Featuring a virtual-reality computer flight through Aladdin's Agrabah, this attraction is currently being previewed in Epcot's Innoventions.

The Disney Tours

Disney offers a small assortment of programs and tours designed to give participants a behind-the-scenes look into the workings of Walt Disney World. To make arrangements for them, call (407) 939-8687. There are discounts to each tour for American Express cardholders.

- The Backstage Magic Tour will take you behind the scenes in the theme parks. It includes the Utilidor tunnel under the Magic Kingdom and several attraction operation centers. The tour lasts eight hours and costs $150. Minimum age is 16. It is offered only on Monday and Wednesday.
- The Gardens of the World Program is a three-hour tour of the landscapes of Epcot and is conducted by Disney horticulturists. Offered Monday, Tuesday, and Thursday, this program costs $25. Participants must be at least 16 years old.
- The Hidden Treasure Tour is a three-hour adventure that will give you a look into the architecture, design, history, and costuming of the countries of Epcot. Offered on Sunday, Wednesday, Friday, and Saturday, this program costs $20 for persons 16 years and older.
- The Keys to the Kingdom Tour is designed to give participants both a backstage and an on-stage Disney experience. It includes the Utilidor tunnel and the Disney Production Center and runs only during off season. It begins at 10 A.M. and ends at 2 P.M. You can sign up for it at City Hall in the Magic Kingdom.
- The Inside the Animation Tour will take you right into the working studios to give you a look at how animation is created. You'll even get a chance to make your own cel. The two-hour tour costs $45, and participants must be at least 16 years old.
- D.E.E.P: The Dolphin Exploration and Education Program is a three-hour experience that will take you behind the scenes at the Living Seas Pavilion and give you an opportunity to interact with dolphins. Space is limited, and the cost is $45 per person. The program is offered Monday through Friday for those 16 years of age and older.

Index